THE TRIAL

HON. CLEMENT L. VALLANDIGHAM,

BY A

Military Commission:

AND THE

PROCEEDINGS UNDER HIS APPLICATION

FOR A

WRIT OF HABEAS CORPUS

IN THE

CIRCUIT COURT OF THE UNITED STATES FOR THE
SOUTHERN DISTRICT OF OHIO.

PUBLISHED BY
RICKEY AND CARROLL,
73 WEST FOURTH STREET, (OPERA-HOUSE BUILDING,)
CINCINNATI.
1863.

STEREOTYPED AT THE FRANKLIN TYPE FOUNDRY, CINCINNATI, O.

PREFACE.

In issuing this Report of the Trial of the Hon. Clement L. Vallandigham, by a Military Commission, convened in Cincinnati by order of Major-General Burnside, for language in violation of General Order No. 38, used at Mount Vernon, Ohio, and of the proceedings before the Hon. H. H. Leavitt, in the Circuit Court of the United States for the Southern District of Ohio, under the application for a writ of Habeas Corpus, the publishers are influenced, in part, by the expressed desire of many members of the bar to have such publication made, but chiefly because the great principles involved in the investigation, and the ability and learning displayed in the arguments of counsel and the opinion of the Court, give the cases sufficient interest and importance to justify their preservation in the substantial form of a book.

The military orders and the proceedings of the Military Commission are published with the consent of Major-General Burnside; while, through the courtesy of Brigadier-General Cox, the publishers have been enabled to verify their report by a careful comparison with the original record.

The arguments of counsel and the opinion of the Court in the Habeas Corpus case have been prepared for the press by their respective authors.

Thus the book obtains that authenticity which makes it perfectly reliable both in its historical and judicial aspects.

RICKEY & CARROLL,
Publishers.

CONTENTS.

THE TRIAL

OF

HON. CLEMENT L. VALLANDIGHAM,

BY A

MILITARY COMMISSION.

GENERAL ORDER No. 38.

HEAD-QUARTERS DEPARTMENT OF THE OHIO,
Cincinnati, O., April 13, 1863.

General Orders,
No. 38.

The Commanding General publishes, for the information of all concerned, that hereafter all persons found within our lines who commit acts for the benefit of the enemies of our country will be tried as spies or traitors, and, if convicted, will suffer death. This order includes the following class of persons:

Carriers of secret mails.

Writers of letters sent by secret mails.

Secret recruiting officers within the lines.

Persons who have entered into an agreement to pass our lines for the purpose of joining the enemy.

Persons found concealed within our lines belonging to the service of the enemy, and, in fact, all persons found improperly within our lines, who could give private information to the enemy.

All persons within our lines who harbor, protect, conceal, feed, clothe, or in any way aid the enemies of our country.

The habit of declaring sympathies for the enemy will not be allowed in this Department. Persons committing such offenses will be at once arrested, with a view to being tried as above stated, or sent beyond our lines into the lines of their friends.

It must be distinctly understood that treason, expressed or implied, will not be tolerated in this Department.

All officers and soldiers are strictly charged with the execution of this order.

By command of Major-General BURNSIDE.

LEWIS RICHMOND,
Assistant Adjutant-General.

Official:
D. R. LARNED,
Captain and Assistant Adjutant-General.

ORDER OF ARREST.

HEAD-QUARTERS DEPARTMENT OF THE OHIO,
Cincinnati, O., May 4, 1863.

Captain CHAS. G. HUTTON, A. D. C., etc.:

Captain—You will proceed at once to Dayton, Ohio, by special train, and cause the arrest of the Hon. Clement L. Vallandigham, after which you will return at once to these Head-quarters.

You will confer with the Provost Marshal, who will await your arrival at Dayton, and see that the arrest is made as quietly as possible. Captain Murray will accompany you, and will render you any assistance you may request of him.

The superintendent of the C., H. and D. Railroad will make all the necessary arrangements for trains, upon your showing him this order. You should endeavor to arrive here before daylight to-morrow morning.

Much discretion is allowed to your good judgment in this matter.

By command of Major-General A. E. BURNSIDE.

D. R. LARNED,
Captain and Assistant Adjutant-General.

Official.

TRIAL OF

HON. CLEMENT L. VALLANDIGHAM,

BY THE

MILITARY COMMISSION.

Proceedings of a Military Commission, convened at Cincinnati, Ohio, by virtue of the following Order:

HEAD-QUARTERS DEPARTMENT OF THE OHIO,
Cincinnati, O., April 21 1863.

Special Orders,
No. 135.

4. A Military Commission is hereby appointed, to meet at Cincinnati, Ohio, at 10 o'clock A. M., on Wednesday, the 22d instant, or as soon thereafter as practicable, for the trial of such prisoners as may be brought before it.

DETAIL FOR THE COMMISSION.

1. Brig.-Gen. R. B. POTTER, U. S. Vols.
2. Lieut.-Col. E. R. GOODRICH, C. S., U. S. Vols.
3. Major J. L. VAN BUREN, A. D. C.
4. " J. M. BROWN, 10th Kentucky Cavalry.
5. " R. M. CORWINE, A. D. C.
6. " A. H. FITCH, 115th Ohio Vols.
7. Captain E. GAY, 16th U. S. Infantry.
8. " P. M. LYDIG, A. D. C.
9. " W. H. FRENCH, C. S., U. S. Vols.

Captain J. M. CUTTS, 11th U. S. Infantry, is appointed Judge-Advocate.

By command of Major-General BURNSIDE.

W. P. ANDERSON, *A. A. General.*

[The Commission met and adjourned from time to time, disposing of such business as was brought before it, till May 6, which was, of its sittings, the]

TWELFTH DAY.

Cincinnati, O., Wednesday, May 6, 1863.

The Commission met pursuant to adjournment.

HEAD-QUARTERS DEPARTMENT OF THE OHIO,
Cincinnati, O., May 5, 1863.

Special Orders, }
No. 161. }

3. Captain W. H. FRENCH, C. S., is hereby relieved from duty as a member of the Military Commission convened by P. 4 of S. O. 135, current series, from these Head-quarters, and of which Brigadier-General ROBERT B. POTTER is President.

4. Colonel JOHN F. DE COURCY, 16th Regiment Ohio Vol. Inf., is hereby assigned to duty as a member of the Military Commission, convened by P. 4 of S. O. 135, current series, from these Head-quarters, and of which Brigadier-General ROBERT B. POTTER is President.

By command of Major-General BURNSIDE.

W. P. ANDERSON, *A. A. General.*

PRESENT:

General POTTER,	Colonel DE COURCY,
Lieut.-Col GOODRICH,	Major VAN BUREN,
Major BROWN,	Major FITCH, and
Captain LYDIG,	JUDGE-ADVOCATE.

The Judge-Advocate stated that the absence of Major Corwine and Captain Gay is sufficiently explained by the fact that they had recently been ordered on other duty by the General commanding the Department.

The proceedings of the preceding day were read by the Judge-Advocate, and approved.

The Commission then proceeded to the trial of CLEMENT L. VALLANDIGHAM, a citizen of the State of Ohio, who, being called into Court, and having heard the foregoing orders read; was asked if he had any objection to any of the members named therein, to which he replied in the negative.

The Commission was then duly sworn by the Judge-Advocate, and the Judge-Advocate was sworn by the President, in the presence of the accused, and Clement L. Vallandigham was arraigned on the following charge and specification of charge:

CHARGE.

Publicly expressing, in violation of General Orders No. 38, from Head-quarters Department of the Ohio, sympathy for those in arms against the Government of the United States, and declaring disloyal sentiments and opinions, with the object and purpose of weakening the power of the Government in its efforts to suppress an unlawful rebellion.

SPECIFICATION.

In this, that the said Clement L. Vallandigham, a citizen of the State of Ohio, on or about the first day of May, 1863, at Mount Vernon, Knox County, Ohio, did publicly address a large meeting of citizens, and did utter sentiments in words, or in effect, as follows, declaring the present war "a wicked, cruel, and unnecessary war;" "a war not being waged for the preservation of the Union;" "a war for the purpose of crushing out liberty and erecting a depotism;" "a war for the freedom of the blacks and the enslavement of the whites;" stating "that if the Administration had so wished, the war could have been honorably terminated months ago;" that "peace might have been honorably obtained by listening to the proposed intermediation of France;" that "propositions by which the Northern States could be won back, and the South guaranteed their rights under the Constitution, had been rejected the day before the late battle of Fredericksburg, by Lincoln and his minions," meaning thereby the President of the United States, and those under him in authority; charging "that the Government of the United States was about to appoint military marshals in every district, to restrain the people of their liberties, to deprive them of their rights and privileges;" characterizing General Orders No. 38, from Head-quarters Department of the Ohio, as "a base usurpation of arbitrary authority," inviting his hearers to resist the same, by saying, "the sooner the people inform the minions of usurped power that they will not submit to such restrictions upon their liberties, the better;" declaring "that he was at all times, and upon all occasions, resolved to do what he could to defeat the attempts now being made to build up a monarchy upon the ruins of our free government;" asserting "that he firmly believed, as he said six months ago, that the men in power are attempting to establish a despotism in this country, more cruel and more oppressive than ever existed before."

All of which opinions and sentiments he well knew did aid, comfort, and encourage those in arms against the Government, and could but induce in his hearers a distrust of their own Government, sympathy for those in arms against it, and a disposition to resist the laws of the land.

The accused asked delay to procure counsel, stating that he was engaged in preparing his plea, and required advice.

The Commission was duly cleared for deliberation, and on its reopening, the Judge-Advocate announced, as its decision, that the Commission would require the accused to plead "Guilty," or "Not Guilty," to the charge and specification, and would then adjourn for half an hour to permit the accused to procure counsel, when the Commission would proceed to hear the evidence for the prosecution.

The accused, denying the jurisdiction of the Commission, and refusing to plead as directed by the Commission, the Commission directed that the plea of "Not Guilty" to the specification and charge be entered for him by the Judge-Advocate.

The Commission then adjourned for half an hour.

The Commission reassembled pursuant to its adjournment.

All persons required to give evidence were directed to withdraw and remain in waiting till called for.

Captain H. R. Hill, of the 115th Regiment Ohio Volunteer Infantry, a witness for the prosecution, being duly sworn, testifies as follows:

Question by the Judge-Advocate.—What is your rank and regiment?

Answer.—Captain, 115th Regiment Ohio Volunteers.

Q.—Were you present at a meeting of citizens held at Mount Vernon on or about May 1, 1863?

A.—I was.

Q.—Did you hear the accused address that meeting?

A.—I did.

Q.—How near were you to him while speaking?

A.—I was leaning on the end of the platform on which he was speaking. I was about six feet from him.

Q.—Was this your position during the whole of the time he was speaking?

A.—Yes.

Q.—State what remarks he uttered in relation to the war now being waged, and any remarks he may have made in that connection.

A.—The witness stated that, in order to state his remarks in the order in which they were made, he would refresh his memory from manuscript notes made on the occasion. These the witness produced, and held in his hands.

The speaker commenced by referring to the canopy under which he was speaking—the stand being covered by an American flag—"the flag which," he said, "had been rendered sacred by Democratic Presidents—the flag under the Constitution."

After finishing his exordium, he spoke of the designs of those in power being to erect a despotism; that "it was not their intention to effect a restoration of the Union; that previous to the bloody battle of Fredericksburg an attempt was made to stay this wicked, cruel, and unnecessary war." That the war could have been ended in February last. That, a day or two before the battle of Fredericksburg, a proposition had been made for the readmission of Southern Senators into the United States Congress, and that the refusal was still in existence over the President's own signature, which would be made public as soon as the ban of secrecy enjoined by the President was removed. That the Union could have been saved, if the plan proposed by the speaker had been adopted; that the Union could have been saved upon the basis of reconstruction; but that it would have ended in the exile or death of those who advocated a continuation of the war; that "Forney, who was a well-known correspondent of the *Philadelphia Press*, had said that some of our public men (and he, Forney, had no right to speak for any others than those connected with the Administration), rather than bring back some of the seceded States, would submit to a permanent separation of the Union." He stated that "France, a nation that had always shown herself to be a friend of our Government, had proposed to act as a mediator;" but "that her proposition, which, if accepted, might have brought about an honorable peace, was insolently rejected." It may have been "instantly rejected;" that "the people had been deceived as to the objects of the war from the beginning;" that "it was a war for the liberation of the blacks, and the enslavement of the whites. We had been told it would be terminated in three months—then in nine months, and again in a year—but that there was still no prospect of its being ended. That Richmond was still in the hands of the enemy; that Charleston was theirs, and Vicksburg was theirs; that the Mississippi was not opened, and would not be so long as there was cotton on its banks to be stolen, or so long as there were any contractors or officers to enrich." I do not remember which word, contractors or officers, he used. He stated that a Southern paper had denounced himself and Cox, and the "Peace Democrats," as having "done more to prevent the establishing of the Southern Confederacy than a thousand Sewards." That "they proposed to operate through the masses of the people, in both sections, who were in favor of the Union." He said that "it was the purpose or desire of the Administration to suppress or prevent such meetings as the one he was addressing." That "military marshals were about to be appointed in every district, who would act for the purpose of restricting the liberties of the people;" but that "he was a freeman;" that he "did not ask David Tod, or Abraham Lincoln, or Ambrose E. Burnside for his right to speak as he had done, and was doing. That his authority for so doing was higher than General Orders No. 38—it was General Orders No. 1—the Constitution. That General Orders

No. 38 was a base usurpation of arbitrary power; that he had the most supreme contempt for such power. He despised it, spit upon it; he trampled it under his feet." That only a few days before, a man had been dragged down from his home in Butler County, by an outrageous usurpation of power, and tried for an offense not known to our laws, by a self-constituted court-martial—tried without a jury, which is guaranteed to every one; that he had been fined and imprisoned. That two men had been brought over from Kentucky, and tried, contrary to express laws for the trial of treason, and were now under the sentence of death. That an order had just been issued in Indiana, denying to persons the right to canvass or discuss military policy, and that, if it was submitted to, would be followed up by a similar order in Ohio. That he was resolved never to submit to an order of a military dictator, prohibiting the free discussion of either civil or military authority. "The sooner that the people informed the minions of this usurped power that they would not submit to such restrictions upon their liberties, the better." "Should we cringe and cower before such authority?" That we "claimed the right to criticise the acts of our military servants in power." That there never was a tyrant in any age who oppressed the people further than he thought they would submit to or endure. That in days of Democratic authority, Tom Corwin had, in face of Congress, hoped that our brave volunteers in Mexico "might be welcomed with bloody hands to hospitable graves," but that he had not been interfered with. It was never before thought necessary to appoint a captain of cavalry as Provost Marshal, as was now the case in Indianapolis, or military dictators, as were now exercising authority in Cincinnati and Columbus. He closed by warning the people not to be deceived. That "an attempt would shortly be made to enforce the conscription act;" that "they should remember that this war was not a war for the preservation of the Union;" that "it was a wicked Abolition war, and that if those in authority were allowed to accomplish their purposes, the people would be deprived of their liberties, and a monarchy established; but that, as for him, he was resolved that he would never be a priest to minister upon the altar upon which his country was being sacrificed."

Q.—Will you state what other flags or emblems decorated the platform than the American flag?

A.—There were frames covered with canvas, all of which were decorated with "butternuts." One banner, which was borne at the head of a delegation, bore the inscription, "The Copperheads are coming."

Q.—Did you see any badges worn by the citizens? How many, and what were those badges?

A.—Yes: I saw hundreds of them wearing butternuts, and many of them wearing copperheads cut out of cents.

Q.—Did you hear many, and how many, cheering for Jeff Davis, or expressing sympathy for him?

A.—I heard no cheers for Jeff Davis, but I heard a shout in the crowd, that "Jeff Davis was a gentleman, and that was what the President was not."

CROSS-EXAMINED BY THE ACCUSED.

Prisoner—Q.—Did not the speaker refer to the Crittenden propositions, and condemn the rejection of them?

A.—In endeavoring to show that the restoration of the Union was not the object of the war, he stated a number of means, this among others, by which the war could have been ended; he considered, from the fact that none were adopted, that this was proof that the restoration of the Union was not the object of the war.

Q.—Did I not quote Judge Douglas's declaration that the responsibility for the rejection of those propositions was with the Republican party?

Objected to by the Judge-Advocate.

The Commission was duly cleared for deliberation; and on its reopening, the Judge-Advocate announced as its decision, that the question would not be admitted.

Q.—When speaking in connection with Forney's *Press*, did I not say that "if other Democrats in Washington and myself had not refused all ideas and suggestions from some prominent men of the party in power, to make peace on terms of disunion, that I believed the war would have been ended in February?

A.—When speaking of the proposition, viz: "That it was not a war for the restoration of the Union," he stated that, if the Democrats in Washington had united in a plan for the permanent separation of the Union, the thing would have been accomplished in February.

Q.—Did I not expressly refer to myself in that connection, and say that I had refused, and always would refuse, to agree to a separation of the States—in other words, to peace, on terms of disunion?

A.—He stated something to that effect. He stated that he wished to have a voice in the manner in which the Union was to be reconstructed, and that he wished also our Southern brethren to have a voice.

Q.—Referring to the *Richmond Enquirer* article, did I not say that "it, Jeff Davis's organ, had called upon Dictator Lincoln" to lock up Mr. Cox, Senator Richardson, and myself in one of his military prisons, because of our doing so much against Southern recognition and independence?

A.—Yes, substantially, he did say so.

Q.—Referring to General Orders No. 38, did I not say that, in so far as it undertook to subject citizens not in the land or naval forces or militia of the United States, in actual service, to trial by court-martial or military commission, I believed it to be unconstitutional, and a usurpation of arbitrary power?

A.—He did, except the words "in so far."

Q.—Referring to two citizens of Kentucky tried by Military Court in Cincinnati, did I not say that what they were charged with was actual treason, punishable by death, and that, if guilty, the penalty by statute was hanging, and they ought to be hung, after being tried by a judicial court and a jury—instead of which they had been tried by a military court, as I understood, and sentenced to fine and imprisonment—one of them a fine of three hundred dollars?

A.—That was, in substance, what he said.

Q.—Did I not also say, in that connection, that the rebel officer who was tried as a spy by the Military Court at Cincinnati was legally and properly tried and convicted, according to the rules and articles of war; that that was a clear case where the Court had jurisdiction?

A.—It is my recollection that he denounced the Court as an unlawful tribunal, and that he did use the above language, and then gave the instances referred to in my direct testimony. He probably did refer to Campbell's case.

The Judge-Advocate stated that the accused did distinguish in his speech the different cases for the purpose of showing jurisdiction, condemning those cases in which he held the Court to have no jurisdiction, and approving the case of the spy.

Q.—Did I not distinctly, in the conclusion of the speech, enjoin upon the people to stand by the Union at all events, and that, if war failed, not to give the Union up; to try, by peaceable means, by compromise, to restore it as our fathers made it, and that though others might consent, or be forced to consent, I would not myself be one of those who would take any part in agreeing to a dissolution of the Union?

A.—Yes. He said he and the peace men were the only ones who wished the restoration of the Union.

Q.—Did not one of the "banners" you refer to as decorated with "butternuts" bear the inscription, "The Constitution as it is, and the Union as it was?"

A.—One of them bore that inscription.

Q.—Do you mean to be understood to say that *I* heard the reference to Jeff Davis, or gave any assent to it whatever?

A.—I can not say that he did. It was said loud enough for him to hear, if his attention had been directed that way. He gave no assent; neither did he give any dissent.

Q.—What was the size of the crowd assembled there that day?

A.—It was very large.

The Commission adjourned to meet again at 9½ o'clock A. M., on Thursday, the 7th instant.

ROBERT B. POTTER, Brig.-Gen. Vols.,
President.

J. M. CUTTS, Capt. 11th Inf., *Judge-Advocate.*

THIRTEENTH DAY.

Cincinnati, O., Thursday, May 7, 1863.

The Commission met pursuant to adjournment.

PRESENT:

Brig.-Gen. POTTER,	Col. DE COURCY,
Lieut.-Col. GOODRICH,	Major VAN BUREN,
Major BROWN,	Major FITCH, and
Capt. LYDIG,	JUDGE-ADVOCATE.

The proceedings of the preceding day were read by the Judge-Advocate, and approved.

All persons required to give evidence were directed to withdraw and remain in waiting until called for.

The cross-examination of Captain Hill was continued by the accused.

Q.—In speaking of the character of the war, did I not expressly say, as Mr. Lincoln, in his proclamation, July 1, 1862, said: "This *unnecessary* and injurious civil war?"

A.—I do not recollect that he did. The language he made use of I understood to be his own.

Q.—Again, in speaking of the character of the war, did I not expressly give, as proof, the President's proclamation of September 22, 1862, and January 1, 1863, as declaring emancipation of the slaves in Southern seceded States, and as a proof that the war was now being waged for that purpose?

The accused stated that he offered this question as an explanation of the purpose and object of his declarations as to the present character of the war, and as his authority for his statement. If he stated what the President stated, he (the accused) could not be held disloyal for so doing.

The Judge-Advocate stated that the question was one which clearly put in question, not the utterance of certain words, opinions, and sentiments, but their propriety, truth, and justice when uttered, and required the Commission to pass judgment, not upon sentiments uttered by the accused, but upon certain proclamations of the President of the United States. He further objected to the question as one designed, in his belief, not to meet the merits of this case, but to prepare a record in this case of a political character, and for political uses.

The Commission was duly cleared for deliberation, and on its reopening the Judge-Advocate announced, as its decision, that the question would not be admitted.

Q.—Did you continue at the same place during the delivery of the whole speech?

A.—I did.

Q.—Were your notes taken at the time, or reduced to writing after the speech was over?

A.—They were taken at the time. All I used before the Court were just as they fell from his lips.

Q.—Were you not in citizen's clothes; and how came you to be at Mount Vernon that day? Did you go to Mount Vernon for the purpose of taking notes and reporting the speech?

The accused insisted on the question on the ground that it would show the temper and spirit of the witness, and his prejudices, and as showing that the notes were taken with reference to arrest and prosecution before this Commission, he being in the service as Captain, and his regiment in Cincinnati.

The question was objected to by the Judge-Advocate, and the Commission was duly cleared for deliberation; and, on its reopening, the Judge-Advocate stated that he had withdrawn his objection, and the question would be admitted.

The question was then put to the witness.

A.—I was in citizen's clothes, and I went up for the purpose of listening to any speech that might be delivered at that meeting. I had no order to take notes or report.

Q.—Did you take notes of any other speech?

A.—I commenced taking notes of the speech of Mr. Cox, but I considered it harmless after listening to him a short time, and stopped. I took no notes of any other speeches.

Q.—Were you not expressly sent to listen to my speech on that occasion?

A.—I was not, any more than to the other speeches.

Q.—By whom were you sent?

A.—By Captain Andrew C. Kemper, Assistant Adjutant-General of the military commandant of the city of Cincinnati, Ohio.

Q.—Did you make report to him on your return?

A.—I did not. I reported first to Colonel Eastman himself, and from there went to Head-quarters Department of the Ohio.

Captain JOHN A. MEANS, 115th Ohio Volunteers, a witness for the prosecution, being duly sworn, testifies as follows:

Judge-Advocate.—Q.—What is your rank and regiment?

A.—Captain, 115th Ohio Volunteers.

Q.—Were you present at a meeting of citizens, held at Mount Vernon, Ohio, on or about May 1, 1863.

A.—I was.

Q.—Did you hear the accused address that meeting?

A.—I did.

Q.—How near were you; and state your position with reference to the speaker, and state whether you heard the whole or a part of his speech?

A.—I was in two or three positions. Most of the time about ten feet in front of the stand—directly in front. I heard the whole of his speech.

Q.—State what, if any remarks, you heard the accused make with reference to the war, or upon subjects in that connection? Give, as near as you can, his language.

A.—He stated, at one time, that the war was not waged for the preservation of the Union. That it was an Abolition war. That it might have been stopped, or peace restored, some time ago, and the Union restored, if the plan which had been submitted had been accepted.

Objected to by the accused, on the ground that he had applied for a subpœna, summoning Fernando Wood, Esq., of New York, and directing him to bring with him a letter signed by the President, referring to this plan, which had been refused by the Judge-Advocate.

The Judge-Advocate stated that he would withdraw so much

of the specification as related to remarks alleged to have been made by the accused with reference to the termination of the war.

The witness was directed to omit any testimony he might possess on that point.

The witness continued: The accused stated, that "if the plan he had proposed himself had been adopted, peace would have been restored, the Union saved by a reconstruction, the North won back, and the South guaranteed in their rights. That our army had not been successful; that Richmond was not taken, Charleston, nor Vicksburg; that the Mississippi was not opened, and would not be so long as there was cotton to sell, or contractors to enrich. He spoke in regard to the rebuke of the Administration at the last fall election; that no more volunteers could be had—that the Administration had to resort to the French conscription law. That he would not counsel resistance to military or civil law; that was not needed. That a people were unworthy to be freemen who would submit to such encroachments on their liberties. He was then speaking of the conscription act. He said he believed the Administration was attempting to erect a despotism. That in less than one month Mr. Lincoln had plunged the country into this cruel, bloody, and unnecessary war. He stated that General Orders No. 38 was a usurpation of power; that he despised it, spit upon it, and trampled it under his feet; and that he, for one, would not regard it. He styled the officers of the Administration, and the officers of the army, as minions of the Administration, or as Lincoln's minions. I do not recall any thing else. I will add that he said he did not ask Tod, or Lincoln, or Burnside, whether he might speak as he was doing, and had done; that he was a free man; that he spoke as he pleased, and where he pleased. He said that proclamations and military orders were intended to intimidate the people, and to prevent them from meeting as they were then that day doing. That he claimed the right to discuss and criticise the actions of civil and military men in power. He advised, at the close of his speech, to come up together at the ballot-box and hurl the tyrant from his throne. In one part of his speech he styled the President as "King Lincoln."

CROSS-EXAMINED BY THE ACCUSED.

Prisoner.—Q.—Did you make any notes at all of my speech, or are you testifying solely from memory?

A.—I took no notes at the delivery of the speech; but, after Pendleton commenced speaking, went to the hotel and made minutes. I made those minutes an hour and a half, or thereabouts, after I heard the speech.

Q.—About what was the length of the speech?

A.—I think about an hour and a half.

Q.—You speak of my saying the *North* might be won back. Was it not that the *South* might be won back, her rights being guaranteed under the Constitution?

A.—No: I noticed this particularly. It struck me very forcibly.

Q.—You say that I said that I would not counsel resistance to military or civil laws. Did I not expressly counsel the people to obey the Constitution and all laws, and to pay proper respect to men in authority, but to maintain their political rights through the ballot-box, and to redress personal wrongs through the judicial tribunals of the country, and in that way put down the Administration and all usurpations of power?

A.—He said, at the last of his speech, to come up united at the ballot-box and hurl the tyrant from his throne. I did not understand him to counsel the people to submit to the authorities at all times. I do not remember the language as stated, but part of it I remember.

Q.—Did I not say that my authority to speak to the people in public assemblages on all public questions was not derived from General Orders No. 38, but from General Orders No. 1, the Constitution of the United States—George Washington, commanding.

A.—I understood him to say, that his authority to speak to the people was higher than General Orders No. 38, by that military despot, Burnside. It was Orders No. 1, signed Washington.

Q.—Were not the words "Tod, Lincoln and Burnside" used, and that I did not ask their consent to speak?

A.—He did use these words at one time.

Q.—Were not the remarks you say I made, about spitting and trampling under foot, expressly applied in reference to arbitrary power generally, and did I not in that connection refer to General Orders No. 9 in Indiana, signed by General Hascal, denying the right to criticise the war policy of the Administration.

A.—The remarks in reference to spitting upon, etc., were made in direct reference to General Orders No. 38. He some time afterward, in speaking of the tyranny of the Administration, said that a General Order had been issued in Indiana denying the rights of the people to criticise the military power of the Administration, and, if submitted to, would be followed by a similar one in Ohio.

Q.—Do you undertake to give any connected or methodical statement of my speech of an hour and a half on that occasion?

A.—I do not pretend to give his speech just as he spoke it. I only remember part.

Q.—Were you not present in citizen's clothes? How came you to be at Mount Vernon that day—by whose order, and were you sent for the purpose of listening to and reporting the speech?

A.—I was present in citizen's clothes, by order of Colonel Eastman. I was sent there to listen to the speech, and report his language as near as I could, and I did make report to Colonel Eastman.

Q.—Did you make report of any other speech on that occasion?

A.—I related the substance of Mr. Cox's and of Mr. Kenny's speeches.

Q.—Were you directed to go to Mount Vernon and make a report of the speech, with reference to the prosecution under General Orders No. 38?

A.—I was not.

Q.—Was any object stated to you, and if so, what, for your

going there in citizen's clothes, listening to, and reporting the speech?

A.—Not any.

The Judge-Advocate stated that he did not propose to re-examine the witness, and having no other witnesses, would here close the testimony for the prosecution.

The accused asked to consult with his counsel, who did not appear, and had not appeared in the court-room during the trial, before entering upon his defense.

The Commission adjourned for fifteen minutes to enable the accused to consult with his counsel.

The Commission reassembled pursuant to adjournment.

Hon. S. S. Cox, a witness for the defense, being duly sworn, testifies as follows:

Prisoner.—Q.—Were you present at a public political meeting of citizens of Ohio, at Mount Vernon, on Friday, May 1, 1863, and, if so, in what capacity?

A.—I was present as one of the speakers.

Q.—Did you hear the speech of Mr. Vallandigham that day?

A.—I did. I heard the whole of it.

Q.—State where your position was during its delivery; what your opportunity for hearing was; whether you heard it all, and whether and why your attention was particularly directed to it?

A.—Before the speaking began, I was on the stand a few feet from Mr. Vallandigham, most of the time standing near him, so that I could not fail to hear all that he said. I do not think my attention was distracted but for perhaps a few moments during the entire speech. I had not heard Mr. Vallandigham speak since the adjournment of Congress, and as I came in from the West, I did not know that he was to be there. I took an especial interest in listening to his speech throughout. Having to follow him, I naturally noted the topics which he discussed.

Q.—Did you hear allusions to General Burnside, by name, and if so, what were they?

A.—The only allusion he made to the General was, I think,

near the beginning of his speech, in which he said he was not there by the favor of Abraham Lincoln, Governor Tod, or Ambrose E. Burnside.

Q.—Was any epithet applied to him during the speech?

A.—No, sir. If there had been I should have noticed it, because General Burnside is an old friend of mine, and I should have remembered any odious epithet applied to him.

Q.—Did you hear the references to General Orders No. 38, and if so, what were they? State fully.

A.—The only reference made to that order in that speech was something to this effect: that he did not recognize (I do not know that I can quote the language) Order No. 38 as superior to Order No. 1, the Constitution, from George Washington commanding.

Q.—Were any insolent epithets, such as spitting upon, trampling under foot, or the like, used at any time in the speech, in reference to this Order 38; and if any criticism was made upon it, what was that criticism?

A.—I can not recall any denunciatory epithets applied to that order. I did not hear any that I can remember. The only criticism I heard was that in reference to the Constitution. Mr. Vallandigham discussed these matters very briefly, taking up the larger portion of his speech with another proposition. The other proposition was in connection with closing of the war by separation. He charged that men in power were willing to make peace by separation. He exhausted some time in reading proofs from publications of Montgomery Blair and Forney. He also stated there were private proofs yet to be disclosed, which time would disclose. He said they pursued this thing until they found that Democrats were unwilling to make peace, except upon a basis of the restoration of the whole Union. He denounced bitterly any attempts to restore peace by a separation of the States.

Q.—Do you remember to what, if at all, in connection with future usurpations of power, he applied his strongest language?

A.—I can not say as to his "strongest language," for he always speaks pretty strongly. He denounced, in strong language, any usurpations of power to stop public discussions and the suffrage. He appealed to the people to protect their rights, as a remedy for every grievance of a private nature. He counseled no resistance except such as might be had at the ballot-box.

Q.—Was any thing said by him at all looking to forcible resistance of either laws or military orders?

A.—Not as I understand it. He stated the sole remedy to be in the ballot-box, and in the courts. I remember this distinctly, for I had been pursuing the same line of remark at Chicago and Fort Wayne, and other places where I had been speaking, and with the purpose of repressing any tendency toward violence among our Democratic people.

Q.—Was any thing said by me on that occasion in denunciation of the conscription bill, or looking in any way to resistance to it?

A.—My best recollection is that Mr. Vallandigham did not say a word about the conscription.

Q.—Did he refer to the French conscription bill, and, if not, was such reference made, and by whom?

A.—He did not. I did.

Q.—Do you remember his quotation from President Lincoln's proclamation of July 1, 1862, of the words "unnecessary and injurious war?"

A.—I do not. He may have done so.

Q.—Did you hear similar language used by him?

A.—I did not.

Q.—Do you remember his comments on the change of the policy of the war some year or so after its commencement, and what references were made by him in that connection?

A.—He did refer to the change in the policy of the war, and I think devoted some time to show that the war had been deviated from a war for the restoration of the Union into a war for the abolition of slavery.

Q.—What did he claim to have been its original purpose as avowed, and how show it?

A.—He referred, in that connection, to the Crittenden Resolutions, declaring the war to be one for the restoration of the Union, and not to break up the "institution" of a State.

Q.—Did he counsel any other mode in that speech of resisting usurpations of arbitrary power, except by free discussion and the ballot-box?

A.—He did not.

Q.—Were any denunciations of the officers of the army indulged in by him, or any offensive epithets applied to them?

A.—He occasionally used the words "the President and his minions," but I did not understand him to use them in connection with the army. It was not in that connection. It was in connection with arbitrary arrests.

Q.—Do I understand you to say that the denunciations to which you refer were chiefly in reference to arbitrary arrests?

A.—My recollection is that that is the connection in which they were used. He applied some pretty strong epithets to spies and informers, whom he did not seem to like very much.

Q.—Do you remember the connection in which some words to this effect were used at the close of the speech, with regard to the possibility of a dissolution of the Union, and of his own determination in regard to such a contingency?

A.—I could not give the exact words. I remember the metaphor, that "he would not be a priest to minister at the altar of disunion." He was speaking about the Union, and his attachment to it. I can not give the words of the metaphor.

Q.—What counsel did I give at the close of my speech upon that subject?

A.—He invoked the people under no circumstances to surrender the Union.

Q.—Do you remember any rebuke, in connection with the Butler County case, of men who hurrahed for "Jeff Davis?"

A.—Yes, I do. He denounced the applause of Davis.

Q.—Was any thing said, in that speech, in reference to the war, except in condemnation of what he claimed to be the policy upon which it was now being waged, and as a policy which he insisted could not restore the Union, but must end, finally, in disunion?

A.—I can only give my understanding. I do not know about inferences people might draw. I understood his condemnation of the war to be launched at its perversion from its original purpose.

The Court here adjourned to meet at 4½ o'clock P. M. of the same day.

4½ O'CLOCK P. M.

The Court met pursuant to adjournment.

The witnesses, Locky Harper, J. T. Irvine, and Frank H. Hurd, summoned for the defense, not having appeared, the Judge-Advocate stated that if it would avoid an adjournment he would admit that they, if present, would, under oath, testify substantially the same as Hon. S. S. Cox.

Thereupon the accused stated that he would close his defense, and offer no further testimony.

The Judge-Advocate stated that he did not propose to offer any further testimony.

The accused then read to the Commission a statement (of which Mr. Vallandigham has a copy).

[The statement here referred to does not appear in the record of the trial. It is as follows:]

PROTEST OF MR. VALLANDIGHAM.

Arrested without due "process of law," without warrant from any judicial officer, and now in a military prison, I have been served with a "charge and specifications," as in a Court-martial or Military Commission.

I am not in either "the land or naval forces of the United States, nor in the militia in the actual service of the United States," and therefore am not triable for any cause, by any such Court, but am subject, by the express terms of the Constitution, to arrest only by due process of law, judicial warrant, regularly issued upon affidavit, and by some officer or Court of competent jurisdiction for the trial of citizens, and am now entitled to be tried on an indictment or presentment of a Grand Jury of such Court, to speedy and public trial by an impartial jury of the State of Ohio, to be confronted with witnesses against me, to have compulsory process for witnesses in my behalf, the assistance of counsel for my defense, and evidence and argument according to the common laws and the ways of Judicial Courts.

And all these I here demand as my right as a citizen of the United States, and under the Constitution of the United States.

But the alleged "offense" is not known to the Constitution of the United States, nor to any law thereof. It is words spoken to the people of Ohio in an open and public political meeting, lawfully and peaceably assembled, under the Constitution and upon full notice. It is words of criticism of the public policy of the public servants of the people, by which policy it was alleged that the welfare of the country was not promoted. It was an appeal to the people to change that policy, not by force, but by free elections and the ballot-box. It is not pretended that I counseled disobedience to the Constitution, or resistance to laws and lawful authority. I never have. Beyond this protest I have nothing further to submit.

C. L. VALLANDIGHAM.

CINCINNATI, OHIO, *May* 7, 1863.

The Judge-Advocate stated that he had no reply to make to the statement of the accused. In so far as it called in question the jurisdiction of the Commission, that question had been decided by the authority convening and ordering the trial, and he was not called upon to discuss it, nor had the Commission been willing at any time to entertain it. In so far as any implications or inferences, designed or contemplated in the statement, of his right of counsel, and to have witnesses summoned for his defense, were involved, the Judge-Advocate had summoned such witnesses as the accused had requested, and he had had the benefit of three lawyers of his own choice as counsel, who had, however, remained continuously in an adjoining room during the continuance of the trial—the accused, himself, for some reason unknown, not having introduced them before the Commission, though the Commission had expressly authorized him to do so, and had adjourned to permit his obtaining their presence.

The facts alleged in the specification were to be decided upon the evidence before the Commission, and he believed it unnecessary to comment thereon.

The question of the criminality of the facts alleged, if proved, was also a question purely for the Commission, and which the Judge-Advocate deemed it unnecessary to enforce by argument. He, therefore, without further comment, submitted the case to the consideration of the Commission.

The Commission was duly cleared for deliberation.

HEAD-QUARTERS DEPARTMENT OF THE OHIO,
Cincinnati, O., May 16, 1863.

General Orders,
No. 68.

I. At a Military Commission which convened at Cincinnati, Ohio, on the 6th day of May, 1863, pursuant to Special Orders No. 135, of April 21, 1863, current series, from these Head-quarters, and of which Brigadier-General Robert B. Potter, U. S. Vols., is President, was arraigned and tried, Clement L. Vallandigham, a citizen of the State of Ohio, on the following charge and specification of charge, to-wit:

CHARGE.

Publicly expressing, in violation of General Orders No. 38, from Head-quarters Department of the Ohio, sympathy for those in arms against the Government of the United States, and declaring disloyal sentiments and opinions, with the object and purpose of weakening the power of the Government in its efforts to suppress an unlawful rebellion.

SPECIFICATION.

In this, that the said Clement L. Vallandigham, a citizen of the State of Ohio, on or about the first day of May, 1863, at

Mount Vernon, Knox County, Ohio, did publicly address a large meeting of citizens, and did utter sentiments in words, or in effect, as follows, declaring the present war "a wicked, cruel, and unnecessary war;" "a war not being waged for the preservation of the Union;" "a war for the purpose of crushing out liberty and erecting a depotism;" "a war for the freedom of the blacks and the enslavement of the whites;" stating "that if the Administration had so wished, the war could have been honorably terminated months ago;" that "peace might have been honorably obtained by listening to the proposed intermediation of France;" that "propositions by which the Northern States could be won back, and the South guaranteed their rights under the Constitution, had been rejected the day before the late battle of Fredericksburg, by Lincoln and his minions," meaning thereby the President of the United States, and those under him in authority; charging that "the Government of the United States was about to appoint military marshals in every district, to restrain the people of their liberties, to deprive them of their rights and privileges;" characterizing General Orders No. 38, from Head-quarters Department of the Ohio, as "a base usurpation of arbitrary authority," inviting his hearers to resist the same, by saying, "the sooner the people inform the minions of usurped power that they will not submit to such restrictions upon their liberties, the better;" declaring "that he was at all times, and upon all occasions, resolved to do what he could to defeat the attempts now being made to build up a monarchy upon the ruins of our free government;" asserting "that he firmly believed, as he said six months ago, that the men in power are attempting to establish a despotism in this country, more cruel and more oppressive than ever existed before."

All of which opinions and sentiments he well knew did aid, comfort, and encourage those in arms against the Government, and could but induce in his hearers a distrust of their own Government, sympathy for those in arms against it, and a disposition to resist the laws of the land.

To which charges and specifications, the prisoner refusing to plead either "Guilty," or "Not Guilty," the Commission directed the Judge-Advocate to enter on the records the plea of "Not Guilty."

FINDING AND SENTENCE.

The Commission, after mature deliberation on the evidence adduced, and the statement of the accused, find the accused, Clement L. Vallandigham, a citizen of the State of Ohio, as follows:

Of the specification (except the words, "That propositions by which the Northern States could be won back, and the South guaranteed their rights under the Constitution, had been rejected the day before the battle of Fredericksburg, by Lincoln and his minions," meaning thereby the President of the United States, and those under him in authority, and the words, "asserting that he firmly believed, as he asserted six months ago, that the men in power are attempting to establish a despotism in this country, more cruel and more oppressive than ever existed before,") "Guilty."

And as to these words, "Not Guilty."

Of the charge, "Guilty."

And the Commission do, therefore, sentence him, the said Clement L. Vallandigham, a citizen of the State of Ohio, to be placed in close confinement in some fortress of the United States, to be designated by the commanding officer of this Department, there to be kept during the continuance of the war.

II. The proceedings, finding, and sentence in the foregoing case are approved and confirmed, and it is directed that the place of confinement of the prisoner, Clement L. Vallandigham, in accordance with said sentence, be Fort Warren, Boston Harbor.

By command of Major-General Burnside.

LEWIS RICHMOND,
Assistant Adjutant-General.

Official:

W. P. ANDERSON,
Assistant Adjutant-General.

ORDER OF THE PRESIDENT.

U. S. MILITARY TELEGRAPH,
Cipher.] May 19, 1863.

[By Telegraph from Washington, 9.40 P. M., 1863.]

TO MAJOR-GENERAL BURNSIDE,
Commanding Department of the Ohio:

SIR—The President directs that, without delay, you send C. L. Vallandigham, under secure guard, to the Head-quarters of General Rosecrans, to be put by him beyond our military lines, and that in case of his return within our lines he be arrested and kept in close custody for the term specified in his sentence.

By order of the PRESIDENT.

ED. M. CANBY,
Brig.-Gen. and A. A. G.

Please acknowledge receipt of this, and time when received, by request of BRIG.-GEN. CANBY.

THE PROCEEDINGS

UNDER THE APPLICATION OF

HON. CLEMENT L. VALLANDIGHAM

FOR A

WRIT OF HABEAS CORPUS

IN THE

CIRCUIT COURT OF THE UNITED STATES FOR
THE SOUTHERN DISTRICT OF OHIO.

PROCEEDINGS

ON

APPLICATION FOR WRIT OF HABEAS CORPUS.

THE UNITED STATES OF AMERICA, ON THE RELATION OF CLEMENT L. VALLANDIGHAM *v.* AMBROSE E. BURNSIDE, MAJOR-GENERAL IN THE ARMY OF THE UNITED STATES, COMMANDING, ETC.

ON Saturday, May 9, 1863, in the Circuit Court of the United States for the Southern District of Ohio, Judge LEAVITT presiding, the Hon. GEORGE E. PUGH made an application on behalf of Hon. CLEMENT L. VALLANDIGHAM, for the allowance of a writ of Habeas Corpus, to be directed to Major-General AMBROSE E. BURNSIDE, Commanding the Department of the Ohio, which application was as follows:

UNITED STATES OF AMERICA,
SOUTHERN DISTRICT OF OHIO, TO-WIT:

To the Honorable the Judges of the Circuit Court of the United States within and for the District aforesaid:

Your petitioner, Clement L. Vallandigham, says that he is a native-born citizen of the State of Ohio, residing in Montgomery County, and not enlisted or commissioned in the land or the naval forces of the United States, nor called into actual service as one of the militia of any State. Nevertheless, on the fifth day of May, instant, between two and three o'clock in the morning of said day, his dwelling-house (in which he and his family then were) in the city of Dayton, and county of Montgomery aforesaid, was surrounded by about one hundred soldiers, armed, and in uniform as such, and acting under the direction of Ambrose E. Burnside, a Major-General in the army of the United States; which soldiers then and there violently broke the outer door and two inner doors of your petitioner's said house, and entered the same, and then and there seized your petitioner by overpowering numbers, and thence carried him to the city of Cincinnati, in Hamilton County, in the State and Southern District of Ohio, where they imprisoned him, against his will, in a building on Second or Columbia street, then used as a military prison. And your petitioner says that he has ever since been, and now is, detained, in said city of Cincinnati, under a military guard of which said Ambrose E. Burnside is commander.

Your petitioner alleges that he was thus violently seized in his own house, in the night time, without any warrant issued upon probable cause supported by oath or affirmation, and in contempt of his rights as an American citizen. He says, also, that since his imprisonment, as aforesaid, a paper has been delivered to him (of which a true copy is herewith annexed) purporting to contain a charge and a specification against him, signed by J. M. Cutts, Captain and Judge-Advocate, on which charge and specification he has been arraigned, against his will, before a number of officers of the army of the United States, assembled in a room of the St. Charles Exchange, on East Third street, in the city of Cincinnati, styling themselves a Military Commission, and assuming to exercise judicial authority at the instigation of said Ambrose E. Burnside as Major-General aforesaid. But your petitioner denies that he is subject to any such mode of arraignment or of trial, and claims that all proceedings of that description are, in his case, forbidden by the Constitution and laws of the United States.

Therefore, and to the end that he may be relieved from manifest oppression under color of military authority, and that he may be charged in due course of law, in this Court or some other, with whatsoever crime is intended to be imputed by the charge and specification above mentioned, your petitioner moves your Honors to grant him a writ of Habeas Corpus directed to said Ambrose E. Burnside, and all persons assuming to act in obedience to his orders, commanding him and them forthwith to bring the body of your petitioner before this Court, together with the cause (if any) of his caption and detention. And your petitioner submits hereby to whatsoever the Constitution of the United States in this behalf may require.

C. L. VALLANDIGHAM,
By G. E. PUGH, his Attorney.

SOUTHERN DISTRICT OF OHIO, TO-WIT:

George E. Pugh, being duly sworn, says that he makes this application for a writ of Habeas Corpus at the request of Clement L. Vallandigham, the petitioner above named, and that he believes the matters alleged in the foregoing petition to be true.

G. E. PUGH.

Sworn to before me, and subscribed in my presence, this 9th day of May, A. D. 1863.

JOSEPH H. GEIGER,
Clerk C. C. U. S. Southern District of Ohio.

Cincinnati, O., May 11, 1863.

The application on my behalf, on May 9, 1863, to the Circuit Court of the United States, for a writ of Habeas Corpus to release me from illegal military custody, was made by Hon. George E. Pugh at my express instance and request.

C. L. VALLANDIGHAM.

The Court inquired if there was any one present representing the United States in this behalf; whereupon Flamen Ball, Esq., District Attorney of the United States, said that, as he was the attorney of the United States in their legitimate legal business in this district, he felt called upon to answer the inquiry of the Court, by saying he had no express authority to appear either for Major-General Burnside or the War Department; that he considered it would be indelicate in him to volunteer to act, and he felt sure if he should do so, all his acts might justly be held to be void. He declined appearing, but, as *amicus curiæ*, suggested that, in accordance with the practice of the Court, notice should be given to General Burnside, that there might be a hearing on the application.

Mr. Pugh objected, and insisted on the prompt issue of the writ, and that the hearing could be had when the body of the prisoner should be brought into Court.

The Court took the matter under advisement, and in the afternoon decided to hear the argument on the application, and directed the Clerk to notify Major-General Burnside that the hearing would be had on Monday, May 11.

On the opening of the Court, May 11, Hon. Aaron F. Perry and District-Attorney Ball appeared for General Burnside, and Hon. George E. Pugh appeared for Mr. Vallandigham.

The District-Attorney presented to the Court the following:

STATEMENT OF MAJOR-GENERAL BURNSIDE.

HEAD-QUARTERS DEPARTMENT OF THE OHIO,
Cincinnati, O., May 11, 1863.

To the Honorable the Circuit Court of the United States within and for the Southern District of Ohio:

The undersigned, commanding the Department of the Ohio, having received notice from the Clerk of said Court that an application for the allowance of a writ of Habeas Corpus will be made this morning before your Honors, on behalf of Clement L. Vallandigham, now a prisoner in my custody, asks leave to submit to the Court the following

STATEMENT.

If I were to indulge in wholesale criticisms of the policy of the Government, it would demoralize the army under my command, and every friend of his country would call me a traitor. If the officers or soldiers were to indulge in such criticisms, it would weaken the army to the extent of their influence; and if this criticism were universal in the army, it would cause it to be broken to pieces, the Government to be divided, our homes to be invaded, and anarchy to reign. My duty to my Government forbids me to indulge in such criticisms; officers and soldiers are not allowed so to indulge, and this course will be sustained by all honest men.

Now, I will go further. We are in a state of civil war. One of the States of this Department is at this moment invaded, and three others have been threatened. I command the Department, and it is my duty to my country, and to this army, to keep it in the best possible condition; to see that it is fed, clad, armed, and, as far as possible, to see that it is encouraged. If it is my duty and the duty of the troops to avoid saying any thing that would weaken the army, by preventing a single recruit from joining the ranks, by bringing the laws of Congress into disrepute, or by causing dissatisfaction in the ranks, it is equally the duty of every citizen in the Department to avoid the same evil. If it is my duty to prevent the propagation of this evil in the army, or in a portion of my Department, it is equally my duty in all portions of it; and it is my duty to use all the force in my power to stop it.

If I were to find a man from the enemy's country distributing in my camps speeches of their public men that tended to demoralize the troops or to destroy their confidence in the constituted authorities of the Government, I would have him tried, and hung if found guilty, and all the rules of modern warfare would sustain me. Why should such speeches from our own public men be allowed?

The press and public men, in a great emergency like the present, should avoid the use of party epithets and bitter invectives, and discourage the organization of secret political societies, which are always undignified and disgraceful to a free people, but now they are absolutely wrong and injurious; they create dissensions and discord, which just now amount to treason. The simple names "Patriot" and "Traitor" are comprehensive enough.

As I before said, we are in a state of civil war, and an emergency is upon us which requires the operations of some power that moves more quickly than the civil.

There never was a war carried on successfully without the exercise of that power.

It is said that the speeches which are condemned have been made in the presence of large bodies of citizens, who, if they thought them wrong, would have then and there condemned them. That is no argument. These citizens do not realize the effect upon the army of our country, who are its defenders. They have never been in the field; never faced the enemies of their country; never undergone the privations of our soldiers in the field; and, besides, they have been in the habit of hearing their public men speak, and, as a general thing, of approving of what they say; therefore, the greater responsibility rests upon the public men and upon the public press, and it behooves them to be careful as to what they say. They must not use license and plead that they are exercising liberty. In this Department it can not be done. I shall use all the power I have to break down such license, and I am sure I will be sustained in this course by all honest men. At all events, I will have the consciousness, before God, of having done my duty to my country, and when I am swerved from the performance of that duty by any pressure, public or private, or by any prejudice, I will no longer be a man or a patriot.

I again assert, that every power I possess on earth, or that is given me from above, will be used in defense of my Government, on all occasions, at all times, and in all places within this Department. There is no party—no community—no State government—no State legislative body—no corporation or body of men that have the power to inaugurate a war policy that has the validity of law and power, but the constituted authorities of the Government of the United States; and I am determined to support their policy. If the people do not approve that policy, they can change the constitutional authorities of that Government, at the proper time and by the proper method. Let them freely discuss the policy in a proper tone; but my duty requires me to stop license and intemperate discussion, which tends to weaken the authority of the Government and army: whilst the latter is in the presence of the enemy, it is cowardly so to weaken it. This license could not be used in our camps—the man would be torn in pieces who would attempt it. There is no fear of the people losing their liberties; we all know that to be the cry of demagogues, and none but the ignorant will listen to it; all intelligent men know that our people are too far advanced in the scale of religion, civilization, education, and freedom, to allow any power on earth to interfere with their liberties; but this same advancement in these great characteristics of our people teaches them to make all necessary sacrifices for their country when an emergency requires. They will support the constituted authorities of the Government, whether they agree with them or not. Indeed, the army itself is a part of the people, and is so thoroughly educated in the love of civil liberty, which is the best guarantee for the permanence of our republican institutions, that it would itself be the first to oppose any attempt to continue the exercise of military authority after the establishment of peace by the overthrow of the rebellion. No man on earth can lead our citizen soldiery to the establishment of a military despotism, and no man living would have the folly to attempt it. To do so would be to seal his own doom. On this point there can be no ground for apprehension on the part of the people.

It is said that we can have peace if we lay down our arms. All sensible men know this to be untrue. Were it so, ought we to be so cowardly as to lay them down until the authority of the Government is acknowledged?

I beg to call upon the fathers, mothers, brothers, sisters, sons, daughters, relatives, friends, and neighbors of the soldiers in the field to aid me in stopping this license and intemperate discussion, which is discouraging our armies, weakening the hands of the Government, and thereby strengthening the enemy. If we use our honest efforts, God will bless us with a glorious peace and a united country. Men of every shade of opinion have the same vital interest in the suppression of this rebellion; for, should we fail in the task, the dread horrors of a ruined and distracted nation will fall alike on all, whether patriots or traitors.

These are substantially my reasons for issuing "General Order No. 38;" my reasons for the determination to enforce it, and also my reasons for the arrest of Hon. C. L. Vallandigham for a supposed violation of that order, for which he has been tried. The result of that trial is now in my hands.

In enforcing this order I can be unanimously sustained by the people, or I can be opposed by factious, bad men. In the former event, quietness will prevail; in the latter event, the responsibility and retribution will attach to the men who resist the authority, and the neighborhoods that allow it.

All of which is respectfully submitted.

A. E. BURNSIDE, Major-General,
Commanding Department of the Ohio.

OPENING ARGUMENT

OF

HON. GEORGE E. PUGH.

MAY IT PLEASE YOUR HONOR:

I INSIST on my motion for a writ of Habeas Corpus, notwithstanding the defense attempted by General Burnside. And here I must be allowed to complain of the hardship to which Mr. Vallandigham has been subjected by the Court on this occasion. The statement we have just heard is, in effect, a return to the writ: it avows the caption and detention of the petitioner in manner and form as alleged by the petition; it proclaims the fact that he has been tried by a Military Commission, and for an offense unknown to the laws of the land; and yet, without having the body of the petitioner in Court, so as to prevent the execution, possibly, of an illegal sentence, without any writ or order compelling General Burnside to stay the execution of such a sentence until your Honor can determine this application, I am now required to proceed in the discharge of my duty as an advocate.

[Here Judge Leavitt observed that it was the settled practice of the Court to give notice to the defendant, in cases of military arrest, before issuing a writ of Habeas Corpus; and that Judge Swayne had so announced, in a case from Champaign County, at the last term.]

MR. PUGH—His Honor may have intended that as a rule in future; but, inasmuch as the question was not then argued at the bar, I wish to be heard in opposition to the establishment of any such rule. I know that the practice of the Court has been otherwise: I know that your Honor granted me a writ of Habeas Corpus, at chambers, without any notice to General Mitchel, the defendant, less than two years ago; and that, sitting here, at October term, 1861, your Honor commanded him to show cause why he should not be attached for contempt in disobeying the writ. And I feel confident that no decision or authority can be found, in America or in England, to countenance the rule which Judge Swayne has suggested. The petitioner is clearly entitled, if need be, to call upon the Supreme Court of the United States to review the proceedings of this Court; and how can he do that effectually, according to the doctrine of Kaine's case, 14 Howard, 103, until a writ has been issued, or, at least, some determination made of record?

And furthermore, as all authorities agree, the writ of Habeas Corpus is a writ of right; by which I do not mean that a petitioner can sue it out of the Clerk's office, as he may a writ of summons or of subpœna, but that whenever, by his own showing or that of others, on affidavit, it appears that he is unlawfully imprisoned, the Court has no choice, no latitude, no right even of postponement.

Judge Leavitt observed that the granting or refusing of the writ was a matter of judicial discretion.

Mr. Pugh—Of *judicial* discretion, assuredly; but that means a discretion guided by the principles of the law, not by considerations of convenience or favor.

Judge Leavitt—Certainly.

Mr. Pugh—The doctrine is well announced by Mr. Justice Wilmot in his opinion to the House of Lords, May 9, 1758:

> "A writ which issues upon a probable cause, verified by affidavit, is as much a writ of right as a writ which issues of course."—*Wilmot's Notes*, 82.

In the same opinion (pp. 83, 84) the learned Judge declares that writs of Habeas Corpus, Mandamus, Prohibition, Supplicavit, and the writ of Homine Replegiando, are all writs of right; "but," he adds, "a proper case must be laid before the Court, by affidavit, before the parties praying such writs may be entitled to them." And he continues:

> "*They are* THE BIRTHRIGHT *of the people, subject to such provisions as* THE LAW *has established for granting them.* THOSE PROVISIONS ARE NOT A CHECK UPON JUSTICE, BUT A WISE AND PROVIDENT DIRECTION OF IT."

Anterior to the Revolution of 1688, in England, judges were appointed by the Crown, and held their offices only during its pleasure. The consequence was, and naturally, that while the writ of Habeas Corpus could be obtained, in term time, on application to the Court of King's Bench, individual judges would not grant it in vacation, or delayed, under various pretexts, to hear and determine upon the cause of imprisonment. To remedy these evils, and thus render the writ effectual in every case, the famous act or statute of 31 Charles II, ch. 2, was proposed and adopted.

> "It is a very common mistake," observes Dr. Hallam, "and that not only among foreigners, but many from whom some knowledge of our constitutional laws might be expected, to suppose that this statute of Charles II enlarged in a great degree our liberties, and forms a sort of epoch in their history. But, though a very beneficial enactment, and eminently remedial in many cases of illegal imprisonment, it introduced no new principle, nor conferred any right upon the subject. From the earliest records of the English law, no freeman could be detained in prison except upon a criminal charge, or conviction, or for a civil debt. In the former case, it was always in his power to demand of the Court of King's Bench a writ of Habeas Corpus ad subjiciendum directed to the person detaining him in custody, by which he was enjoined to bring up the body of the prisoner with the warrant of commitment, that the Court might judge of its sufficiency, and remand the party, admit him to bail, or discharge him, according to the nature of the charge. This writ issued of right, and could not be refused by the Court. It was not to bestow an immunity from arbitrary imprisonment, which is abundantly provided in Magna Charta, if indeed it were not much more ancient, that the statute of Charles II was enacted; but to cut off the abuses by which

the Government's lust of power and the servile subtlety of Crown lawyers had impaired so fundamental a privilege."—*Constit. His. of England, ch.* 8.

This appears, also, from the language of the Court in Bushell's case, Vaughan, 135, decided nine years before the statute.

Bushell and eleven others were the jury which acquitted Penn and Mead, at the Old Bailey sessions, upon an indictment for holding an unlawful assembly; Penn having attempted to preach in Great-Church street, and Mead having accompanied him. The Recorder of London was so exasperated at this verdict that he fined all the jurymen; sentencing Bushell, as foreman, to pay forty marks, and to be imprisoned in Newgate until they had been paid. Bushell sued out a writ of Habeas Corpus from the Court of Common Pleas, and was thereupon discharged from imprisonment. The Court said:

"The writ of Habeas Corpus is now the most usual remedy by which a man is restored again to his liberty if he have been, against law, deprived of it.

"Therefore, the writ commands the day and the cause of the caption and the detaining of the prisoner to be certified upon the retorn; which, if not done, the Court can not possibly judge whether the cause of the commitment and detainer be according to law, or against it.

"Therefore, the cause of the imprisonment ought, by the retorn, to appear as specifically and certainly to the judges of the retorn as it did appear to the Court or person authorized to commit."

One peculiar excellence of the Habeas Corpus Act, so called, was that it required the Courts of Westminster in term time, and every judge in vacation, to grant the writ immediately, without excuse or evasion, and immediately proceed to examine and decide upon the cause of imprisonment. Another excellence was that, being the united act of King, Lords, and Commons, it could not be repealed, or superseded, or suspended in any manner, without the consent of all. Afterward, to be sure, James II asserted, and attempted to exercise, what was called a "dispensing" power—a power, namely, to dispense with the operation of an act of Parliament in the case of particular individuals. But this arbitrary assumption was rebuked, and forever put to rest, by the famous case of the Seven Bishops, 4 State Trials, 304, and cost King James the throne of his ancestors.

The Declaration of Rights adopted, as a solemn covenant, when William and Mary were called to the place from which James had been expelled, condemns the "dispensing power" in every shape and form; since which time, for now almost two hundred years, the writ of Habeas Corpus never has been refused, or successfully evaded, or trifled with, in England, except in pursuance of an act of Parliament suspending its privilege for a limited period, and in particular cases.*

Our act of Congress, entitled "An act to establish the Judicial Courts of the United States," approved September 24, 1789, declares:

"SECTION 14. That all the before-mentioned Courts of the United States shall have power to issue writs of Scire Facias, Habeas Corpus, and all other writs not specially provided for by statute, which may be necessary for the exercise of their respective jurisdictions, and agreeably to the principles and usages of law. And that either of the Justices of the Supreme Court, as well as Judges of the District Courts, shall have power to grant writs of Habeas Corpus for the purpose of an inquiry into the cause of commitment: *Provided*, That writs of Habeas Corpus shall, in no case, extend to prisoners in gaol, unless where they are in custody under or by color of the authority of the United States, or are committed for trial before some Court of the same, or are necessary to be brought into Court to testify." (U. S. Stat. at Large, vol. 1, pp. 81, 82.)

This act was construed by the Supreme Court of the United States in the case of Tobias Watkins, *ex parte*, 3 Peters, 193.

MARSHALL, C. J.—"No law of the United States prescribes the cases in which this great writ [Habeas Corpus] shall be issued, nor the

---

* Case of Leonard Watson and others, 9 Ad. and Ellis, 731; Crowley's case, 2 Swanston, 70, 71, 72; The King *v.* Hobhouse, 2 Chitty, 207.

Even the privilege of Parliament affords no protection against an attachment for disobeying the writ.—Rex *v.* Earl Ferrers, 1 Burrow, 631.

power of the Court over the party brought up by it. The term is used in the Constitution as one which was well understood; and the judicial act authorizes this Court, and all the Courts of the United States, and the judges thereof, to issue the writ for the purpose of inquiring into the cause of commitment. This general reference to a power which we are required to exercise, without any precise definition of that power, imposes on us the necessity of making some inquiries into its use according to that law which is, in a considerable degree, incorporated into our own. *The writ of Habeas Corpus is a high prerogative writ, known to the common law, the great object of which is the liberation of those who may be imprisoned without sufficient cause.* It is in the nature of a writ of error to examine THE LEGALITY of the commitment.

"The English judges, being originally under the influence of the Crown, neglected to issue this writ where the Government entertained suspicions which could not be sustained by evidence; and the writ, when issued, was sometimes disregarded or evaded, and great individual oppression was suffered in consequence of delays in bringing prisoners to trial. To remedy this evil, the celebrated Habeas Corpus Act of the 31st of Charles II was enacted, for the purpose of securing the benefit for which the writ was given. *This statute may be referred to as describing the cases in which relief is, in England, afforded by this writ to a person detained in custody.* IT ENFORCES THE COMMON LAW."

[Mr. Pugh then read from Blackstone's Commentaries, vol. 3, pp. 136, 137, 138, the several provisions of the act of 31 Charles II, ch. 2, known as the Habeas Corpus Act.]

And then, sir, we have an act of the Congress lately in session, entitled "An act relating to Habeas Corpus and regulating judicial proceedings in certain cases," approved March 3, 1863.

"SECTION 1. That, during the present rebellion, the President of the United States, whenever, in his judgment, the public safety may require it, is authorized to suspend the privilege of the writ of Habeas Corpus, in any case, throughout the United States, or any part thereof. And whenever and wherever the said privilege shall be suspended, as aforesaid, no military or other officer shall be compelled, in answer to any writ of Habeas Corpus, to return the body of any person or persons detained by him by authority of the President; but, upon the certificate, under oath, of the officer having charge of any one so detained by him, as a prisoner, under authority of the President, further proceedings under the writ of Habeas Corpus shall be suspended by the Judge or Court having issued the said writ, so long as said suspension by the President shall remain in force, and said rebellion continue."

This act does not apply, in terms, to the present case; and for the obvious reason that the President of the United States, in whom (solely) the discretion of suspending the privilege of the writ of Habeas Corpus now resides, has not found it necessary to adopt a measure so unusual and extreme. He can not exercise the authority thus conferred by a delegation of it to others: he must employ his own judgment, and in view of all the responsibilities of his great office. I take it for granted, also, that he will not decide a matter of such importance by writing a private letter, or sending a telegraphic dispatch: he ought to give notice by a formal proclamation, or in some manner equally authentic; so that all may be advised of the emergency, and govern themselves accordingly. For that is the true object of an executive proclamation. (12 Rep. 76.) But, even then, as we have seen, the writ must be issued: it is the *privilege* of the writ only, that is, the right to be discharged or admitted to bail, which the President may suspend, and not the right of demanding the writ. And the officer, military or civil, holding a prisoner by the President's immediate authority, must so certify under oath, as a return to the writ when issued; and, thereupon, proceedings are to be stayed, but the writ is not to be dismissed, and far less, in the first instance, wholly denied. If the oath should be a false one, the officer would be liable to an indictment for perjury, and, of course, would be convicted.

If this be the law, as clearly it is, when the privilege of the writ has been duly suspended, why must a prisoner languish in illegal confinement, day after day, and week after week, under peril of his life by a military sentence, at a time when the public safety does not, in the opinion of the President of the United States, require any obstruction of the ordinary course of justice?

Respectfully, therefore, but none the less firmly, in the discharge of my duty as an advocate, I deny the right of this Court to establish any rule of practice, in regard to the writ of Habeas Corpus, at all variant from the practice of the Courts of England in modern times. That subject has been passed upon, adjudicated, and conclusively determined by the Supreme Court of the United States as the tribunal of last resort.

The real question, and the only question, at present, is whether, upon the allegations of his petition, admitting them to be true, Clement L. Vallandigham is lawfully or unlawfully imprisoned.

I repeat, sir, that General Burnside does not deny those allegations, or any of them. On the contrary, in the statement which has been read, he says:

"These are substantially my reasons for issuing General Order No. 38, my reasons for the determination to enforce it, *and, also, my reasons for the arrest of the Hon. C. L. Vallandigham for a supposed violation of that order*, FOR WHICH HE HAS BEEN TRIED. The result of THAT trial is now in MY hands."

The case before us, then, is the case of a citizen exempted from military arrest and jurisdiction, but who has, nevertheless, been arbitrarily and violently subjected to them. Can this be, sir, according to the Constitution of the United States?

General Burnside assumes, throughout the statement which has been read, that *he* is charged, personally, and above all other citizens, with the maintenance of the Federal authority in this neighborhood—an assumption which, with proper respect to him, is most erroneous and unwarrantable. His duties, as a Major-General in the army, are undoubtedly extensive: far be it from me to speak lightly of them, or to detract, in any manner, from their importance. But they do not include many subjects to which, in this statement, he has invited our attention; and they can not excuse him for what he has done, and what he avows that he has done, in the case of the petitioner. And first, that we may have a distinct view of his duties, as well as of our own duties, I will read the preamble and enacting clause in virtue of which the Federal Government exists:

"WE, THE PEOPLE OF THE UNITED STATES, *in order to form a more perfect Union, establish justice, insure domestic tranquillity, provide for the common defense, promote the general welfare, and secure the blessings of* LIBERTY *to ourselves and our posterity*, do ordain and establish this CONSTITUTION for the United States of America."

There can be no UNION except as intended by that compact. The People have not agreed to any other; and, without their consent, it is impossible that any other should be legitimately established. The justice to be administered in this Court, and in all other tribunals, military and civil, must be such as the Constitution requires. Domestic tranquillity is a condition greatly to be envied; but it must be secured by observing the Constitution in letter and in spirit. General Burnside admonishes us of a certain "quietness" which might prevail as the consequence of enforcing his military order: I answer him that quietness attained by the sacrifice of our ancestral rights, by the destruction of our constitutional privileges, is worse than the worst degree of confusion and violence. Touch not the liberty of the citizen; and we, in Ohio, at least, will be unanimous. We may not concur as to the causes which induced so mighty a rebellion; we may differ as to the best methods of subduing or of mitigating it; we may quarrel as partisans, or even as factionists; but we will, nevertheless, with one accord, sustain the General in the darkest hour of his despondency as well as in the day of triumph—sustain him by our counsels, by all our means, and, if necessary, at the expense of our lives. But we can not give him our liberties. That sacrifice would be of no advantage to him; and it would render us and our posterity forever miserable. It is not necessary to the common defense; it would not—it can not—promote the common welfare.

I know that General Burnside affects to scorn these and all similar suggestions. "There is no fear," he asserts, "of the people *losing* their liberties"—but I will read his argument at large:

"There is no fear of the people losing their liberties; we all know that to be the cry of demagogues, and none but the ignorant will listen to it; all intelligent men know that our people are too far advanced in the scale of religion, civilization, education, and freedom, to allow any power on earth to interfere with their liberties; but this same advancement in these great characteristics of our people teaches them to make all necessary sacrifices for their country, when an emer gency requires."

I not only fear, but I am well assured by the examples of history, that our liberties can not survive a patient submission to arbitrary power. It is not the "cry" of demagogues: it is the voice of wisdom in all ages; it speaks to us from the tombs of an hundred republics, once happy, and proud, and confident of perpetuity. It is the watchword of patriots, and the testament of martyrs; it should be the first lesson of youth, the last injunction of the aged to their children. "ETERNAL VIGILANCE IS THE PRICE OF LIBERTY!" We can have it for no less, and upon no other terms. "Religion, Civilization, Education!" These do not supply the place of liberty at all; nor have they been found sufficient to preserve it. Other nations, living under despotic forms of government, are quite as religious, and quite as thoroughly civilized, as we are; some of them are much better educated. The rude Roman was free; the Roman of the highest civilization became an abject slave:

"Sævior armis,
Luxuria incubuit, victumque ulcisitur orbem."

I will not intrust my sacred birthright to any man—let him be ever so great or good—upon his promise that, by and by, when he shall have conquered an enemy, or put down a rebellion, he will give it back to me. He may take it without my consent; he may be so strong that I can not resist; these are misfortunes which I may not be able to avoid: but no words of flattery, no power on earth, can deceive me, or compel me into any measure of compliance. Better the sharpest pangs of death; or, sharper than death, a life of exile, and poverty, and constant hardship! Give me the crust of bread and the cup of water, with liberty, rather than the amplest luxury with servitude. Give me, instead of this genial climate, this fertile soil, this prosperous community, under an arbitrary government, the bleakest Arctic or Antarctic region, the almost insufferable winter, the night of one half-year in duration, the day which can hardly be called a day; but give me, withal, the consciousness—the proud, the noble, the priceless, the inexpressible consciousness—of being a free man!

Whenever General Burnside speaks, therefore, of the GOVERNMENT of the United States, I respond that such a Government exists only, and only can exist, in virtue of the Constitution. To that my allegiance and his allegiance are both due; by that I will stand firmly, and at all hazards; and in the name of that, uttering its very language, I now address him:

"Congress shall make no law respecting an establishment of religion, or prohibiting the free exercise thereof; or abridging the freedom of speech, or of the press, or the right of the people peaceably to assemble and to petition the Government for a redress of grievances."

General Burnside holds an office created by act of Congress alone—an office which Congress may, at any time, abolish. His title, his rank, his emoluments, his distinction above his fellow-citizens, are all derived from that source. I take it to be absolutely certain, therefore, that he can make no "law" which Congress could not make. He can not abridge the freedom of speech, or of the press, or the right of the people to assemble and to consider of their grievances. And yet, sir, of what does he accuse Mr. Vallandigham? Let the specification of Captain Cutts answer: Of having addressed a public assembly of the electors of Ohio, at Mount Vernon, in Knox County, on the first day of this month. Nothing more; nothing whatsoever. It was an assembly of the people to deliberate upon their grievances, and to advise with each other in what way those grievances could be redressed. Into that forum—the holiest of holy in our political system—has General Burnside intruded his military dictation. Need I say more? What avails a right of the people to assemble, or to consult of their public affairs, if, when assembled, and that peaceably, they have no freedom of speech?

General Burnside appears to think, because he can not behave with contempt or disrespect toward the President of the United States, that a similar restraint applies to every citizen. He forgets, possibly, that the President, as commander-in-chief of the army, is his superior in military rank; at all events, that is the reason governing his case. The President is protected, as against him, by the very words of the sixth Article of War:

"Any officer or soldier who shall behave himself with contempt or disrespect toward his commanding officer, shall be punished, according to the nature of his offense, by the judgment of a court-martial."

And so in respect of words written or spoken:

"ARTICLE 5. Any officer or soldier who shall use contemptuous or disrespectful words against the President of the United States, against the Vice-President thereof, against the Congress of the United States, or against the Chief Magistrate or Legislature of any of the United States in which he may be quartered, if a commissioned officer, shall be cashiered, or otherwise punished as a court-martial shall direct; if a non-commissioned officer, or soldier, he shall suffer such punishment as shall be inflicted on him by the sentence of a court-martial."

The General argues entirely, in the statement which has been read, from the premises of his own example. He commences by that

"If I were to indulge in wholesale criticisms of the policy of the Government, it would demoralize the army under my command, and every friend of his country would call me a traitor. If the officers or soldiers were to indulge in such criticisms, it would weaken the army to the extent of their influence; and if this criticism were universal in the army, it would cause it to be broken to pieces, the Government to be divided, our homes to be invaded, and anarchy to reign. My duty to my Government forbids me to indulge in such criticisms; officers and soldiers are not allowed to so indulge, and this course will be sustained by all honest men."

Assuredly so; and, therefore, such conduct as he reprobates can not be tolerated on the part of soldiers and military officers. But General Burnside has overlooked an essential fact in this connection. The Articles of War comprise a code for the regulation of soldiers and officers exclusively: that is declared by the first section of the act of Congress which ordains them, approved April 10, 1806. (U. S. Statutes at Large, vol. 2, p. 359.) It must be remembered, also, that those articles constitute an express contract between the Government of the United States as one party, and each soldier and each officer as the other party; and are, in law, obligatory as a contract. This can not be doubted after reading the famous opinion of Lord Loughborough, Chief-Justice, in Grant *v.* Gould, 2 H. Bla. 69. The soldier is enlisted by his own agreement; he has the articles read to him at that time, and he distinctly swears that he will obey them. (Article 10.) The officer—every officer—must sign the articles before entering upon his duties. (Article 1.) But neither as a statutory regulation, nor as a matter of contract, are citizens of the United States, other than those engaged in the military or the naval service, excluded from the privilege of speaking ever so disrespectfully, or contemptuously, of men in public station. It is, with them, entirely a matter of taste, or of individual discretion. I know of but a single excepted case: it is when the citizen has been called into the actual service of the United States as one of the militia of the State in which he resides. Then, sir, and for a reason too obvious to require any especial argument, his privilege as a mere citizen is temporarily suspended, and he becomes amenable to the Articles of War until discharged from such service. The Constitution expressly authorizes the Congress of the United States to ordain this as a part of the law of the land; and it is ordained by Congress, accordingly, in the 97th article:

"The officers and soldiers of any troops, whether militia or others, being mustered and in pay of the United States, shall, at all times, and in all places, when joined or acting in conjunction with the regular forces of the United States, be governed by these Rules and Articles of War, and shall be subject to be tried by courts-martial in like manner with the officers and soldiers in the regular forces;

save, only, that such courts-martial shall be composed entirely of militia officers."

I can not here, without abandoning the line of my argument, especially observe the language employed by Congress in this article; and much that I would say has occurred to others, probably, upon hearing it.

Beyond the terms of exception thus defined by statute, and in obedience to the Constitution of the United States, article first, section eighth, clauses fifteenth and sixteenth,* the right of the American people to deliberate upon and freely to speak of what General Burnside calls the "Policy of the Government" at all times—whether of peace or of war, of safety or of peril, of ease or of difficulty—is a right supreme, and absolute, and unquestionable. They can exhort each other to impeach the President or any executive officer; to impeach any magistrate of judicial authority; to condemn Congressmen and legislators of every description. They can, at pleasure, indulge in criticism, by "wholesale" or otherwise, not only upon "the policy" adopted or proposed by their servants, military as well as civil, but upon the conduct of those servants in each and every particular, upon their actions, their words, their probable motives, their public characters. And, in speaking of such subjects, any citizen addressing his fellow-citizens, by their consent, in a peaceable assembly, may use invective, or sarcasm, or ridicule, or passionate apostrophe or appeal, or—what is, ordinarily, much better—plain, solid, unostentatious argument. There is no style of rhetoric to be prescribed for the people. They are the masters of every style, and of every art and form of utterance. General Burnside suggests that "the press and public men, in a great emergency like the present, should avoid

* "To provide for calling forth the militia to execute the laws of the Union, suppress insurrections, and repel invasions.

"To provide for organizing, arming, and disciplining the militia, and for governing such part of them as may be employed in the service of the United States; reserving to the States, respectively, the appointment of the officers, and the authority of training the militia according to the discipline prescribed by Congress."

the use of party epithets and bitter invectives." I esteem that as excellent advice on all occasions; but, unfortunately, the General and I must both succumb, with what grace we can, to the choice or fancy of the people. They will render his advice or my advice effectual, if they approve it, by not reading such papers and not listening to such orators as habitually violate or trifle with decorum. There is no other way; there can be no censorship, civil or military, in this regard. That would inevitably, and at once, destroy the liberty of speech and of the press: that presupposes an incapacity of the people to distinguish right from wrong, truth from falsehood, reason from intemperance, or decency from outrage. And, if we can not confide in the good sense of the people as to these things, how can we confide in them at all?

I know that much is written and spoken every day, and in the most public manner, at which honorable men feel indignant, or, at least, annoyed. But does it really affect the people at large? Does it alienate them from the Government under which they live? Does it induce them to think less dearly of their kinsmen, their friends, their neighbors, in military service; or to be unmindful of the toils of any soldier in camp, or on the march, or of his sufferings in the awful day of battle? Does it palsy the ministering hand? Does it prevent the sympathizing tear? O, sir, no, no! General Burnside errs, and errs greatly, in supposing that. Our people are often excited by some false or foul word; but, by and by, assertion meets contradiction, violence encounters violence; and so, at length, slowly perhaps, but certainly, will justice achieve her victory, and conclude the contest.

I regret very much to learn, by one paragraph in his statement, that General Burnside can not appreciate the force of what all the great politicians of this country, in every generation, and with no distinction of parties, have unhesitatingly accepted as the fundamental doctrine of our system:

"It is said," he observes, "that the speeches which are condemned, have been in the presence of large bodies of citizens, who, if they thought them wrong, would have then and there condemned them. That is no argument."

I crave the General's pardon. That is an argument: it is the whole argument, and it is perfectly conclusive. Let us hear what he can say in opposition:

"These citizens do not realize the effect upon the army of our country, who are its defenders. They have never been in the field; never faced the enemies of their country; never undergone the privations of our soldiers in the field; and, besides, they have been in the habit of hearing their public men speak, and, as a general thing, of approving of what they say."

It is generally true that the majority of those who attend a public meeting approve the greater part of what is there said: they agreed substantially, if not entirely, before they came—and they came because they agreed. As to the speaker—in addition to the fact that much of what is said, in any meeting, is not objectionable—it should be remembered that his hearers have known him personally, or by reputation, for years; that they have probably voted for him, or, at all events, sustained him; that they admire his character and cherish his good name. He knows all this; and knows, therefore, that he must speak to them upon the confidence of honorable men. This obligation is not as rigidly observed as it should be; but I can say, as well of my opponents as of my friends, in Ohio, that the consciousness of being trusted by their fellow-partisans, together with a real desire to be worthy of such affection, is quite sufficient, ordinarily, to insure an honest, candid, and reasonably temperate discussion of political questions. I do not say that I agree with the conclusions of every speaker; but I say that he has declared what he honestly believes, and what a large majority of his hearers believed, or wished to believe, at all events, before they heard him. I can say, furthermore, that although it is not usual for an audience to contradict the speaker, they are apt to lose interest in him, and to depart summarily, when they discover that he is inimical to the cause of the country, to its essential glory, to the perpetuity of its free institutions.

But, perhaps, I have not yet sufficiently answered General Burnside's objection. I ask him, then, whether he means to argue that citizens who have not experienced military service—"never been in the field, never faced the enemies of their country, never undergone the privations of our soldiers"—are, on that account, so devoid of intelligence, so spiritless in patriotism, that they can not be trusted to discharge their duties at home, as citizens, in the way to which they and their fathers before them, for almost a century, have been accustomed? If so, what becomes of his other assertion, in a later paragraph, "that our people are too far advanced in the scale of religion, civilization, education, and freedom, to allow any power on earth to interfere with their liberties."

O!—but the effect on the soldiers. Well, sir, let us inquire into that. The soldiers have been citizens; they have been in the habit of attending public meetings, and of listening to public speakers. They are not children, but grown men—stalwart, sensible, and gallant men—with their hearts in the right place, and with arms ready to strike whenever and wherever the cause of their country demands. The General assures us of more, even, than this: "No man on earth," he says, "can lead our citizen-soldiery to the establishment of a military despotism." And are these the men to be discouraged, and, especially, to feel weary in heart or limb—unable to cope with an enemy in the field—because Mr. Vallandigham, or any other public speaker, may have said something, at Mount Vernon or elsewhere, with which they do not agree? The soldiers have not chosen me for their eulogist; but I will say, of my own accord, that they are no such tender plants as General Burnside imagines. They know, exactly, for what they went into the field; they are not alarmed, nor dissatisfied, nor discouraged, because their fellow-citizens, at home, attend public meetings, and listen to public speeches, as heretofore; they have no serious misgiving as to the estimation in which they are holden by the people of the Northern and North-western States, without any distinction of sects, parties, or factions.

Let the officers, and especially those of highest degree, observe their military duties; let them see to it, as General Burnside has well said, and as, I doubt not, he has well done, so far as his authority extends, that the soldiers are "fed, clad, and armed," and kept "in the best possible condition" for service. Allow them to vote as they please; allow them to read whatever newspapers they like; cease any attempt to use them for a partisan advantage: I do not accuse General Burnside of this—but others, and too many, have been guilty of the grossest tyranny in regard to it. Protect the soldier against the greed of jobbers and knavish contractors—against dealers in shoddy, in rotten leather, in Belgian muskets, in filthy bread and meat—against all the hideous cormorants which darken the sky and overshadow the land in times of military preparation. Let the party in administration discharge these duties; and my word for it, sir, that the volunteers from Ohio, from Indiana, from Illinois, from every other State, will do and dare as much, at least, as the best and bravest soldiers in the world can accomplish.

One more commentary on the statement of General Burnside, and it shall be as brief as possible. Undoubtedly, as he observes, a great responsibility attaches to public men and to the conductors of the public press; but their responsibility is toward the people, and not toward him. "They must not," he declares, "they must not use license, and plead that they are exercising liberty." But every definition of "liberty" excludes the idea of his censorship; so that the distinction which he has attempted neither expresses nor admits of any imaginable difference.

I might say more, and much more, of this extraordinary statement; but having disposed of its principal suggestions, I leave the rest unanswered.

The "charge" against Mr. Vallandigham, as defined by Captain Cutts, the Judge-Advocate, is this:

> "Publicly expressing, in violation of General Orders No. 38, from Head-quarters Department of the Ohio, his sympathy for those in arms against the Government of the United States, declaring disloyal sentiments and opinions, with the object and purpose of weakening the power of the Government in its efforts to suppress an unlawful rebellion."

But the "charge" is only a conclusion supposed, or invented, by the Judge-Advocate, from the premises of fact alleged in the specification. I have merely to say, therefore, that it assumes, as indisputable, an authority at "Head-quarters Department of the Ohio" to enact a LAW abridging the freedom of speech; and this in palpable defiance of the Constitution of the United States. Let us proceed, however, to the language of the specification:

"In this, that the said Clement L. Vallandigham, *a citizen of the State of Ohio*, on or about the first day of May, 1863, at Mount Vernon, Knox County, Ohio, did publicly address a large meeting of citizens, and did utter sentiments in words, or in effect, as follows."

One or the other—"in words, or in effect"—as the Judge-Advocate, at his pleasure, may regard equivalents. And here follows no connected form of speech, but merely disjointed phrases and sentences, taken from the context of a public address, and with no relation to what preceded, or accompanied, or otherwise explained or mitigated them. Is that the style of accusation by which, in this country, or in any civilized country, a man is put in peril of his life or his liberty? Is that the way in which my learned friend, the District Attorney of the United States, would think of indicting a prisoner? But I will read the sentences which, "in words, or in effect," are so eminently disloyal. Mr. Vallandigham, as we are told, declared "the present war" to be "a wicked, cruel, and unnecessary war." And so President Lincoln, by one of his proclamations, declares it "unnecessary" as well as injurious; and is not every "unnecessary" war both cruel and wicked? I do not say on which side, or to which of the two parties, a condemnation thus grievous should be wholly, or for the most part, applied; I will speak to that question, if at all, when I have not in charge the interests of an imprisoned client. But Mr. Vallandigham said, in addition, that it is "a war not being waged for the preservation of the Union." Observe those words carefully; they do not mean that "the preservation of the Union" is not the avowed object, nor even that the Administration may not so intend, but only that the war is "not being waged" in such a manner as to accomplish the object. Again, as we are told, he declared it to be "a war for the purpose of crushing out liberty and erecting a despotism." Well, if the proceedings in his case, in virtue of General Orders No. 38, are to become a precedent for other cases, and to be sustained by judicial authority, that declaration will prove to be substantially true. But he said, also, that it is "a war for the freedom of the blacks, and the enslavement of the whites." We know that President Lincoln has, by two proclamations, dated September 22, 1862, and January 1, 1863, undertaken, "as a fit and necessary war measure," to emancipate millions of black slaves; whether he intends, if possible, to enslave white men, will be ascertained when he shall have acted on this particular case.

Mr. Vallandigham said, furthermore, as the Judge-Advocate assures us, "that, if the Administration had so wished, the war could have been honorably terminated months ago." That allegation may be true; I have no means, except from what is alleged subsequently, of deciding whether it be true or false. Nor do I find myself much enlightened by the next sentence imputed to Mr. Vallandigham: that "peace might have been honorably obtained by listening to the proposed intermediation of France." I do not know what terms, if any, the Emperor of the French suggested; but they would have to be very advantageous, as well as unmistakably honorable, before I would consent to his interference, or the interference of any other monarch, with the affairs of our distracted republic. And yet, if Mr. Vallandigham thinks otherwise, he has the same right to declare and to maintain his opinion as I have to maintain or to declare mine. But he made another accusation, and of much more serious importance: he said "that propositions by which the Southern States could be won back, and the South be guaranteed their rights under the Constitution, had been rejected, the day before the late battle at Fredericksburg, by Lincoln and his minions"—"meaning thereby," as the Judge-Advocate kindly informs us, "the President of the United States and those under him in authority." I never heard that it was actionable, at common law, to say of one man, orally, that he was the minion of another; and, far less, that it could be a matter of State prosecution. As to the rest, the accusation is one of fact—positive, distinct, with addition of time and circumstances. Is it true, or is it false? Sir, I do not know; but I do know that *that* is a vital question to the American people. Was it for making such an accusation that Mr. Vallandigham has been arrested; and is it by imprisoning him, or otherwise stopping his mouth, that Mr. Lincoln would answer to such an accusation in the face of his countrymen, of the civilized world, of the tribunal of God and of history? As to General Burnside, whose personal sincerity in these proceedings, as well as at the battle of Fredericksburg, I do not intend to question, what living man is more interested to have the truth, or the falsehood, of that accusation publicly ascertained?

The next sentence imputed to Mr. Vallandigham, by the specification, is this: "That the Government of the United States were about to appoint military marshals, in every district, to restrain the people of their liberties, to deprive them of their rights and privileges." That refers to the appointment of a Provost Marshal in each Congressional district, as provided in the act of March 3, 1863, commonly called the Conscription Act. I have no time, at present, to argue whether the act be, or be not, open to such interpretation; but I have to say this: Mr. Vallandigham not only voted against it, while a Representative in the Congress of the United States, but characterized it more severely, more harshly, more bitterly, in a speech delivered to the House of Representatives, on the 23d day of February, 1863. Did the House regard his words, on that occasion, as words which, by the dictionary of General Burnside, "must now amount to treason." He was not expelled; he was not censured; he was not even accused of having overstepped the limits of his privilege as a Representative; but when he returned to his constituents (for every Representative in Congress, although chosen by the people of a district, represents the whole State) he is not allowed, in giving them an account of his stewardship, to repeat such language as he uttered, without any

5

objection, in the hearing of the President, of the Cabinet, of the two houses of Congress, of the General commanding the whole army, of the Army of the Rappahannock almost immediately at hand.

Then, sir, as we are told, Mr. Vallandigham spoke of General Order No. 38, Head-quarters Department of the Ohio, as "a base usurpation of arbitrary authority." Well, except the first adjective, which is a flower of speech in reference to which, considering his own style of rhetoric, in the charge and specification before us, I should hardly have expected any complaint on the part of the Judge-Advocate, those words are literally true. It is authority usurped, because it is contrary to the Constitution and laws of the land; and that it is arbitrary, *ex vi termini*, appears from the whole tenor of General Burnside's statement. But Mr. Vallandigham invited his "hearers to *resist* the same." Ah!—and how? By telling them to take up arms against it?—to fall into ranks for the purpose of obstructing its execution?—by committing any act of violence or disorder whatsoever? O, no, sir!—but "by saying" that "the sooner the people inform the minions of usurped power that they will not submit to such restrictions upon their liberties the better." To give this information by their resolutions in primary meetings, by the voices of their favorite orators, by their votes in the ballot-box. Nothing else is alleged; nothing else is pretended; nothing else could reasonably have been imagined. I quote the remaining sentences:

"Declaring 'that he was, at all times, and upon all occasions, resolved to do what he could to defeat the attempts now being made to build up a monarchy upon the ruins of our free government.'

"Asserting 'that he firmly believed, as he said six months ago, that the men in power are attempting to establish a despotism in this country, more cruel and more oppressive than ever existed before.'"

These are obviously conclusions of the speaker—correctly or incorrectly drawn—from premises of which little, very little indeed, is narrated by the specification. I do not undertake to say, and I can not say, at present, whether such conclusions are correct or incorrect; but what are they—and, in asking this question, I would lay my hand, if possible, upon the heart of every freeman—what are they but the impassioned appeals of a sincere, conscientious, honorable, and, if you please, over-vigilant citizen? Granted—if you will have it so—that he is in error, and greatly in error: I do not ask you to approve his conclusions, or in any manner to accept his opinions; but I do ask you, in all truthfulness, whether these words bear any taint of treason or disloyalty? They were intended, most evidently, to arouse the people to a sense of the vast peril in which all of us now stand; and, although they are startling, and seem very bitter, should we not err upon the side of jealousy rather than upon the side of laxity and too much confidence in our rulers, at a time when, month by month, day by day, the Union of our fathers, the Constitution by which that Union was ordained, and the Liberty of which the Constitution and the Union were intended as perpetual guarantees, are fading into a dim, a broken, and a most sorrowful vision?

Mr. Judge-Advocate appears to have felt the difficulty of sustaining his "charge" upon the words, simply, as quoted in his specification. He has added to them, therefore, this remarkable conclusion:

> "All of which opinions and sentiments he well knew did aid, comfort, and encourage those in arms against the Government, and could but induce in his hearers a distrust of their own Government and sympathy for those in arms against it, and a disposition to resist the laws of the land."

Here is what lawyers would call the *scienter* of an offense—the imputation, that is, of guilty knowledge. But, clearly, unless the words themselves, simply as spoken, have the effect of aiding, comforting, and encouraging those in arms against the Government, and of inducing such as hear them, at any time, not only to distrust the Government, but, also, to sympathize with those in arms against it, or, at all events, to resist the laws of the land, no guilt ever existed, and there could be, of course, no knowledge of any such guilt. Now, as to those in arms, not one of them attended the meeting at Mount Vernon, or would have known of Mr. Vallandigham's speech on that occasion, but for the arrest and imprisonment which ensued. In the next place, although his language may have induced (as he had the perfect right, if he could, to induce) all his hearers to distrust the persons who are now administering the Government of the United States, and to seize the first constitutional opportunity of putting other persons into their places, I can not, for the life of me, discover one syllable directed against the "Government" as such, and far less—that being necessary, also, by the terms of the Judge-Advocate's conclusion—inducing the slightest degree of sympathy for those who, anterior to the transactions of which Mr. Vallandigham spoke, and without any regard to the grievances which he enumerated, but wholly for excuses of their own, and manifestly against his wishes, had openly and formidably arrayed themselves in rebellion. And so, even admitting General Order No. 38 to be, as certainly it is not, a part of the law of the land, no resistance whatsoever was suggested except by the ordeal of a peaceable election.

The burden of complaint, therefore, as to Mr. Vallandigham, is, that he opposes, whether for a good reason or a bad one, the prosecution of this war; that he is greatly dissatisfied with the manner in which it has been conducted; that he believes, with or without sufficient evidence, that it might have been brought to an "honorable" conclusion—"by which the Southern States could be won back"—months ago; and that, consequently, he is in favor of electing other men than those at present in office to administer our public affairs. That is all; standing upon the very words quoted in Captain Cutts's specification—garbled even as they are—I repeat, sir, that is all. And for the supposed offense of entertaining such opinions, and of declaring them to an audience of his fellow-citizens, by their request, at Mount Vernon, has Mr. Vallandigham experienced the tender mercy of General Orders No. 38; the outer and inner doors of his dwelling-house have been violently battered and broken, between midnight and day-dawning, by a multitude of soldiers, without any warrant or even color of legal process; his person has been seized by overpowering numbers, in the presence of his terrified family, and secretly hurried to this city and here confined in a military prison, in order to his trial by a "Commission" of army officers, and according to some hitherto unknown course of judicial procedure. And this, America, is thy boasted freedom! Verily, to accept the consolation of General Burnside, thou needst have no "fear" of losing it.

Since what time, I would inquire, has it become an offense of such magnitude for any citizen to propose the cessation of a war which he believes to be unnecessary and injurious? I am not advised of any alteration of our Federal Constitution since the 22d of February, 1848, when the General Assembly of Ohio adopted resolutions denouncing President Polk for his prosecution of the war against Mexico, and calling upon Congress to withhold further supplies of money and of men. I will read those resolutions as they appear in the statute-book, Local Laws, vol. 46, page 299:

"That the State of Ohio repudiates, as a libel upon the Constitution of the United States, the degrading and pernicious dogma which asserts that when the nation is once involved in a war with a foreign country, no matter by what means or for what ends, it is the prerogative of the President to determine the purposes for which it shall thenceforth be carried on, and the measure of its duration.

"That Congress does possess, and may exercise, the right to interfere with this kingly attribute when asserted or claimed by the President; and that it can never be the duty of the representatives of the States and of the people tamely and submissively to bow to the dictates of Executive will, and humbly to subserve its behests by transcribing into the form of legal enactments the imperious requisitions of the President for supplies of money and of men.

"That when an administration shall have become so reckless of the moral sentiment of the nation that, lured by the lust of personal or even of national aggrandizement, it avowedly prosecutes and procrastinates a war for the purpose of wringing from a reluctant adversary, already prostrate and in the dust, the whole or any portion of his rightful territory, it becomes the imperative duty of Congress, upon the failure for that purpose of all other constitutional means, to put a stop to the effusion of blood by withholding all supplies for the further prosecution of the war; and doubly imperative does that duty become when, as in the case of the present contest with Mexico, the war was begun for questionable objects, by a most palpable Executive usurpation of power, and, more especially, when the acquisition of the coveted territory would most fearfully threaten the disruption of the Union itself."

War existed then, as it exists now; the same bitterness of crimination and recrimination prevailed; designs at once arbitrary and unconstitutional were imputed to those in power by their political opponents, and were answered, as at present, by charges of treason, disloyalty, and so forth. But no man was arrested, or even called to account for his opinions, by the civil, and, far less, by the military power.

How is it possible—I would ask General Burnside, or his counsel, in view as well of the statement which has been read as of the order (No. 38) therein mentioned—how is it possible that words, merely as such, should "amount" to treason? The crime requires an overt act; and not only must the particular act be charged in the indictment, but it must be proven, as charged, by the concurrent oath of two witnesses. Jefferies told the jury, in Algernon Sidney's case, 3 State Trials, 817, that writing a letter was an overt act, "sufficient to prove a man guilty of high treason," for that to write is to act—"*scribere est agere*"—but even he had not the audacity to pretend that words spoken would, by themselves, be sufficient. Sir Matthew Hale, discoursing upon the Statute of Treason, 25 Edward III, says:

"Regularly, words, unless they are committed to writing, are not an overt act within this statute; and the reason given is because they are easily subject to be mistaken, or misapplied, or misrepeated, or misunderstood by the hearers.

"And this appears by those several acts of Parliament which were temporary only, or made some words of a high nature to be but felony. The statute of 3 H. 7, cap. 14, makes conspiring the king's death to be felony; which it would not have done if the bare conspiring, without an overt act, had been treason." (1 P. C. 111, 112.)

Again:

"Words may expound an overt act to make good an indictment of treason of compassing the king's death; which overt act possibly, of itself, may be indifferent, and unapplicable to such an intent. And, therefore, in the indictment of treason, they may be joined with such an overt act, to make the same applicable, and expositive of such a compassing." (1 P. C. 115.)

To this effect, only, is the instruction of Lord Chief-Justice Holt to the jury in the case of Charnock, King, and Keyes, 4 State Trials, 593.

I read now from the Institutes of Sir Edward Coke:

"Divers latter acts of Parliament have ordained that compassing, by bare words or sayings, should be high treason; but all they are either repealed or expired. And it is commonly said that bare words may make an heretick, but not a traytor without an overt act. And the wisdome of the makers of this law [25 Edw. III] would not make words only to be treason; seeing such variety amongst the witnesses are, about the same, as few of them agree together." (3 Inst. 14.)

And he glorifies the statute of 1st Mary, sess. 1, ch. 1, as declaring the true intent of the statute of 25th Edward III. on this subject: that there must be an overt act, and not merely words—*per apertum factum, non per apertum dictum.*

Sir William Blackstone says:

"How far mere words spoken by an individual, and not relative to any treasonable act or design then in agitation, shall amount to treason, has been formerly matter of doubt. We have two instances, in the reign of Edward the Fourth, of persons executed for treasonable words; the one a citizen of London, who said he would make his son heir of the Crown, being the sign of the house in which he lived; the other a gentleman whose favorite buck the king killed in hunting, whereupon he wished it, horns and all, in the king's belly. These were esteemed hard cases; and the Chief-Justice Markham rather chose to leave his place than assent to the latter judgment. But *now* it seems clearly to be agreed that, by the common law and the statute of Edward III, words spoken amount only to a high misdemeanor, and no treason. For they may be spoken in heat, without any intention, or be mistaken, perverted, or misremembered by the hearers; their meaning depends always on their connection with other words and things; they may signify differently even according to the tone of voice with which they are delivered, and sometimes silence itself is more expressive than any discourse. As, therefore, there can be nothing more equivocal and ambiguous than words, it would, indeed, be unreasonable to make them amount to high treason. And, accordingly, in 4 Car. I, on a reference to all the judges, concerning some very atrocious words spoken by one Pyne, they certified to the king that, though the words were as wicked as might be, yet they were no treason; *for, unless it be by some particular statute, no words will be treason.*" (4 Comm. 80.)

And Sir Michael Foster, agreeing to the same doctrine, thus comments on two statutes of Queen Anne's time (4 Ann. ch. 3, and 6 Ann. ch. 7) for the punishment of such as "maliciously and directly, by preaching, teaching, or advised speaking," should deny her royal title:

"1. The positions condemned by them had as direct a tendency to involve these nations in the miseries of an intestine war, to incite her majesty's subjects to withdraw their allegiance from her, and to deprive her of her crown and royal dignity, as any general doctrine and declaration, not relative to actions or designs, could possibly have; and yet, in the case of bare words, positions of this dangerous tendency, though maintained maliciously, advisedly, and directly, and even in the solemnities of preaching and teaching, are not considered as overt acts of treason.

"2. In no case can a man be *argued* into the penalties of the acts by inferences and conclusions drawn from what he hath affirmed. The criminal position must be *directly* maintained, to bring him within the compass of these acts.

"3. Nor will every rash, hasty, or unguarded expression, owing, perhaps, to natural warmth, or thrown out in the heat of disputation, render any person criminal within these acts; the criminal doctrine must be maintained *maliciously* and *advisedly.*

"Such caution did the Legislature use in framing these statutes, made in the zeal of the times—a most laudable zeal it was—for purposes of no less importance than the security of her then majesty's person and government, and of the succession to the crown in his present majesty's royal house—a caution formerly used in similar cases, and not unworthy of imitation in framing future acts of the like kind, if any such shall be thought necessary, and which may serve as a faithful monitor in the conduct of prosecutions for words or writings supposed to be treasonable, but not relative to any treasonable measure then on foot, or intended to be taken." (Foster's Discourse of High Treason, ch. 1, sec. 7.)

Sidney was prosecuted upon the clause of the English statute (25 Edw. III) which defines compassing of the king's death; and, as appears from the language of Hale, Coke, and Blackstone, already quoted, it was only in cases arising upon *that* clause—few as the cases are, and of no authority—that even the worst judges, in the very worst times, pretended to regard the speaking of words as an overt act of treason.

Our Federal Constitution, article third and section third, employs this plain language:

"Treason against the United States shall consist ONLY in levying war against them, or in adhering to their enemies, giving them aid and comfort.

"No person shall be convicted of treason, unless on the testimony of two witnesses to the same overt act, or on confession in open Court."

Two definitions are intended here, and both taken from the English statute: first, levying war; second, adhering to public enemies, giving them aid and comfort.

As to the latter, it has no reference to any rebellion or insurrection; but only applies in a time of war with some other nation. So it was decided by this Court in Chenoweth's case, at April term, 1862, after examining all the authorities, English and American, and ascertaining them to be unanimous on the subject.

At present, therefore, treason can not be committed against the United States in any other manner than by "LEVYING WAR" against them. (U. S. *v.* Hoxie, 1 Paine, 269.) I do not allege that each conspirator must have joined the warlike array; but I do allege that no prisoner can be convicted, or even charged, except by proving, or charging, what the law denominates an "overt" act. And what are *such* acts, in legal contemplation, Mr. Justice Foster has clearly defined in his Discourse of High Treason, ch. 2, sec. 8:

"The joining with rebels in an act of rebellion, or with enemies in acts of hostility, will make a man a traitor; in the one case, within the clause of levying war; in the other, within that of adhering to the king's enemies."

"Furnishing rebels or enemies with money, arms, ammunition, or other necessaries, will, *prima facie*, make a man a traitor. But if enemies or rebels come with a superior force, and exact contributions, or live upon the country at free quarter, submission in these cases is not criminal."

"And the bare sending money or provisions, except in the case just excepted, or sending intelligence to rebels or enemies, which, in most cases, is the most effectual aid that can be given them, will make a man a traitor, though the money or intelligence should happen to be intercepted. For the party, in sending, did all he could: the treason was complete on his part, though it had not the effect he intended."

As to this, however, the learned author next intimates some degree of uncertainty; inasmuch as in all the reported cases, before his time, the prisoners had been charged, also, with compassing the queen's death.

Again, same chapter, sections 9, 10, and 11:

"An assembly armed and arrayed in a warlike manner, for any treasonable purpose, is *bellum levatum*"—war levied—"though not *bellum percussum*. Listing and marching are sufficient overt acts, without coming to a battle or action. So, cruising on the king's subjects, under a French commission, France being then at war with us, was holden to be adhering to the king's enemies, though no other act of hostility was laid or proved.

"Attacking the king's forces, *in opposition to his authority*, upon a march, or in quarters, is levying war against the king. But if, upon a sudden quarrel, from some affront given or taken, the neighborhood should rise and drive the forces out of their quarters, that would be a great misdemeanor, and, if death should ensue, it may be felony in the assailants; but it will not be treason, because there was no intention against the king's person or government.

"Holding a castle or fort against the king or his forces, if actual force be used in order to keep possession, is levying war. But a bare detainer, as suppose by shutting the gates against the king or his forces, without any other force from within, Lord Hale conceiveth (1 P. C. 146) will not amount to treason. But, if this be done *in confederacy with* enemies, or rebels, that circumstance will make it treason; in the one case, under the clause of adhering to the king's enemies; in the other, under that of levying war. So, if a person, having the custody of a castle or fort, deliver it up to the rebels, or enemies, *by treachery and in combination with them*, this is high treason within the act: in the former case, it is levying war; in the latter, it is adhering to the king's enemies."

Once more, in the same chapter, section 13:

"In prosecutions for these treasons, as well as for that of compassing the death of the king, an overt act of the treason must, as I have already observed, be charged in the indictment, and proved."

No act of less degree than those just enumerated, and no act which does not *immediately* relate to an assemblage of men, in warlike array, for the purpose of subverting the Government, or, by such means, resisting its authority, can amount to the levying of war. So said the Supreme Court of the United States in the case of Bollman and Swartwout, 4 Cranch, 126:

"However flagitious may be the crime of conspiring to subvert, by force, the Government of our country, such conspiracy is not treason. To *conspire* to levy war, and *actually* to levy war, are distinct offenses. The first must be brought into open action by the assemblage of men for a purpose treasonable in itself, or the fact of levying war can not have been committed. So far has this principle been carried that, in a case reported by Ventris, and mentioned in some modern treatises on criminal law, it has been determined that the actual enlistment of men to serve against the Government does not amount to levying war. It is true that, in that case, the soldiers enlisted were to serve without the realm, but they were enlisted within it; and, if the enlistment for a treasonable purpose could amount to levying war, then war had been actually levied.

"It is not the intention of the Court to say that no individual can be guilty of this crime who has not appeared in arms against his country. On the contrary, if war be actually levied, that is, if a body of men be actually assembled for the purpose of effecting by force a treasonable purpose, all those who perform any part, however minute, or however remote from the scene of action, *and who are actually leagued in the general conspiracy*, are to be considered as traitors. But there must be an actual assembling of men for the treasonable purpose to constitute a levying of war."

Again:

"To complete the crime of levying war against the United States, there must be an actual assemblage of men for the purpose of executing a treasonable design. In the case now before the Court, a design to overturn the Government of the United States in New Orleans, by force, would have been unquestionably a design which, if carried into execution, would have been treason; and the assemblage of a body of men for the purpose of carrying it into execution would amount to levying of war against the United States. But no *conspiracy* for this object, *no enlisting of men to effect it*, would be an *actual* levying of war." (4 Cranch, 127.)

Mr. Chief-Justice Marshall, who delivered this opinion, explained it, afterward, upon the trial of Aaron Burr, before the Circuit Court, at Richmond, August 31, 1807:

"Some gentlemen have argued as if the Supreme Court had adopted the whole doctrine of the English books on the subject of accessories to treason. But, certainly, such is not the fact. *Those* ONLY *who perform a part*, AND WHO ARE LEAGUED IN THE CONSPIRACY, *are declared to be traitors*. To complete the definition, both circumstances must concur. They must perform a part, *which will furnish the overt act*, and they must be leagued in the conspiracy. The person who comes within this description, in the opinion of the Court, levies war." (Burr's Trial, vol. 2, page 406.)

And he proceeded, at length, to demonstrate that even "the advising or procurement" of treason, unless the party had *also* joined the warlike array, or done some overt act *in pursuance* of the conspiracy, would not amount to levying war. (2 Burr's Trial, 436, 437, 438, 439.)

How superfluous, then, is that portion of General Orders No. 38 which denounces the penalty of death for an overt act of treason! The same penalty has been denounced by the Constitution of the United States, and by the laws of Congress in pursuance of it; only, instead of a military arrest, of charges and specifications, of a trial by captains, lieutenants, or other officers, and upon rules of evidence which are in effect no rules at all, the party accused must be arrested by a warrant in due form, upon probable cause supported by oath or affirmation—must be indicted by a grand jury of the district in which the crime is supposed to have been committed—must be tried in the Circuit Court of the United States for that district, by a petit jury of his countrymen, and according tô the rule of evidence which the Constitution itself has prescribed. For so the Constitution, article third, section second, clause third, expressly requires:

> "The trial of ALL crimes, except in cases of impeachment, shall be by jury; and such trial shall be held in the State where the said crimes shall have been committed; but when not committed within any State, the trial shall be at such place or places as the Congress may, *by law*, have directed."

As to the residue of General Orders No. 38, including "the habit of declaring sympathies for the enemy," if such a "habit" ever existed in this community or neighborhood, I must say, once for all, that the acts or utterances intended to be embraced, whatever their moral complexion, or how objectionable soever in any respect, do not and can not amount to treason. The Constitution of the United States forbids that as plainly as language can be written.

And the Constitution is full of wisdom in this regard. It does not even intrust to CONGRESS the definition of a crime so perilous, so easily imputed, so apt to be imputed in times of great disorder. It even restrains Congress in prescribing the measure of punishment.* The bloody experience of their English ancestors, commencing with the civil war between the adherents of Stephen and those of the Empress Matilda, before the middle of the twelfth century, and extending thence, with brief intermissions, almost to the epoch of American independence, had sufficiently admonished the people of the eleven States which consented to the establishment of a UNION consecrated to Civil and Religious Liberty, that they must incorporate in its organical law, as things unalterable and unavoidable, in any circumstances, as well the provisions of the statute defining treason, 25 Edward III, as the provisions of Magna Charta and of the Habeas Corpus Act. I call upon the writers of "The Federalist" to bear me witness of this:

"As treason may be committed against the United States, the authority of the United States ought to be enabled to punish it; but, *as new-fangled and artificial treasons have been the great engines by which violent factions*, the natural offspring of free governments, *have usually wreaked their alternate malignity on each other*, the Convention have, with great judgment, opposed a barrier to this peculiar danger by inserting a constitutional definition of the crime, fixing the proof necessary for conviction of it, and restraining the Congress, even in punishing it, from extending the consequences of guilt beyond the person of its author." (*Federalist, No.* 43, written by Madison.)

Such admonition, also, the sages of the Common Law had previously, and most heartily, delivered. Lord Chief-Justice Hale, after speaking of the diversities of judicial opinion before the statute of 25 Edward III, and the consequent unhappy condition of the people, says:

"Now, although the crime of high treason is the greatest crime against faith, duty, and human society, and brings with it the greatest and most fatal dangers to the government, peace and happiness of a kingdom or State, and therefore is deservedly branded with the

---

* "Congress shall have power to declare the punishment of treason; but no attainder of treason shall work corruption of blood, or forfeiture, except during the life of the person attainted."

highest ignominy, and subjected to the greatest penalties that the law can inflict; yet, by these instances, and more of this kind that might be given, it appears: First, how necessary it was that there should be some fixed and settled boundary for this great crime of treason, and of what great importance the statute of 25 Edward III was in order to that end. Second, how dangerous it is to depart from the letter of that statute, and to multiply and enhance crimes into treason by ambiguous and general words, as accroaching of royal power, subverting of fundamental laws, and the like. And, third, how dangerous it is by construction and analogy to make treasons where the letter of the law has not done it. *For such a method admits of no limits or bounds, but runs as far as the wit and invention of accusers, and the odiousness and detestation of persons accused, will carry men.*" (1 P. C. 86, 87.)

And Lord Chief-Justice Coke tells us (3 Inst. 2) that the Parliament which enacted the statute was called, on that account, the Blessed Parliament—BENEDICTUM PARLIAMENTUM.

But, sir, what become of our safeguards—what avails the experience of seven hundred years—where is that CONSTITUTION which declares itself to be the supreme law of the land—if a Major-General commanding the Department of the Ohio, or any other officer, civil or military, can create and multiply definitions of treason at his pleasure? The ancient Ruminalis put forth new leaves when all men supposed it to be dying;* whether the tree of American liberty will be able to supply the place of that splendid foliage which has been stripped from its branches, and scattered beneath our feet, by this rude blast of arbitrary and unlimited authority, is a question hereafter to be determined. That question does not concern my distinguished client any more than it concerns every other citizen. The partisans in power to-day will be the partisans in opposition to-morrow; then military command will be shifted from those who oppress to those who have been oppressed; and so, with

---

* "Eodem anno (A. U. C. 811) Ruminalem arborem in comitio, quæ octingentos et quadraginta ante annos Remi Romulique infantiam texerat, mortuis ramalibus et arescente trunco deminutam prodigii loco habitum est, donec in novos fetus revivesceret." TACITUS: Ann. Lib. XIII, 58.

the mutations of political fortune, must the personal rights and rights of property, and even the lives, of all be in constant hazard. I pray that my learned friends upon the other side will consider this in time; that they will use their influence not only with the defendant, but with those to whom at present he is amenable, to revoke—ere it be too late—the dreadful fiat of tyranny, of hopeless confusion, of ultimate anarchy, which has been sounded in our midst.

May it please your Honor! Although the argument on the part of the petitioner might well be concluded here, I am nevertheless under the necessity, from his instruction, of commenting upon another article of the Constitution of the United States:

"The right of the people to be secure in their persons, houses, papers, and effects, against unreasonable searches and seizures, shall not be violated; and no warrants shall issue but upon probable cause, supported by oath or affirmation, and particularly describing the place to be searched, and the persons or things to be seized."

This declares, first, as an *universal* prohibition, that no man's house—it being his castle and place of abode—shall be entered, nor his person, or papers, or effects be seized, at the pleasure of any individual whomsoever. Such an entry or seizure, unless it can be justified or, at least, excused by the authority of the law, is a trespass; for which the party aggrieved is entitled to his action of damages, and which is punishable, also, by indictment. An act of the General Assembly of Ohio, passed on the 8th of March, 1831, declares:

"SECTION 1. That if any person shall, in the night season, unlawfully break open and enter any mansion-house, shop, store, ship, boat or other water-craft, in which any person shall reside or dwell, and shall commit, or attempt to commit, any personal violence or abuse, or shall be so armed with any dangerous weapon as to indicate a violent intention, the person so offending shall, upon conviction thereof, be fined in any sum not exceeding three hundred dollars and be imprisoned in the cell or dungeon of the jail of the county, and be fed on bread and water only, not exceeding thirty days, at the discretion of the Court."

The second section declares the unlawful breaking open and entering, "in the day time," of any mansion-house, shop, etc., "in which any person shall or may dwell or reside," to be an offense punishable by a fine not exceeding one hundred dollars, and by imprisonment in the cell or dungeon of the jail of the county, with sustenance of bread and water only, for a term not exceeding twenty days. (3 Chase's Stat. 1729.)

Therefore, to justify or even excuse the breaking and entering of the petitioner's house, and especially in the night season, it must be shown that those who did so, whether officers or private men, soldiers or citizens, had a *legal* authority to arrest him; without this, all who participated in the act are liable to the penalties I have just recited, and all who abetted and procured the act are liable, also, as accessories.

Undoubtedly, an arrest may be made, in some cases, without any warrant. For examples:

"1. By a justice of the peace, who may himself apprehend, or cause to be apprehended, by word only, any person committing a felony, or breach of the peace, in his presence. 2. The sheriff, and (3) the coroner, may apprehend any felon, within the county, without warrant. 4. The constable . . . hath great original and inherent authority with regard to arrests. He may, without warrant, arrest any one for a breach of the peace committed in his view, and carry him before a justice of the peace. And, in case of felony actually committed, or a dangerous wounding, whereby felony is like to ensue, he may, upon probable suspicion, arrest the felon; and, for that purpose, is authorized (as upon a justice's warrant) to break open doors, and even to kill the felon if he can not otherwise be taken. And if he or his assistants be killed in attempting such arrest, it is murder in all concerned. 5. Watchmen, either those appointed by the statute of Winchester, 13 Edward I, c. 4, to keep watch and ward in all towns from sunsetting to sunrising, or such as are mere assistants to the constable, may, *virtute officii*, arrest all offenders, and commit them to custody till the morning." (4 Bla. Com. 292.)

So much as to officers; in which it will be observed that an arrest, without a warrant, can be made only in cases of felony or breach of the peace. It can not be made for a *misdemeanor* unaccompanied by a breach of the peace, nor upon *suspicion* of felony as distinguished from a felony "actually" committed.

Blackstone continues:

"Any private person, and, a fortiori, a peace-officer, that is *present* when a felony is committed, is bound by law to arrest the felon, on pain of fine and imprisoment if he escapes through the negligence of the standers-by. And they may justify breaking open doors upon *following* such felon; and if they kill him, provided he can not be otherwise taken, it is justifiable; though, if they are killed in endeavoring to make such arrest, it is murder.

"Upon probable suspicion, also, a private person may arrest the felon, or other person so suspected. But he can not justify breaking open doors to do it; and if either party kill the other, in the attempt, it is manslaughter, and no more. It is no more, because there is no malicious design to kill; but it amounts to so much, because it would be of most pernicious consequence if, under pretense of suspecting felony, any private person might break open a door, or kill another, and, also, because such arrest upon suspicion is barely *permitted* by the law, and not enjoined as in the case of those who are present when a felony is committed." (4 Bla. Com. 293.)

The pretended offense of Mr. Vallandigham is the speaking of certain words; which words, even if they were scandalous, or seditious, or treasonable, would only amount to a misdemeanor at common law. We have no such crimes in this State, nor by the laws of the United States; but, if we had, and if Mr. Vallandigham were ever so guilty, no sheriff, coroner, or constable—and, a fortiori, no other person than such an officer—could justify or excuse the breaking into his house, nor the arresting him without a warrant.

The residue of the article which I have quoted from the Constitution prescribes what a warrant shall contain, and in what circumstances (only) it can be issued. It must "particularly" describe the place to be searched, or the person or thing to be seized; and it must be founded upon a complaint in writing, whereby "probable cause" of guilt appears, and be supported by oath or affirmation. Every man who sets the law thus in motion against his neighbor, without any probable cause, is liable to an action of damages; for the jury will be directed to infer malice from the want of probable cause. And, as an additional safeguard to the rights of a citizen, the party making a false oath or affirmation, knowing it to be false, or having no sufficient reason to believe that it is true, may be prosecuted for perjury.

A warrant must *specify* the alleged crime: otherwise, it will not protect even a constable in breaking open a door. (Foster *v.* Hill, 1 Bulstrode, 146.)

To the same effect is the case of Burford, *ex parte*, 3 Cranch, 448. He had been committed on a warrant under the hands and seals of eleven justices of the peace for Alexandria County, in the District of Columbia, in default of a recognizance with sureties "for his good behavior toward the citizens of the United States and their property." The Supreme Court awarded writs of Habeas Corpus and Certiorari; on the return of which, after an argument, the petitioner was discharged.

"The judges of this court," says the reporter, "were unanimously of opinion that the warrant of commitment was illegal, *for want of stating some good cause certain, supported by oath.*" (Page 453.)

It must specify, also, the person to be arrested—or, if it be a search-warrant, the place to be searched, and the things to be seized. On this subject we have the authority of a great and memorable series of cases.

On the 30th of April, 1763, John Wilkes and divers others were taken into custody, and their houses searched, by virtue of a warrant from Lord Halifax, Secretary of State, for the arrest of the editors, publishers, and printers of the *North Briton*, No. 45, as a seditious and treasonable paper. Wilkes was discharged by the Court of Common Pleas (Rex *v.* Wilkes, 2 Wilson, 151) upon Habeas Corpus; he being a member of Parliament, and the publication of a libel not amounting, in law, to a breach of the peace. The other prisoners were released, by order of the Privy Council, after various terms of imprisonment; and then commenced their actions, severally, for this violation of their personal rights.

Huckle *v.* Money, 2 Wilson, 205, is the first reported case. It was tried before Lord Chief-Justice Pratt, afterward Lord Camden, and the plaintiff obtained a verdict of three hundred pounds. The king's counsel, who defended the action, moved for a new trial upon the ground that the damages were excessive, and, especially, as fourteen other verdicts, of £200 each, had been rendered against the same defendants for executing the same warrant. The plaintiff (Huckle) was in custody about six hours, and was treated with the utmost forbearance and even kindness.

PRATT, C. J.—"If the jury had been confined, by their oath, to consider the mere personal injury only, perhaps £20 damages would have been thought damages sufficient. But the small injury done to the plaintiff, and the inconsiderableness of his station and rank in life, did not appear to the jury in that striking light in which the great point of law touching the liberty of the subject appeared to them at the trial. They saw a magistrate over all the king's subjects exercising arbitrary power, violating Magna Charta and attempting to destroy the liberty of the kingdom by insisting upon the legality of this general warrant before them; they heard the king's counsel and saw the Solicitor of the Treasury endeavoring to support and maintain the legality of the warrant in a tyrannical and severe manner: These are the ideas which struck the jury on the trial, and I think they have done right in giving exemplary damages. To enter a man's house by virtue of a nameless warrant, in order to procure evidence, is worse than the Spanish Inquisition—*a law under which no Englishman would wish to live an hour.* IT WAS A MOST DARING PUBLIC ATTACK MADE UPON THE LIBERTY OF THE SUBJECT. . . . I can not say what damages I should have given if I had been upon the jury." *Motion overruled.*

The next action reported is Beardmore *v.* Carrington, 2 Wilson, 250. It was by an attorney, who had been arrested, against the four messengers of the Privy Council, for executing Lord Halifax's warrant—entering the house of the plaintiff;

searching and reading his papers, and carrying some away; and for imprisoning him six days. Verdict: £1,000. Motion by the king's serjeants to set aside the verdict as excessive.

PER CURIAM.—"The nature of the trespass, in the present case, is joint and several; and the plaintiff has still another action against Lord Halifax, who, it is said, is still more culpable than the defendants, who are only servants, and have done what he commanded them to do, and, therefore, the damages are excessive as to them. But we think this is no topic for mitigation; and, for any thing we know, the jury might say, 'We will make no difference between the minister who executed, and the magistrate who granted this illegal warrant.' So the court must consider these damages as given against Lord Halifax; and can we say that £1,000 are monstrous damages as against him who has granted an illegal warrant to a messenger who enters into a man's house and prys into all his secret and private affairs, and carries him from his house and business, and imprisons him for six days? IT IS AN UNLAWFUL POWER ASSUMED BY A GREAT MINISTER OF STATE. CAN ANY BODY SAY THAT A GUINEA, PER DIEM, IS SUFFICIENT DAMAGES IN THIS EXTRAORDINARY CASE, WHICH CONCERNS THE LIBERTY OF EVERY ONE OF THE KING'S SUBJECTS? We can not say the damages of £1,000 are enormous; and, therefore, the rule to shew cause why a new trial should not be granted, must be discharged."

One of the cases (Money *v.* Leach, 1 W. Bla. 555) was taken to the Court of King's Bench by Sir Charles Yorke, Attorney-General, upon writ of error. Lord Mansfield, who was extremely favorable to the ministry, and anxious to sustain them, if possible, thus endeavored to palliate a proceeding which he could not judicially support:

"How do the *ordinary* magistrates, who are conservators of the peace, usually act in such cases? It is not contended that *they* can issue such a warrant. If the secretary acts in *that* capacity, the law must be the same, unless a different reason can be assigned. It is said that usage will justify it; and it appears that the same form subsisted at the Revolution, and has been continued ever since. Usage has great weight, but will not hold against clear and solid principles of law."

The other judges had no interest as partisans, and thus exclaimed in chorus:

WILMOT, J.—"I have not the least doubt, nor ever had, that these warrants are illegal and void."

YATES, J.—"So totally bad, that an usage, even from the foundation of Rome itself, would not make them good."

ASTON, J.—"I am of the same opinion, that this is a void and illegal warrant."

Thus the law was, in England, before the American Revolution had even commenced; and it is so, without the least shadow of question, this very hour.

The rights of individual citizens, as declared in the first eight amendments to the Constitution of the United States, had not only been secured, but were perfectly understood, at the time when the Thirteen Colonies of North America revolted from British dominion. They were rights which every colonist had brought with him, AS INALIENABLE, to the shores and wildernesses of the Western Hemisphere.

The Federal Constitution being only a delegation of specific powers by the people of the several States, and not the creation of an unlimited government, its authors deemed a BILL OF RIGHTS unnecessary and superfluous. But, with that jealousy which ought ever to distinguish freemen, our ancestors required the addition of ten amendments; and these were added, at the first session of the first Congress, without any opposition.

Two other of those amendments I proceed next to consider:

"No person shall be held to answer for a capital or otherwise infamous crime, unless on a presentment or indictment of a grand jury, except in cases arising in the land or naval forces, or in the militia when in actual service in time of war or public danger; nor shall any person be subject, for the same offense, to be twice put in jeopardy of life or limb; nor shall be compelled, in any criminal case, to be a witness against himself; nor be deprived of life, liberty, or property, without due process of law; nor shall private property be taken for public use without just compensation."

"In all criminal prosecutions, the accused shall enjoy the right to a speedy and public trial by an impartial jury of the State or district wherein the crime shall have been committed (which district shall have been *previously* ascertained by law) and to be informed of the nature and cause of the accusation; to be confronted with the witnesses against him; to have compulsory process for obtaining witnesses in his favor, and to have the assistance of counsel for his defense."

These two articles (amendments) were added only from abundant caution; for, as we have seen, the original text of the Constitution, article third, section second, clause third, expressly declares:

"The trial of all crimes, *except in cases of impeachment*, shall be by jury; and such trial shall be held in the State where the said crimes shall have been committed," etc.

But the judgment in cases of impeachment extends no further than to a removal from office, and, if necessary, a disqualification to hold any other office: so that, in effect, as the Constitution originally was, no man's life or limb, or even his liberty, could have been legally endangered except by the verdict of a jury, and the sentence of a court upon that verdict. Nevertheless, and, as I have said, from abundance of caution, these other declarations of rights were added by amendment:

I. No man shall be put on his defense for any capital or infamous crime except by the indictment or presentment of a grand jury of the district wherein such crime is supposed to have been committed.

This, too, is the result of a long and very memorable struggle in the experience of our English ancestors. It takes away the power of prosecuting for treason, felony, and such like offenses, by information of the Attorney-General, or at the relation of any private individual. That was the process by means of which the Court of the Star Chamber inflicted such oppression and misery; and it was for their servile habit of employing that process, at the expense of the privileges of the people, that two infamous lawyers, Empson and Dudley, were doomed to death.

II. No man shall twice be put on trial, "in jeopardy of life or limb," for the same offense.

By this, therefore, as at common law, a verdict of acquittal is conclusive; it can not be set aside by the judges, nor altered, reviewed, or questioned in any manner. But such is not the rule of military law. The sentence of a court-martial, whether it be of acquittal or of conviction, may be disregarded, wholly or in part, by the commanding officer. It has no validity without his confirmation. He can order a prisoner once acquitted to be again tried, upon the same charge and specification, by the court which acquitted him, or by a court composed of other officers. A military sentence, therefore, is the sentence of the military commander; the proceedings of the court-martial being only intended to inform his judgment or conscience, and so enable him to decide upon the particular case.

III. No man shall be compelled to be a witness against himself in any criminal prosecution.

IV. No man shall be deprived of his life, liberty, or property, except by due process of law.

This repeats the twenty-ninth chapter of Magna Charta, as expounded by Lord Coke (2 Inst. 50) and, after him, by all the writers, English and American, upon constitutional construction:

"NISI PER LEGEM TERRÆ. The words 'law of the land' import due process of law—that is, by indictment or presentment of good and lawfull men, where such deeds be done in due manner, or by writ originall of the common law."

Again:

"Without being brought in to answere, but by due process of the common law."

"No man be put to answer without presentment before justices, or thing of record, or by due process, or by writ originall according to the old law of the land."

V. No man's property shall be taken, upon the excuse or

pretense of a public necessity, without compensating him for its loss or deterioration.

The sixth article of amendment, which I have quoted also, prescribes the essential requisites of a trial upon indictment or presentment:

1. It must be a *public* trial as well as a speedy one.

2. It must be by an impartial jury of the State and the district wherein the crime is alleged to have been committed.

3. The prisoner must be informed of the nature and cause of the accusation; that is to say, of what crime he has been accused, and of the particular transaction, with time, place, and material circumstances, which is supposed to constitute that crime.

4. He must be confronted or brought face to face, while they are testifying, with the witnesses against him.

5. He must have, on demand, such a writ as will compel any person, anywhere within the jurisdiction of the United States, to attend the trial and give testimony in his favor.

6. He must have, as a matter of absolute right, the assistance of counsel learned in the law.

These, except the third, fourth, and fifth, are not the rules of procedure in military tribunals. It is at the discretion of the commanding officer when a prisoner shall be arraigned for trial; and, at his discretion, also, or that of the court-martial, whether a trial shall be public or secret. Counsel are not allowed to address the court in defense of a prisoner, or upon any question of evidence: they are not even allowed to be present except by indulgence or special favor.

The greatest objection yet remains: a trial by court-martial is not a trial by jury, nor its equivalent. The court may consist of thirteen officers, or it may consist of only five; and those officers are chosen by the military commander without any regard to the question of their residence in the State or district wherein the crime is alleged to have been committed. The prisoner has no peremptory challenge.

But, sir, why do I waste time on so plain a distinction? Every man knows that trial by jury is a form peculiar to the common law; and that it has no equivalent in any other form of procedure, or in any other system of jurisprudence.

I have already explained the cases of exception allowed by these two articles—"cases arising in the land or naval forces, or in the militia when in actual service in time of war or public danger"—as well as the reason which dictated such exceptions. I might say, in addition, that the Rules and Articles of War do not assume to punish, as a crime, any act which is declared to be criminal by the ordinary law of the land. They define what are known as military offenses, or offenses in violation of discipline and the good order of the service. Even an officer or a soldier can not be tried by court-martial for a crime against the laws of his country: he must be delivered to the civil magistrate, and tried by a court of civil judicature. So the thirty-third Article of War distinctly provides:

> "When any commissioned officer or soldier shall be accused of a capital crime, or of having used violence or committed any offense against the person or property of any citizen of any of the United States, such as is punishable by the known laws of the land, the commanding officer and officers of every regiment, troop, or company, to which the person or persons accused shall belong, are hereby required, upon application duly made by or in behalf of the party or parties injured, to use their utmost endeavors to deliver over such accused person or persons to the civil magistrate, and, likewise, to be aiding and assisting to the officers of justice in apprehending and securing the person or persons so accused, in order to bring him or them to trial. If any commanding officer or officers shall willfully neglect, or shall refuse upon the application aforesaid, to deliver over such accused person or persons to the civil magistrates, or to be aiding and assisting to the officers of justice in apprehending such person or persons, the officer or officers so offending shall be cashiered."

Instead of which, General Burnside has undertaken to extend the jurisdiction of a court-martial over citizens not in military service, and to arrest, accuse, try, and condemn them for offenses alike unknown to the Articles of War and to the ordinary laws of the land. That all the proceedings of the court are void; that every officer who participates in them, including the members of the court and the judge-advocate, and, also, the provost marshal who executes any such sentence, is liable to an indictment as well as to an action for damages: these are propositions so clearly established—so entirely indisputable—that I should not conceive it decorous, in other circumstances, to urge them upon your Honor's attention.

Wise *v.* Withers, 3 Cranch, 331, was an action of trespass, *vi et armis*, for entering the plaintiff's house, and taking away his goods. The defendant justified as the collector of a fine imposed on the plaintiff by sentence of a court-martial for not serving as a militiaman; to which the plaintiff replied that he was a justice of the peace for Alexandria County, in the District of Columbia, and, as such, exempted by statute from service in the militia. The Circuit Court sustained a demurrer to this replication, as insufficient, and thereupon gave judgment in favor of the defendant.

On writ of error by the plaintiff, in the Supreme Court of the United States, it was contended for the defendant (first) that a justice of the peace was not one of the officers exempted by statute, and (second) that the court-martial had exclusive authority to hear and determine his claim of exemption. The Supreme Court overruled both propositions; and as to the second, with which only I have to deal at present, said:

"It follows from this opinion that a court-martial has no jurisdiction over a justice of the peace: he could never be legally enrolled. *And it is a principle that a decision of such a tribunal, in a case clearly without its jurisdiction, can not protect the officer who executes it.* THE COURT AND THE OFFICER ARE ALL TRESPASSERS." (P. 337.)

To the same effect is the language of the Supreme Court in the case of Tobias Watkins, 3 Peters, 208, 209.

Courts-martial may be restrained by writ of prohibition from the courts of common law—"the general ground of prohibition being an access of jurisdiction," as Lord Loughborough termed it, "where they assume a power to act in matters not within their cognizance." (Grant *v.* Gould, 2 H. Bla. 100.)

But the most remarkable case is that which resulted in the

conviction of Governor Wall for murder, at the Old Bailey sessions, in January, 1802. Before narrating it, in the language of Lord Campbell, I must observe that the court-martial had jurisdiction of the party accused, and of the offense with which he was charged; but, inasmuch as all such courts are of special and limited authority, a defect which would not impair the sentence of a court of general jurisdiction, will suffice to annul their sentences even upon collateral examination.

"Joseph Wall, who had served, from early youth, as an officer in the army, and had always been distinguished for gallantry and good conduct, was, during the American war, appointed Governor of Goree, on the coast of Africa. With a very insufficient garrison, and with very slender military supplies, he had to defend this island from the French, who planned expeditions against it from their neighboring settlement of Senegal. Governor Wall performed his duty to his country, in the midst of formidable difficulties, with firmness and discretion; and the place intrusted to him was safely preserved from all perils till peace was re-established. He was then about to return home, in the expectation of thanks and promotion, but great discontents existed among the troops forming the garrison by reason of their pay being in arrear. This grievance they imputed to the Governor, and they resolved that he should not leave the island till they were righted. Benjamin Armstrong, a sergeant, their ring-leader, was brought by him, irregularly, before a regimental court-martial, and sentenced to receive eight hundred lashes. Although this whipping was administered with much severity, he, in all probability, would have recovered from it, if he had not immediately after drunk a large quantity of ardent spirits; but his intemperance, together with the wounds inflicted upon him by the flagellation, and an unhealthy climate, brought on inflammation and fever, of which he died. Order was restored, and the Governor returned to England. However, representations were made to the authorities at home, respecting the irregularity and alleged cruelty which had been practiced, and exaggerated accounts of the proceedings were published in the newspapers; stating, among other things, that the Governor had murdered Armstrong and several other soldiers by firing them from the mouths of cannon. A warrant was issued against him by the Secretary of State; he was arrested by a king's messenger, and he made his escape as they were conveying him from Bath in a chaise-and-four. He immediately went abroad, and he continued to reside on the continent till the peace of Amiens; when, on the advice of counsel, he came to England, wrote a letter to the Secretary of State announcing his return, and surrendered himself to take his trial." (Lives of the Chief-Justices, vol. 3, pp. 149, 150.)

Twenty years had thus elapsed: nevertheless, Wall was put on trial before a special commission; and the jury, after deliberating half an hour, returned a verdict of guilty, and sentence of death was immediately pronounced. Execution was respited until Lord Eldon and others of the ministry could examine the case; but, finally, the Governor was hanged on a gibbet, in front of the jail of Newgate, and, as Lord Campbell informs us, "amidst the shouts and execrations of the most numerous mob ever assembled in England to witness a public execution."

I mention this painful and singular case, not that I approve Wall's execution—for, although he was rightly convicted, I think he ought to have been pardoned—but to show that the sentence of a military tribunal acting irregularly, and, a fortiori, acting upon persons beyond its jurisdiction, can not avail as a defense to those who pronounce the sentence, or those who execute the sentence, when called to account, in due course of law, notwithstanding the lapse of many years.

And thus, if your Honor please, it ought to be. Otherwise, military officers would not only, as now, become too powerful to be restrained by the civil magistrates, but would purchase to themselves an immunity for all transgressions.

The rights of the people, as enumerated in the several clauses of the Constitution which I have read, can not be affected, in any degree, by the suspension of the privilege of the writ of Habeas Corpus. Harsh as that suspension would be, and unnecessary (as I think) except in the States where insurrection and rebellion prevail, it would not authorize any arrest of a citizen by the military power while the ordinary course of justice remains unobstructed, nor even, without a warrant, except in the cases I have already specified, by a civil magistrate. It would not dispense with the necessity of a trial by jury, and upon indictment: it would justify none of the acts of General Burnside in this particular case.

De Lolme, in his celebrated Essay on the Constitution of England, Book II, ch. 17, part second (note), says:

"At the times of the invasions of the Pretender, assisted by the forces of hostile nations, the Habeas Corpus Act was indeed suspended. . . But the executive power did not thus, of itself, stretch its own authority: the precaution was deliberated upon and taken by the representatives of the people; and the detaining of individuals, in consequence of the suspension of the act, was limited to a certain fixed time. Notwithstanding the just fears of internal and hidden enemies, which the circumstances of the times might raise, the deviation from the former course of the law was carried no further than the single point we have mentioned. Persons detained by order of the Government were to be dealt with in the same manner as those arrested at the suit of private individuals; the proceedings against them were to be carried on no otherwise than in a public place; they were to be tried by their peers, and have all the usual legal means of defense allowed to them—such as calling of witnesses, peremptory challenge of juries," etc.

And such Lord Eldon, while Attorney-General, and addressing the jury in Hardy's case, October 28, 1794, declared to be "the true constitutional meaning" of the act of Parliament, then in force, whereby the privilege of the writ of Habeas Corpus had been suspended. Little did he conceive, with all his inclinations toward an arbitrary and irresponsible government, and at the very time when he was endeavoring to maintain the authority of the crown against what he regarded as an extensive and most dangerous conspiracy—a time when the people of England stood aghast at the horrors of the French Revolution, and even doubted, from day to day, whether such anarchy would not extend to them—little, I say, did Lord Eldon conceive that a Major-General or a Field-Marshal could arrest men, other than soldiers, at his pleasure, and for offenses unknown to the law; could confine them in military prisons; could deprive them of the privilege of the writ of Habeas Corpus without any act of Parliament suspending that privilege; could subject them to the form of a trial by courts or commissions composed of military officers, and upon charges and specifications alike indefinite, inconclusive, and frivolous!

And yet, sir, to that we have come—in the first century of our Republic, with a written Constitution less than eighty years old, in a country professing to be civilized, intelligent, refined, and (strangest of all) to be free! It is *our* case—if your Honor please—your own case and mine; and not merely the case of Clement L. Vallandigham. He is the victim to-day; but there will be, and must be, other victims to-morrow. What rights have we, or what security for any right, under such a system as this?

> "Every minist'ring spy,
> That will accuse and swear, is lord of you,
> Of me, of all our fortunes and our lives.
> Our looks are call'd to question, and our words,
> How innocent soever, are made crimes:
> We shall not shortly dare to tell our dreams,
> Or think, but 't will be treason."

And the excuse for it, as given by General Burnside, is that a rebellion exists in Tennessee, in Arkansas, in Louisiana, in Mississippi, in Alabama, in other States a thousand miles distant from us. Does any rebellion exist here? President Lincoln, by his proclamation of January 1, 1863, has undertaken to "designate" the States, and even "parts" of States, at present in rebellion; but I do not find the State of Ohio, nor the county of Montgomery, nor the city of Dayton so designated. How can the rebels, in addition to disclaiming their own rights under the Constitution of the United States, also forfeit the rights of my client? I ask General Burnside, or his counsel, to answer me that question; because, until it has been answered, and answered satisfactorily, there can be no excuse, no apology, not the least degree of palliation, for such extraordinary proceedings as have been avowed here, and vainly attempted to be justified.

You have presided in this Court almost thirty years; and, during that time, have heard and determined a vast number and variety of important controversies. But never, as I venture to affirm, have you been called to the discharge of a greater duty than upon this occasion. I had supposed, in the simplicity of my heart and understanding, that all the propositions for which I have contended were too firmly established in America, as well as in England, to be disturbed or even doubted. It seems otherwise; and, therefore, at unusual length, and without as lucid an order and as close an argument as I could wish, have I descanted upon the mighty themes of contest, in all past ages, between the supporters of arbitrary power and the defenders of popular rights. I pray that you will command the body of my client to be brought before you, in this court of civil judicature, and in the open light of day; to the end that he may be informed here of what he is accused, and may be tried on that accusation, whatever it be, in due form of law. Let us know the worst any man has to allege against him; and then let him stand before a jury of his countrymen, in the face of all accusers, for deliverance, or, if guilty, for condemnation.

I ask this, sir, in the interest of that Constitution which has been violated by his arrest and imprisonment—in the interest of that Union the fortunes of which now depend on the arbitrament of the sword—in the interest of that army which we have sent into the field to maintain our cause—in the interest of peace at home, and of unanimity in waging a battle so bloody and so hazardous—in the interest of liberty, of justice, of ordinary fairness between man and man.

I have tried to say what ought to be said, and no more, in vindication of the rights of the petitioner. God help me if I have said any thing which ought to have been omitted, or omitted any thing which ought to have been said!

ARGUMENT

OF

HON. AARON F. PERRY.

May it Please the Court:

When General Burnside requested me to assist the District Attorney on this occasion, he forebore to give me any instructions, except to present such considerations to the judgment of the Court as should seem to me right and proper. I have a distinct impression that he has no preference that the questions here presented should be heard before any other jurisdiction or tribunal rather than this; and that he wishes his proceedings to be here discussed by his counsel, chiefly on the broad basis of their merits; that they should be made to rest on the solid ground of the performance of a high and urgent public duty. The main argument which I shall present to the Court will, therefore, be founded on the obligations, duties, and responsibilities of General Burnside as a Major-General in command of an army of the United States, in the field of military operations, for the purposes of war, and in the presence of the enemy. I shall not place it on any ground of apology, excuse, or palliation, but strictly and confidently on the ground of doing what he had a lawful, constitutional right to do; and on the ground of performing a duty imposed upon him as one of the necessities of his official position. I shall make no plea of an exigency in which laws are suspended, and the Constitution forgotten, but shall claim that the Constitution is equal to the emergency, and has adequately provided for it; that the act complained of here is an act fully warranted by law, and authorized by the Constitution. I shall support this claim by references to more than one opinion of the Supreme Court of the United States, and to other authorities.

But before advancing to the main argument, I beg leave to invite a few moments' attention to the paper which is offered as a basis for the proposed action of this Court. It is a petition purporting to relate certain incidents or transactions which befell Clement L. Vallandigham, who is stated to be here in the city. No reason is shown why these statements could not have been authenticated by his own signature and affidavit. In the nature of the case, his attorney, Mr. Pugh, could have had little, if any, personal knowledge of the circumstances related. Mr. Vallandigham, if any one, had knowledge of them. Yet Mr. Vallandigham does not sign his own petition, nor make any affidavit. Mr. Pugh, his attorney, makes affidavit that he "believes" the petition to be true. Is there any reason here shown why, if an affidavit be required, as undoubtedly it is, it should not be made by the party knowing the facts? Why should the general rule be set aside in this proceeding, which requires an affidavit to be made by the person who knows the circumstances, or, at least, that good ground be stated for offering the affidavit of another? I do not care to multiply remarks on this part of the case, but refer the Court to *Ex parte* Dorr, 3 How. 103, for an example of great strictness, in applications of this description.

The petition thus vicariously made and sworn to, on behalf of Mr. Vallandigham, presents some peculiarities of structure, partly as matter of rhetoric and partly as matter of substance, which can not be entirely overlooked. It relates that the petitioner is a native-born citizen of the State of Ohio, a fact which may be interesting, but how it can be thought to be material is not apparent. A native-born citizen of South Carolina, or a naturalized citizen, would be entitled to the same legal immunities. The petitioner next informs the Court that he is not enlisted or commissioned in the land or naval forces of the United States, nor called into actual service as one of the militia. On this allegation the main argument for petitioner is grounded. It is implied by the whole argument, if not distinctly admitted, that if he had been enlisted or commissioned in the land or naval forces of the United States, or had been called into actual service as one of the militia, the arrest might have been made. Having thus drawn a broad line of demarkation between himself and those in the actual service of their country in a military capacity, he relates that, "nevertheless" he was arrested. The circumstances of the arrest are rhetorically stated; but, in substance, nothing more is made of it than an arrest. It was done, he says, between two and three o'clock in the morning; done in his dwelling-house; done in his dwelling-house in which his family then were. His house was surrounded; surrounded by about one hundred soldiers; soldiers in uniform and armed, acting under the direction of General Burnside. These soldiers then and there, he says, broke the outer door and two inner doors; not only broke them, but violently did it; that they seized the petitioner, seized him by overpowering numbers, and imprisoned him against his will. If petitioner had imagined it possible there might be those whose good opinion he valued, who might suspect him of want of enterprise, or want of activity in allowing himself to be captured, and who might look upon it as wearing unheroic aspects, and as tending to an anti-climax in his career, then this part of the petition might be useful in his defense. It is graphic and explanatory. He was undoubtedly captured, not with his consent; perhaps unexpectedly. And it must be confessed that the rehearsal carries with it more or less of the sound of aggravation. If these men had not been in uniform; if there had been only seventy-five instead of a hundred; if they had broken open only two doors instead of three, or broken them more gently; if they had merely arrested him, and had not "seized" him, or had not done it by "overpowering numbers," or had acted the little drama at precisely midnight or at sunrise or at noon, I apprehend the legal effect would have been the same as now. This rhetorical literature is, for the purposes of legal inquiry, redundant. But in another particular there is no redundance. It is not stated, nor does the attorney, in his affidavit of belief, venture upon the assertion that any thing of all these circumstances was wanton or unnecessary. It is not charged that more men were there, or that more violence was used in entering the house than was necessary, nor that petitioner has been subjected to harsh treatment or useless rigor. It stands on the petition, after all, as a simple military arrest—no more.

The petition further relates, not that the arrest was made without probable cause, or without a warrant, or without a charge supported by oath or affirmation, but in effect, that all three of these things did not exist together. It was, it is alleged, "without any warrant issued upon probable cause supported by oath or affirmation, and in contempt of his rights as an American citizen." And this is the only part of the affidavit which goes to charge the arrest as illegal. It is stated, in another part of the petition, that petitioner is not, under the Constitution, amenable to be *tried* by a military commission; but unless the seizure "in contempt of his rights" is equivalent to an allegation that the arrest was illegal, there is no allegation of illegality.

The petitioner states further that he was furnished with a copy of the charge and specifications against him, which he exhibits and makes part of his petition, and which will be more particularly referred to in the course of the argument. For the present purpose it is enough to notice that the charge was, in substance, a charge of active disloyalty toward his own government, and of active sympathy with its enemies, now in battle array against it. Neither the petition nor affidavit denies that there was probable cause for the charge, nor that the charge was honestly believed by General Burnside to be true, nor that the charge was, and is in fact, a true charge. But the petition, claiming the arrest to have been made by soldiers, and by the command of a Major-General of the United States, declares it to be "manifest oppression under color of military authority," and invokes the action of this Court for his relief. It appears that a portion of these allegations were made to show that this Court has jurisdiction. By the fourteenth section of the Judiciary Act of 1789, the jurisdiction of this Court, in cases of Habeas Corpus, is confined to instances where the applicant is in custody, "*under or by color of the authority of the United States*," etc. (Dunlop's Dig. 53.) That is to say, this application must be brought under one of two categories, or the Court has no jurisdiction: 1. The applicant must show himself in custody under the authority of the United States. Or, 2. He must show himself in custody by color of the authority of the United States. I submit that this petition shows that petitioner does not place himself in either category. The whole argument of Mr. Pugh is directed to the point that there is no authority in any branch or part or officer of the Government of the United States to make such arrests. If he is correct, the arrest is clearly not under the authority of the United States. His argument is that the act is wholly unauthorized and unconstitutional: in effect, that the United States is a corporation; that the Constitution is its charter; that this arrest is not authorized by the charter, and, in legal phrase, is *ultra vires*. If it be admitted to be legally done under the authority of the United States, the admission takes away all ground for a Habeas Corpus; for the end of a Habeas Corpus is to ascertain whether a commitment is legal. There may be cases where an arrest is made under the authority of the United States, in which all papers are in due form, and the authority indisputable, but where the process was set in motion by some groundless, wanton, or fraudful device. In such cases, I apprehend, the jurisdiction of this Court would be ample. But this is not claimed to be a case of that kind.

Indeed, the counsel for petitioner does not place the jurisdiction on this branch of the alternative. He denies, utterly, thoroughly, and without stint or qualification, that this arrest was, or could have been under the authority of the United States. He places the jurisdiction on the other ground, viz.: that the arrest was "*by color* of the authority of the United States."

What is meant by color in law? An arrest under color of authority would be an arrest by proceedings apparently legal, but which, by reason of some irregularity or defect, would be capable of being shown to be unauthorized. (Wharton's Law Dic. 157; 1 Bouvier's Law Dic. 243.) The case, *Ex parte* Joseph Smith, (3 McLean, 121,) is an example of arrest by *color* of authority. The warrant was in due form. The officer had full power. But the affidavit was defective on which the warrant had been issued. In the present case there was no mistake or defect, no fallacious appearance or pretext, nothing pretended or supposed which has been found to be unreal. The authority was perfect, or it was nothing. It was wholly sufficient, or wholly wanting. It was a perfectly legal arrest, or it was an open, flagrant violation of the peace. Whatever else may be said of it, it can not be said to be by *color* of any thing. The fact that it was done by a Major-General, and by soldiers in uniform, does not give it the *color* of authority. Unlawful and unauthorized acts done by soldiers or officers of the United States are not by *color* of authority. "*To give color to the plaintiff is to assign to him, in the plea, some colorable* (i. e., *defective*) *but fictitious title,*" *etc.* (Gould's Pleadings, 348.) I submit that it would be an abuse of language to call the arrest made by General Burnside a defective or fictitious thing. It was completely authorized, or it had no colorable excuse.

The petition, therefore, makes a case of arrest which was neither "under or by color of the authority of the United States," and consequently not within the jurisdiction of this Court; or it makes a case of arrest every way legal and fully authorized, in which no writ of Habeas Corpus should be granted.

Having sufficiently called attention to these preliminary points, I advance with more satisfaction to the main argument. The careful analysis of the petition, already made, will be found to have its uses and bearings in the argument which I shall now offer, not altogether disproportioned to the time which it has occupied.

Mr. Pugh has correctly argued that a Habeas Corpus is in the nature of a writ of error to examine into the legality of an arrest or commitment. If it appear that the arrest or commitment complained of was a legal act, the writ of Habeas Corpus will not issue; because its whole office is to inquire into the legality of the act, and the Court will not do a nugatory and useless thing.

A Habeas Corpus does not meddle with arrests legally made. There are well-known cases where the civil magistrates and officers of the peace make arrests on sight and without warrant. In such cases the legality depends upon circumstances to make a case where an arrest is allowed by law without a warrant. These circumstances, if they exist, *are* a warrant, or equivalent to it. So, if war or any other state of affairs exist, which by recognized principles authorize, require, and justify an arrest by military force, no Habeas Corpus can meddle with it. The order which sends an army to make war, is all the warrant it needs for every necessary act of war. It may capture and imprison enemies, and not those in arms only. "The whole," says Vattel's Law of Nations, p. 346, "is deduced from one single principle, from the object of a just war, for when the end is lawful, he who has a right to pursue that end has, of course, a right to employ all the means which are necessary for its attainment." One of the undoubted means of war is to take life. As the greater includes the less, the right to take life implies the right to take every thing.

> "All those persons belonging to the opposite party (even the women and children) he may lawfully secure and make prisoners, either with a view to prevent them from taking up arms again, or for the purpose of weakening the enemy." . . . "At present, indeed, this last-mentioned expedient is seldom put in practice by the polished nations of Europe: women and children are suffered to enjoy perfect security, and allowed permission to withdraw wherever they please. But this moderation, this politeness, though undoubtedly commendable, is not in itself absolutely obligatory, *and* if a General thinks fit to supersede it, *he can not be justly accused of violating the laws of war.*" (Vattel, p. 352, 346.)

Persons so captured or arrested are prisoners of war.

> "For the same reasons, which render the observance of those maxims a matter of obligation between State and State, it becomes

equally and even more necessary in the unhappy circumstance of two incensed parties lacerating their common country. (Vattel, 425.)

The application to citizens in revolt of the rules of war, is in the interests of mercy. If they should be put upon trial before a jury in such moments of overwhelming excitement, one of two results would follow.

If the jury should not be so divided by the passions raging through the whole population as to disagree, and thus bring the law into contempt, their passions would take them to one side or the other. Men might be let loose, and certainly would be, whom the safety of the State required to be restrained, or more probably convicted and executed without sufficient evidence. When society is imperiled by intestine war, the passions rage which occasioned the war. The entrails of the volcano, covered for a while, have at length broken forth. Smoke and ashes obscure the sky. Fiery floods pour along the earth. No good man could be impartial. Who claims to be impartial impeaches himself. Believing his government to be in the right, interest, feeling, lawful duty compel him to uphold it with all his power. He has no decent pretext, certainly no lawful excuse, for throwing on others a duty to uphold the government which he shrinks from. It is each man's duty as much as any other's. Its enemies are, and in the nature of the case must be, his enemies; its friends his friends. The law allows him no other position. On the other hand, he who believes the government to be wrong has no choice but to sympathize with its enemies. He must assist them, and will assist them, either openly or by secret and suppressed sympathy. On one side or the other, men go to the jury-box under the influence of deep feeling. The law of nations, or rather the laws of war, which in civil commotions authorize the opposing parties to treat each other as prisoners of war, is not, therefore, an aggravation of dangers, but an amelioration of them. Vattel, p. 426, assigns two reasons for it: One, lest the civil war should become more cruel. The other, the danger of committing great injustice by hastily punishing those who are accounted rebels. "The flames of discord and civil war are not favorable to the proceedings of pure and sacred justice." More quiet times are to be waited for.

It appears, then, that in time of war, the fact of war authorizes and legalizes arrests; and the order for an army to make war is its sufficient warrant for making such arrests as are justified by the laws of war. I am not now inquiring whether the arrest of Clement L. Vallandigham is justifiable by the rules of war. That inquiry will follow in its due course. I am now adverting to the laws of war, and showing that arrests of some kinds are authorized. These principles are, I suppose, undisputed and indisputable. It follows that such arrests are legal; and by showing the existence of circumstances making the arrest legal, a sufficient answer is made to a Habeas Corpus. The writ is not in such case suspended. It is respected, upheld, enforced, and performs all the office a Habeas Corpus can in any case perform.

It is a logical consequence, unavoidably resulting from the premises, that while all wars, insurrectionary or foreign, bring into action the laws of war, they do not, necessarily, suspend the writ of Habeas Corpus. The Legislature may enact a statute making some act a crime which was not so before, and authorizing persons guilty of it to be arrested and held; or authorizing a writ of civil capias, under which the body is seized and held in circumstances not before authorizing such an arrest. These things not only may be done, but are frequently done. No one thinks of them as a suspension or abolishment of Habeas Corpus. So, in war, the laws of war authorize arrests which were not authorized until those laws were brought into play by the fact of war. In these cases Habeas Corpus is no more suspended than in the others. Full force and effect may be given it while enforcing the laws of war. And this is the constitutional view. The power to declare war is broadly given; the power to suspend Habeas Corpus is given distinctly from the war power, and in addition to it, "when in cases of rebellion or invasion *the public safety may require it.*" If the operation of the laws of war were a suspension of Habeas Corpus, every thing had been said when Congress was authorized to declare war. No further declaration was needed. It is against correct rules of construction to hold that Habeas Corpus suspension is intended to be merely one of the means of war. They might as well have provided for making war in one paragraph, and then have provided, as a separate and distinct power, authority to kill and capture enemies in battle. War may be made. In addition to making war, Habeas Corpus may be suspended in certain contingencies.

Learned counsel, on the other side, has called our attention to the act of Congress of March 23, 1863; and to another act of Congress, showing that the offense with which petitioner is charged is an offense against the civil law, and punishable under a law of Congress; one for which he may be held and tried before the civil tribunals. Neither of these acts interferes with my argument. The first section of the act of March 23, 1863, authorizes the President, in contingencies there named, to suspend the writ of Habeas Corpus. The learned counsel says he has not suspended it. Undoubtedly, if he had suspended it, there would be an end of this case. I do not claim that it is suspended. My whole argument proceeds on the ground that it is nöt suspended, but in full force. That act of Congress is based upon the idea that arrests had before that time been made, and might again be made, which could only be sustained by a suspension of Habeas Corpus; in other words, arrests, not sustainable by the laws of war, or by any other law, except the extreme demands of public safety when "in cases of rebellion or invasion the public safety may require." The suspension of Habeas Corpus is a suspension of a right to inquire into the legality of an arrest; for if it can be shown that the arrest was lawful, there is no need to suspend the Habeas Corpus. War had long before been recognized and legalized. Nothing is more certain in law than that military men, in time of war, are legally protected in doing the acts authorized by the laws of war. Such acts are in no sense unlawful. But this act of Congress, sec. 4, provides an indemnity for acts done by the President, or under his authority, which was wholly unnecessary unless it contemplated acts not defensible under the laws of war. The act neither reprobates nor prohibits. It contemplates the necessity, allows the act, and provides for it. One of two constructions is necessary. It refers only to such arrests as have been made under a suspension of Habeas Corpus, in which construction it does not apply to this case; or it provides for irregular arrests, without process or with defective process, which might, if Habeas Corpus were sustained, be discharged under it. But in no event does it contemplate the discharge of an arrest by Habeas Corpus, unless or until the steps there pointed out shall have been first taken, or the contingency there provided for shall have happened. If learned counsel, therefore, bring themselves under the operation of this act, they defeat their application here, and are remitted to another mode of relief. If this act does not apply, it is outside of the case, and need not be further discussed. If it does apply, it is fatal to this petition. I understand learned counsel to admit that it does not apply here, and in this I agree with him. It is an undoubted principle of public law, that persons captured or seized under the laws of war are prisoners of war. They may be guilty of civil offenses, punishable by the civil tribunals. Imprisonment under the laws of war does not discharge them from their offenses. They are or may be held until they can be brought to a legal trial in a time of restored tranquillity. Necessity forbids their running at large; humanity forbids to put them on trial at a time so unfavorable to the proceedings of pure and sacred justice. (Vattel, 426.) The act of March 23, 1863, is expressly limited, in its operations, to prisoners who are held "otherwise than as prisoners of war."

The President's proclamation of September 24, 1862, suspending Habeas Corpus and declaring martial law, is not referred to in the act of March 23, 1863, nor published in the regular edition of laws. I have no knowledge that it has been withdrawn or superseded, otherwise than as a matter of inference from the act of Congress. If it remains in force, it ends this application. I choose rather not to rely upon it. There is no inference to be drawn from the act of Congress against that part of it which proclaims martial law; but in the view I am urging of the principles of public law, such a proclamation can perform no office except to give publicity to a fact before existing. To whatever extent the fact of war brought into play the laws of war, those laws had their full force without a proclamation; to that extent a proclamation was proper, but unnecessary. Beyond that it was nugatory, and could not add one cubit to the stature of war. A proclamation of martial law is often confounded with, and considered equivalent to, a suspension of Habeas Corpus. But this is inaccurate. If the President had authority to issue such a proclamation, and has not rescinded it, nothing can be more clear than that Congress had no power to rescind it. But I do not choose to embarrass the discussion by relying upon a document which there is plausible ground to suppose Congress might not have considered in force.

Having cleared the field of argument from such chances of misapprehension and confusion as prudence required, I recur to the proposition advanced by learned counsel on the other side, and which I had intended to advance myself, though scarcely necessary to be mentioned.

A proceeding of Habeas Corpus is in the nature of a writ of error, to inquire into the legality of the commitment or arrest. If the application shows the arrest complained of was a lawful one, the Court will go no further. It will not put a defendant to show, by his answer, what is already shown by the petition. On this I suppose I have the happiness to agree with learned counsel on the other side. I have also the happiness to agree with him that the right of Habeas Corpus has not, in this case, been suspended, but is to be treated as in full force, with neither more nor less respect than is habitually paid to it in courts of justice.

I claim, then, that the facts before this Court show that the arrest of Clement L. Vallandigham, by Ambrose E. Burnside, a Major-General in the United States service, commanding in the Department of the Ohio, was a legal and justifiable arrest. For the facts showing its legality I rely, 1. On the petition and affidavit of the prisoner; 2. On facts of current public history of which the Court is bound to take judicial cognizance. Among the facts of public history, I need recall but few. Unfortunately, the country is involved in dangers so many and so critical, that its people neither do nor can divert their thoughts to other topics.

There is on foot an organized insurrection, holding by military force a large part of the United States, and controlling the political organization of at least twelve States of the Union. It has put into the field armies of such strength that the armies of the United States have not been able to overcome them. Battles of great magnitude are fought, and prisoners mutually captured and exchanged. In short, we have, for two years, been in a recognized state of civil war, on a scale large and destructive, almost beyond historical comparison. This insurrection claims to have so much power as to be beyond the means of the government to overcome, and to be entitled to be recognized by foreign nations as an independent power. Were it possible to doubt the imminence of the danger, and extremity of peril from what we see around us, we should be warned of it by the admonitions of foreign governments holding the relations of friendly governments, and claiming to be impartial. They freely express the opinion that our danger is not merely extreme, but irremediable; that the Constitution, and all hopes founded upon it, must perish.

This insurrection has for impulse, feelings and opinions growing out of the past civil history of the country. As a matter of course it can not be, and as a matter of fact it is not, limited to places, or described by geographical descriptions. In some parts of the country it dominates society; in other parts it is dominated by the regular civil administration. We hear of no place so dark but that some weak prayers are uttered for the Constitution; and of no place so bright but that lurking treason sometimes leaves its trail, or shows, through all disguises, its sinister unrest.

The power and wants of the insurrection are not all nor chiefly military. It needs not only food, clothing, arms, medicine, but it needs hope and sympathy. It needs moral aid to sustain it against reactionary tendencies. It needs argument to represent its origin and claims to respect favorably before the world. It needs information concerning the strength, disposition, and movements of government force. It needs help to paralyze and divide opinions among those who sustain the government, and needs help to hinder and embarrass its councils. It needs that troops should be withheld from government, and its financial credit shaken. It needs that government should lack confidence in itself, and become discouraged. It needs that an opinion should prevail in the world that the government is incapable of success, and unworthy of sympathy. Who can help it in either particular I have named, can help it as effectually as by bearing arms for it. Wherever in the United States a wish is entertained to give such help, and such wish is carried to its appropriate act, there is the place of the insurrection. Since all these helps combine to make up the strength of the insurrection, war is necessarily made upon them all, when made upon the insurrection. Since each one of the insurrectionary forces holds in check or neutralizes a corresponding government force, and since government is in such extremity as not safely to allow any part of its forces to withdraw from the struggle, it has no recourse but to strike at whatever part of the insurrection it shall find exposed. All this is implied in war, and in this war with especial cogency. "If war be actually levied—that is, if a body of men be actually assembled for the purpose of effecting by force a treasonable purpose—all those who perform any part, however minute, or however remote from the scene of action, and who are actually leagued in the general conspiracy, are to be considered as traitors." (4 Cranch, 126.)

The Constitution being paralyzed and suspended to the extent described, we may notice the situation and condition of the State of Ohio, where the petition states the arrest to have been made. Geographically it is midway between east and west, bordered on the south by Virginia and Kentucky, both States occupied by contending armies, and over which the tide of war advances and recedes according as its fortunes incline to one side or the other. On the north is Lake Erie, over which England and America hold a divided sway. In the event of a war with England, on the very verge of which we have sometimes seemed, a contest for supremacy on that great lake would be inevitable. Such a war is one of the hopes of the insurrection, and has been schemed for with amazing audacity. A military occupation of either line of railroad running through Ohio, from the river to the lake, would sever the North-western from the North-eastern States. The population of the State is made up of all the conflicting elements now lighting the blaze of civil war in the country. The feelings of all are represented here. None of the extremes and none of the means are wanting. That these elements should be carrying on a bloody strife in the immediate neighborhood, and no strife be kindled here, is improbable in theory and untrue in fact. The insurrection in Ohio is dominated by the federal authorities, and operates in disguise, but it meets and receives constant attention. The arguments for insurrection made in South Carolina are openly repeated in Ohio. The charges there made against the government and those who administer it, as a provocation for rebellion, are openly made here, and with not much difference in the degree of animosity. The South Carolina orators, it is true, draw a different conclusion from their arguments and charges from that which is drawn here from the same arguments and charges. There, for the reasons stated, they declare eternal hostility to the Union; here, eternal fidelity to it. The means to accomplish these diverse results, however, are the same. In South Carolina they propose to overthrow Lincoln and his minions, in order to destroy the Union; here it is proposed, in order to save the Union. There and here each foot steps in the other's track; the toes all point in the same way, but they claim to be traveling in opposite directions. It is not very long since the marshal of this district was obliged to call for military force to suppress a revolt in Noble County in this State; still later was a military force necessary to save Dayton from the ravages of a similar revolt. In numerous instances in Indiana military force has been necessary. These are all fingers of the same hand. Your Honor does not forget how recently the records of this Court were removed, in order to save them from the contingencies of an invasion by insurrectionary forces; nor how recently, by voluntary labor, the people of this city raised embankments and forts to protect it from the insurrection. Nor is your Honor uninformed that these defenses are kept, day and night, in a state of preparation, armed and supported. This Court is sitting, as it were, in garrison. We are deliberating under the protection of the guns of Newport and Covington. At various parts of the State are camps. The streets of our cities are patroled by military guards. Has our government nothing to do that it should vex itself, and waste its means by these precautions, if not known to be necessary?

An inference is unavoidably drawn of the importance of a given field of operations, by the officers placed in charge of it. General Wright, who was first sent to command this Department, was a man eminent for military science and clear abilities. His undemonstrative habits and retiring manners prevented the high popular appreciation which he deserved. The next commander sent us is General Burnside, of Hatteras Inlet, of Roanoke Island, of Newbern, of South Mountain, of Antietam, of Fredericksburg; a General not inferior in ability, nor second to any other in the affections of his countrymen. With him comes that famous army corps, young in organization, but already old in sacrifices and in glory. Next in command, for Ohio, they send us the very Bayard of American volunteers, whose cool heroism at South Mountain was looked upon as an ample response to the high expectations formed of him from his accomplishments and previous services, and who crowned them all at Antietam Creek by performing there, with Ohio troops, trained under his own eye, a feat of arms fit to be compared with the far-famed passage of the Bridge of Lodi. If the government can afford such Generals for the safe places, what can it afford to the dangerous places?

Why are these men here? Have they, at any time since the war begun, sought any other but the place of danger? They are here—they are sent here for war: to lay the same military hand upon this insurrection wherever they can find it, in small force or large .force, before them or behind them, which they have laid upon it elsewhere. They are not here to cry peace, when there is no peace; not here to trifle with danger, or be trifled with by it. They are patriot Generals, commanding forces in the field in the presence of the enemy, constrained by their love of country, and in the fear of God only, to strike. Are they to fold their arms and sleep while the incitements to insurrection multiply around them, and until words shall find their way to appropriate acts? Are they to wait until the wires shall be cut, railroad tracks torn up, and this great base of supplies, this great thoroughfare for the transit of troops, this great center and focus of conflicting elements, is in a blaze, before they can act? Must they wait until apprehended mischief shall become irremediable before they can attempt a remedy? Jefferson Davis would answer "Yes!" Traitors and abettors of treason would everywhere answer "Yes!" I seem to hear a solemn accord of voices rising from the graves of the founders of the Constitution saying "No!" And I seem to hear the response of loyal and true friends of liberty everywhere swelling to a multitudinous and imperative "Amen!"

I may as well here say what I have to say concerning the paper presented by General Burnside. It is eminently respectful to this Court and to the people. It is honorable to the feelings of the General, and creditable to his judgment. Anxious for the cause he represents, and needing the affections of the people to uphold him in his great work, it was natural, and it was proper, that he should desire not to be misunderstood. It was natural and proper that he should give his most sacred assurances of his purpose not to assail liberty but to defend it. But, in my judgment, it was not necessary. The General is modest—I will not say too modest. The people know him better than he seems to think. They know him by acts which speak louder than words. His principles and motives are as visible to them as the shining track of the sun. They know him as one of the first, then unheralded by fame, to bare his bosom to the bolts of this war. They know him as one whose political opinions and prejudices were strong against the present Administration, but who subordinated these to a sense

8

of the necessity of saving the Constitution. They know him as one who has passed through perils innumerable, and has borne, with equal constancy, victory and defeat; who, in all vicissitudes, has stood as a rock against which the waves of sedition dash and are broken. His acts are his explanation. He needed and will need no other.

I have listened with interest and attention to the comments and criticisms of the eloquent advocate for Mr. Vallandigham, on this paper. Considering his zeal, his ingenuity, and his duty as an advocate, I am gratified to see how little he found to complain of. We are entitled, since it has passed this ordeal, to rest upon it as not only substantially unobjectionable, but in form and language prudent. It was, of course, the duty of the advocate to imply, in his criticism, if he did not state, that liberty of speech is chiefly in danger from the Generals who fight to uphold it, and not from the politicians who seek to render the services of the Generals ineffectual. It was properly within the arts of advocacy to drop out of sight the fact that liberty of speech, with other sacred and indispensable rights, has no adequate guarantee or defense except in the safety of the government ordained to establish justice and secure the blessings of liberty to ourselves and our posterity. It was not in the line of his duty to remind us that the only way now to save liberty of speech is to save the government which was made to protect it. Let us imagine that at the large meeting addressed by Mr. Vallandigham, and during the delivery of his speech, an individual had risen from the audience and commenced there a harangue in favor of the liberty of speech. Who, then, would be the defender of free speech, the man who raised for it an untimely clamor, or the constable who should seize him and suppress the disturbance? The right of free speech is only one of the rights secured by civil liberty, and, like other rights, is subjected to some limitations necessary for the safety of all. Civil liberty is defined to be, "the liberty of men in a state of society, or natural liberty, so far only abridged and restrained as is necessary and expedient for the safety and interest of the society, state, or nation."

I understood the learned counsel to intimate that government would receive the unanimous support of the people of Ohio, if it would do nothing which displeased any of them. "Touch not the liberty of the citizen, and we, in Ohio, at least, will be unanimous." May it please your Honor, the liberty of the citizen is touched when he is compelled, either by a sense of duty, or by conscription, to enter the army. The liberty of the citizen is touched when he is forbidden to pass the lines of any encampment. The liberty of the citizen is touched when he is forbidden to sell arms and munitions of war, or to carry information to the enemy. Learned counsel is under a mistake. We, in Ohio, could not be unanimous in leaving such liberties untouched. The liberty to stay at home from war is at least as sacred as the liberty to make popular harangues. But since all these liberties are assailed by war, they must be defended by war. We, in Ohio, never could be unanimous in approving the action of a government which should force one portion of the population to enter the army, and allow another portion of it to discourage, demoralize, and weaken that army. Unanimity, on such conditions, is impossible. But this suggestion of unanimity is not quite new. The zeal of the advocate, the charming voice, the stirring elocution with which it is now reproduced, do all that is possible to redeem it from its early associations. But we can not forget that the same thing has played a conspicuous part in the history of the last few years. At the last presidential election it happened, as it had on all preceding similar occasions, that a majority of lawful votes, constitutionally cast, elected a President of the United States, and placed the federal administration in the hands of persons agreeing in opinion, or supposed to agree with that majority. It happened, as it had ordinarily happened before, that the minority did not agree with the majority, either as to principles or as to the men selected. It claimed to believe the majority in the wrong, and no minority could find provocation or excuse for being in the minority, unless it did believe the majority in the wrong. It is not now necessary to inquire which were right in their preferences and opinions. The minority were fatally wrong in this, that they refused the arbitrament provided in the Constitution for the settlement of such controversies. The new administration must yield, because the minority found itself unwilling to yield. The old Constitution must be changed by new conditions, or run the risk of overthrow. In other words, it must be overthrown in its most vital principles, by compelling a majority to accept terms from a minority, accompanied by threats of war, or it might be nominally kept alive by consenting to abdicate its functions. All that the secession leaders proposed was, that they should be allowed to administer the government when elected, and, also, when not elected. They were willing to respect the constitutional rights of elections, provided it should be conceded that if they were beaten they should go on with public affairs the same as if they had been elected. They were willing to take the responsibility of judging what they would like to do, and all they asked was the liberty to do it. "Touch not our liberties, and we can be unanimous!" The same old fallacy reappears in every phase of the insurrection; sometimes with and sometimes without disguise. Neither change of wigs, nor change of clothing, nor presence nor absence of burnt cork, can hide its well-known gait and physiognomy. The insurrection will support the government, provided the government will support the insurrection; but the government must consent to abdicate its functions, and permit others to judge what ought to be done, before it can be supported. One of its favorite disguises is to desire to support the government, provided it were in proper hands; but to be unable to support it in its present hands. The proper hands, and the only proper hands for government to be in, are the hands in which the Constitution places it. If the whole country should believe any particular hands to be the most suitable, those hands would be chosen. He who can not support the government on the terms pointed out in the Constitution, by recognizing as the proper hands for its administration the hands in which the law places it, is not a friend, but an enemy of the Constitution. What he means by liberty is not that qualified liberty in which all may share, but a selfish, tyrannical, irresponsible liberty to have his own way, without reference to the wishes or convenience of others. This notion of selfish and irresponsible liberty is an unfailing test and earmark of the insurrection. Whatever other appearances it may put on, it can always be known and identified by this. No darkness can conceal, no dazzling light transform it. Wherever it may be found, there is insurrection, in spirit at least, and, according to different grades of courage, in action also. This kind of liberty can not live at the same time with the liberty which our Constitution was ordained to secure. Government must lay hands upon it or die. Dangerous as its hostility may be, its embrace would be more fatal. Its hostility may, in time, destroy the government, but any government consenting to make terms with it is already dead.

My eloquent friend on the other side desires to know what may be General Burnside's notion concerning the people, that he should fear the effect of Vallandigham's speeches? On this subject I can only exercise my privileges of observation. I infer, from General Burnside's bearing and habits, that his opinions concerning the people are, in an eminent degree, respectful. I have an impression that he regards them and theirs with affectionate and undoubting confidence. I presume he thinks that if the people of Ohio can be persuaded that the war is a wicked one, they will give it a much less cordial support than they otherwise would. I presume he thinks well enough of them to suppose that if they can be persuaded to believe their government is striving to enslave them, they will resist it, with life and means and sacred honor. I do not suppose he is authorized to think so meanly of them as to imagine they would not make forcible resistance to an effort to enslave them. Three years ago, he might have imagined, as many others of us did, that such persuasions could never go beyond words, and would spend themselves in mere political heats. But he has seen the result of such experiments in South Carolina, Virginia, and over a large section of the Union. The people yet loyal to the Constitution have intrusted to him their sons, and he has seen them go down in battle on many contested fields, to counteract the effect of just such persuasions. I infer that it has occurred to him, by this time, that there is danger of the effects of such persuasion. It would not surprise me to learn that he now looks back with regret, and wonders why the instigators and ringleaders could not have been seized before yet their treasonable words bore fruit in treasonable war!—why we ever felt justified in thinking so meanly of the people of any section of the country as to suppose they could be persuaded their liberties were attacked, and yet not make an appropriate resistance! Perhaps he may feel not a little distress when he reflects that all this bloodshed might have been saved, but was not, by a little timely vigor. I have not the least suspicion that he doubts the right of government to protect the people from such calamities. If it may crush treason in its blossom and fruitage, how much more in its beginning. I can imagine a patriot General—for aught I know, General Burnside may be the man—who should say to himself, "I, too, am one of the people. These men, who fight under my command, are my neighbors. Yonder men, who meet us in battle, are our countrymen. Have not these baleful experiments of an unbridled license of tongue been carried far enough? May we not, at length, cease to trifle, and do what is possible to check these rivers of blood, by obstructing the head-waters from which they flow! All other experiments having failed, may we not, as a last resort, listen to the dictates of common sense?"

I do not propose to follow learned counsel in all their comments on General Burnside's statement. I do not complain of criticism. I have said enough not to leave myself open to the suspicion of slighting the remarks offered by counsel. I am now at liberty to pay that statement the practical compliment of trusting it to stand on its own merits. But before I pass from the theme, I must acknowledge the respect paid to General Burnside's patriotism. It seems to be conceded that the purity and nobleness of his motives are unquestionable. Whatever criticism is bestowed on other things, when counsel approaches an allusion to motives, he is conscious of a pure atmosphere and a high presence. Like Moses approaching the burning bush, he seems, as it were, to pull off hat and shoes, and acknowledge himself to be standing on holy ground.

Let us, then, turn to the petition of Clement L. Vallandigham, and see how it presents him. I know nothing, and desire to know nothing, of the man in this case, except what is shown by the papers before us. It is neither my habit nor my pleasure to incumber an argument with personalities. But I may say, and I will say, that if Mr. Vallandigham be a public man, aspiring to lead public opinion in this great crisis, and be, in fact, disloyal to the Constitution, or if he be of that bat-like nature, which flits and flickers in the twilight between patriotism and treason, so that it never can, at a given moment, be certainly known which side he favors, then

> "May shame and dishonor sit
> By his grave ever;
> Blessings shall hallow it,
> Never! No, never!"

The petition exhibits and sets forth a copy of the charge under which he was arrested. It shows us exactly the ground of his arrest. By referring to the charge and specifications, we have before us the case. It is not a little remarkable that no part of the charge or specification is denied. It stands for the purpose of this inquiry, as admitted.

[Mr. Perry read the charge and specifications as published in another place.]

It appears from this that he publicly addressed a large meeting of citizens. He was not expressing in secrecy and seclusion his private feelings or misgivings, but seeking publicity and influence. The occasion and circumstances show the purpose to have been to produce an effect on the public mind, to mold public feeling, to shape public action. In what direction? The charge says, by expressing his sympathies for those in arms against the Government of the United States, by declaring disloyal sentiments and opinions. He declared the war to be wicked and cruel, and unnecessary, and a war not waged for the preservation of the Union: a war for crushing out liberty and erecting a despotism. What is this but saying that those who fight against the United States are in the right, and that it would be cowardly and dishonorable not to fight against the United States? In what more plain or cogent language could he urge his audience themselves to take up arms against their government? If those who heard him could not be incited to fight against a government by persuading them it was making an unjust and cruel war to crush out liberty, how else could he expect to incite them? If he did not hope to persuade them to join their sympathies and efforts with the enemies of the United States, by convincing them that these enemies are in the right, fighting and suffering to prevent the overthrow of liberty, standing up against wickedness and cruelty, what must he have thought of his audience? What else but the legitimate result of his argument can we impute fairly as the object of his hopes? To whatever extent they believe him, they must be poor, dumb dogs not to rally, and rally at once, for the overthrow of their own government, and for the support of those who make war upon it. But he did not leave it to be inferred. He declared it to be a war for the enslavement of the whites and *the freedom of the blacks*. Which of the two was, in his opinion, the greater outrage, he does not appear to have stated. It is one of the unmistakable marks of the insurrection, by which it can always be identified, that its declarations for liberty are for a selfish and brutal liberty, which includes the liberty of injuring or disregarding others. If his white audience were not willing to be enslaved, that is to say, not willing to endure the last and most degrading outrage possible to be inflicted on human nature, they must, so far as they believed him, resist their own government. If he himself believed what he said, he must take up arms to resist the government, or stand a confessed poltroon. A public man, who believes that his government is guilty of the crimes he imputed, and will not take up arms against it, is guilty of unspeakable baseness. If his audience believed what he told them, they must have looked upon advice not to take up arms as insincere or contemptible. No public man, no private man, can make such charges and decently claim not to mean war. All insurrections have their pretexts. The man who furnishes these is more guilty than the man who believes them and acts on them. If the statements of Vallandigham were true, the pretexts were ample, not merely as pretexts, but as justification of insurrection. They were more: they were incitements which it would be disgraceful to resist, and which human nature generally has no power to resist. The place where such things are done is the place of insurrection, or there is not and can not be a place of insurrection anywhere. If these laboratories of treason are to be kept in full blast, they will manufacture traitors faster than our armies can kill them. This cruel process finds no shelter under the plea of political discussion. Whatever might be said about ballots and elections, the legal inference is that it is intended to produce the results which would naturally flow from it. If the President, with all the army and navy, and his "minions," is at work to overthrow liberty and enslave the whites, every good man must fear to see that army victorious, and hail its disasters with joy. Every good man must strike to save himself from slavery now while he can. The elections are far off, and may be too late. It can not be claimed that the motive was to influence elections, because the argument does not fit that motive. It fits to insurrection, and that only. He pronounced General Orders No. 38 to be a base usurpation, and invited his hearers to resist it. How resist it? How could they resist it, unless by doing what the order forbade to be done?

What was there to be complained of except by persons wishing to do, or to have done by others, the acts by that order prohibited? He invited to resist the order. The order thus to be resisted, prohibited the following acts, viz.: Acts for the benefit of the enemies of our country, such as carrying of secret mails; writing letters sent by secret mails; secret recruiting of soldiers for the enemy inside our lines; entering into agreements to pass our lines for the purpose of joining the enemy; the being concealed within our lines while in the service of the enemy; being improperly within our lines by persons who could give private information to the enemy; the harboring, protecting, concealing, feeding, clothing, or in any way aiding the enemies of our country; the habit of declaring sympathies for the enemy; treason. These are the things prohibited in Order No. 38, which Mr. Vallandigham invited his audience to resist. "The sooner," he told them, "the people inform the minions of usurped power that they will not submit to such restrictions on their liberties, the better." The "minions" here referred to were the commanding General of the Department and others charged with official duties under their own government. The "liberties" not allowed to be restricted were liberties to aid the enemies of the United States. He declared his own purpose to do what he could to defeat the attempt now being made to build up a monarchy upon the ruins of our free government. This resistance could mean nothing but resistance to his own government, which he had before declared to be making attempts to enslave the whites. These appeals to that large public meeting are charged to have been made "*for the purpose of weakening the power of his own government in its efforts to suppress an unlawful rebellion*," all of which opinions and sentiments "*he well knew did aid, comfort, and encourage those in arms against the government*, and could but induce in his hearers a distrust of their own government, and sympathy for those in arms against it, *and a disposition to resist the laws of the land*."

Not one syllable of all this is denied, and yet the arrest is complained of as unconstitutional.

It must be so apparent as to need no further demonstration, that an arrest of some kind had become necessary for the preservation of public decency. Either General Burnside and his soldiers should have been arrested, or Vallandigham. The only open question is, which was the proper party, and whether a mistake was made as to the man. If Vallandigham was right, General Burnside and every other officer of the army, or navy, every member of the Cabinet, even the President himself, should be forthwith put under arrest. The Federal Congress, which voted supplies for the army engaged in such a foray on the rights and interests of mankind, ought to be promptly dispersed. On the other hand, if the President and Congress, and the Government of the United States are not all criminals, if our Generals and soldiers are not all minions and pimps of a wicked scheme to enslave the people, Vallandigham ought to have been arrested. The acts which General Burnside was sent here to perform, and the acts of Vallandigham, considered as separate acts, or as lines of action, could not possibly go on together. They were, in their essence and nature, incompatible things, and mutually destructive of each other. If General Burnside might have arrested Jefferson Davis, and held him a prisoner, why not Clement L. Vallandigham? If we suppose the Constitution was intended to authorize two such incompatible and mutually destructive lines of action at the same time, we impute an incredible absurdity. If it authorizes the drafting of one part of the population, the organizing of armies, and marching to battle to suppress insurrection, it can not at the same time authorize the other part of the population to thwart, defeat, and annul their efforts. On the other hand, if it authorize a portion of the people to attack, and resist, and discredit the government, it can not require the other portion to make war to defeat them. If the object of the Constitution was to provide for its own destruction and protect its enemies, the arrest of Vallandigham was a mistake: Burnside was the man. But if the object was to provide for the safety of the Constitution, and protect its friends, no mistake has been made. Vallandigham is the man to be arrested. It never could have been intended to allow them both to take the field at the same time.

It is claimed that, since Vallandigham was not a military man, this arrest should have been made by the civil authorities. I understand the argument of learned counsel to be placed on this ground. Beyond or in addition to the ordinary arrests by civil process, none other are allowed under the Constitution, except such as are authorized by military law. Military law, he shows us, consists chiefly in the Rules and Articles of War, and applies only to persons engaged in the military service of the Government. The objection, therefore, is not one which relates to time, place, or circumstance. It denies authority to make such arrests at any time, in any place, or under any circumstances. I am not aware that language can state it more broadly than it was stated by learned counsel. Any arrest or capture made by the army, of persons not in the military service, or so connected with it as to be subject to the rules of military law, is, he argues, an unlawful arrest. All such arrests must be discharged on Habeas Corpus, unless it happen that Habeas Corpus has been suspended. A state of war, civil or other, does not, of itself, he thinks, suspend Habeas Corpus. It is a part of his theory that Habeas Corpus has not yet been suspended.

The unavoidable result of this argument is, if it be the law, that no prisoner has been taken during the war, who could not have had his discharge on Habeas Corpus. The prisoners taken by General Burnside at Roanoke Island, and by General Grant at Fort Donelson, were dischargeable on Habeas Corpus. General Banks can make no such arrests in Louisiana; Rosecrans none in Tennessee; Grant none in Mississippi; Hooker none in Virginia; Hunter none in South Carolina. Most of the prisoners seized by these Generals are citizens of the United States, not engaged in the military or naval service thereof, nor called into actual service as a part of the militia. They could copy the form of the present petition, and conscientiously make oath to every material fact stated in it. It may be said that in those cases the prisoners taken were taken in the act of war, *flagrante delicto.* But if there was no authority to take them, under any circumstances, the fact supposed can make no difference. In order to rest a distinction on the fact of flagrant war, where it exists, it must be admitted that in some cases the authority does exist, which being admitted, the whole proposition goes into collapse and disappears. The inquiry then comes down to an inquiry as to time, place, and circumstance, which is a very distinct and different inquiry.

In truth, however, much of the supposed difference in circumstances does not exist. As Generals commanding different armies of the United States, all in the field for purposes of war, and engaged in actual war, the authority conferred on them by the Constitution must be the same. One may be limited by special instructions, another not; but without reference to such limitation, their general authority and duties as Generals must be equal. The exigencies of war may press sometimes more heavily on one, sometimes on another. But if this is allowed to make a difference in the general authority exercised, the question is reduced to a question of circumstances, which learned counsel by no means admits. Nor does his proposition allow of an exception, if it happen anywhere that the civil administration, and the judiciary as a part of it, be forcibly obstructed and overthrown. This again would reduce it to a question of circumstances. His argument is that this kind of arrest is absolutely forbidden by the Constitution; and being so forbidden, of course no circumstance can make it lawful. The denial is far-reaching and fundamental.

It follows, as a necessary corollary from the proposition, that, if at any time, in any part of the United States, an insurrection can make so much head as to obstruct or overthrow civil administration, it will have gained impunity. If those engaged in it may not be arrested by the army sent against it, they may not be shot. If they can not be persuaded, nothing can be done. The application of restraint is imprisonment; and unless military imprisonment be allowed, no imprisonment can take place. For in the case supposed, the civil administration is no longer practicable. It may be said that in such instances Habeas Corpus must be suspended. This does not meet the argument. We are inquiring what arrests may be lawfully made. Suspension of Habeas Corpus makes no arrest lawful which was before unlawful. It merely suspends one remedy for unlawful arrests. It does not necessarily suspend other remedies, such as actions for false imprisonment and trespass. These are usually provided for by acts of indemnity which are not needed for lawful arrests. In England, these acts of indemnity may be passed by Parliament *after* the war is over; for there is no constitutional prohibition against *ex post facto* laws. But here an indemnity act must pass *before* the imprisonment, to be available as an indemnity. The question now under consideration is, what acts are lawful and need no indemnity? What need can there be to suspend Habeas Corpus, when the civil tribunals, which alone should issue such writs, are already overthrown? The question is, whether every act of battle or of war by our soldiers against an insurrectionary force, is a civil trespass, and needs an act of indemnity? For if our soldiers may kill their enemies, they may capture them. Reduced to its last analysis, it is a question whether it is lawful, by force, to put down an unlawful and forcible opposition to the civil authorities; whether it is an unconstitutional act to enforce the Constitution. If the gentleman's proposition be true, must it not be also true that every forcible attempt to overthrow the Constitution has the guarantee of that instrument to protect it from harm and insure its success. It is attacked by force, and its friends may not strike without committing trespass.

Let us examine the grounds on which he founds his proposition. He cites several well-known provisions of the Constitution: "The trial of all crimes, except in cases of impeachment, shall be by jury; and such trial shall be held in the State where the said crimes shall have been committed." . . "The right of the people to be secure in their persons, houses, papers, and effects, against unreasonable searches and seizures, shall not be violated; and no warrants shall issue but upon probable cause, supported by oath or affirmation, and particularly describing the place to be searched, and the persons or things to be seized." . . . "No person shall be held to answer for a capital or other infamous crime, unless on a presentment or indictment of a grand jury, except in cases arising in the land or naval forces, or in the militia, when in actual service, in time of war or public danger; nor shall any person be subject, for the same offense, to be twice put in jeopardy of life or limb; nor shall be compelled, in any criminal case, to be a witness against himself, nor be deprived of life, liberty, or property without due process of law; nor shall private property be taken for public use, without just compensation;" and some others.

These are parts of the Constitution, very valuable parts, but not the only ones. If the Constitution had provided no means of enforcing the rights here mentioned it would have been very ineffectual to secure them. Its guarantees of these rights might or might not have been worth the paper on which they were written. The argument of learned counsel leaves the Constitution precisely where the framers of it would have left it, if they had put in it no other clauses but these. I ask him what is to be done if it happen that by civil war the courts are overthrown, juries dispersed, and, in the State where the crime was committed, all civil administration is rendered impossible? I ask him what is to be done if it happen that throughout any large portion of the United States the Constitution, and all the officers under it, all its recognized legal processes and tribunals, be forcibly overcome and defied; and if those claiming the protection of the Constitution are, by unlawful violence there, *not* allowed to be secure in their persons, houses, papers, and effects against unreasonable searches and seizures? What if the enemies of the Constitution, in arms against its authority, *do* attack and seize its friends without probable cause, without charges upon oath, and without warrant? What if they *do* deprive them of life, liberty, or property without due process of law, and take private property for public use without due compensation? In a word, what if the enemies of the Constitution suppress, expel, or demolish every vestige of constitutional administration, and substitute therefor war—war by large armies, war by small bands, war by individual assassinations, hatreds, revenges, physical force, war everywhere, so that not one shred or patch of the Constitution remains in that whole region? The question to be answered here is, what is to be done in such a state of affairs? I have listened to the argument of my learned friend with respectful attention. I have wandered with him over many fine fields of declamation, all about liberty and the Constitution, but I find no answer.

Unfortunately the condition of the country urgently requires an answer. I find that answer in other parts of the Constitution. The instrument would have been nugatory, an idle and perhaps cheerful composition, but wholly unworthy of its framers, if it could furnish no answer. If it could furnish no answer, we should find ourselves involved in a situation unprovided for, never contemplated as possible, and one which would be a law unto itself. Being without law for the situation, we should rightfully act upon the necessity before us. But my argument is that the Constitution does provide an answer—a well-expressed and adequate answer. That answer, in substance, is, to meet war with war. I refuse to be dazzled by glittering fragments of a broken Constitution, or to follow their illusory lights into a bottomless bog of anarchy. On behalf of the people I demand the whole Constitution. On that rock we found our liberty, and the gates of hell shall not prevail against it.

It is not necessary to repeat here the numerous passages of the Constitution intended to establish justice and secure liberty. They do not purport to create, but to guard and secure. Justice existed before, but the concern of the framers of the Constitution was to "establish" it. Domestic tranquillity was an object of general desire, yet government was needed to "insure" it. The common defense might be, indeed, had been, conducted by them successfully without a constitution, but they deemed it expedient to "provide" for it. Liberty had been, by them, successfully asserted, but they felt the necessity of a government to "secure" its blessings. Therefore they did "ordain and establish this Constitution of the United States of America." Its framers understood perfectly that, without it, liberty might exist, but it would have no establishment or security. They would have wasted their many weary years with profitless endeavor, to behold, at last, the object of desire "speed away on cherub pinions — the guide of homeless winds and playmate of the waves."

How, then, did they secure liberty?

In the order of securities we find, first, certain declaratory clauses. It is one step toward establishing and securing rights to agree upon them and declare them. The citizens of each State shall be entitled to all the privileges and immunities of citizens of the several States. Private property shall not be taken for public use without due compensation. No person shall be deprived of life, liberty, or property without due process of law, and other clauses before quoted. It is observable that in these declarations are embraced rights of a different grade—rights called absolute and indefeasible, and rights merely conventional or secondary. But they are all declared with the same solemnity, and secured by the same guarantees. Materials of different degrees of solidity and costliness were fitted to their respective places in the edifice. The whole structure was necessary for the purpose contemplated, and all its parts and details were necessary to the structure. They do not tell us which of them could be taken away without danger to all.

It was necessary to go further and provide for the enforcement of these declarations. The first step was to provide for electing a chief executive officer, to preside over and enforce the laws. Without him the whole machinery would fail. Except in the manner there provided, there can be no President elected. But an election of President implies other things. When elected, he is to perform duties and exercise his faculties. Another practical security is provided by ordaining the election of a legislative body, and prescribing its functions, and declaring "That this Constitution, and the laws of the United States which shall be made in pursuance thereof, and all treaties made or which shall be made under the authority of the United States, shall be the supreme law of the land; and the judges in every State shall be bound thereby, any thing in the constitution or laws of any State to the contrary notwithstanding." But, further than this, the Constitution provides for courts, judges, and marshals, to adjudicate and enforce the laws. It does not stop there. In all ages of the world men have been found not obedient to judicial decisions; sometimes numerous and strong enough to overthrow and defy all the processes of civil administration. The Constitution does not fail to provide for such an emergency. It crowns the guarantees before offered by providing for an adequate physical force to overcome all opposition. It speaks of a well-regulated militia as necessary for the security of a free state. It provides authority to "raise and support armies, to provide and maintain a navy, and to declare war." It provides for organizing, arming, and disciplining the militia; for calling forth the militia to execute the laws of the Union, suppress insurrections, and repel invasions. It makes the President "commander-in-chief of the army and navy of the United

States, and of the militia of the several States when called into the actual service of the United States." Thus placing at his disposal the entire resources of the country, it requires of him, before entering upon his office, to invoke the sanction of Almighty God, and clothe himself with an oath: "I do solemnly swear (or affirm) that I will faithfully execute the office of President of the United States, and will, to the best of my ability, preserve, protect, and defend the Constitution of the United States."

The President is no longer a free man in the chimerical sense of freedom which we hear so much of. But he is not less free than other citizens, who are all bound to support the Constitution. It is not one of the liberties secured by the Constitution, to select some particular right there guaranteed, to maintain it as distinct from and in opposition to the rest, or to hold fast to that one and let go the rest. Each holds his rights upon one ineradicable condition, that he shall, to the extent of his ability, maintain and defend every part of the Constitution. He can not throw off his allegiance, defy the government, make war upon it, and, at the same time, claim its protection. When he lifts his arm against the Constitution, the arm may be cut off without giving him a right to complain of cruel and unusual punishments. When he lifts his voice against the liberties of his countrymen, his voice may be silenced in the interests of freedom of speech. When he arms himself to assail the defenders of the Constitution, those arms may be taken from him in the interest of the general right to bear arms. When he makes of his house a shelter for traitors, and barricades it from the approach of patriots, it may be broken open and searched in the general interest of freedom from unreasonable searches and seizures.

In the civil administration different remedies are applied, each after its kind. A writ of capias seizes the body, but it does not violate the constitutional guarantees of personal liberty; an attachment lays hold of goods, but does not violate property rights; a replevin breaks open houses, but does not conflict with the right to be protected from unreasonable searches and seizures. The common law furnishes redress in some instances; equity in others; maritime law in others. Each of these is so far exclusive as, when properly appealed to, not to be interfered with by any other; and, while in progress, to be governed exclusively by its own rules. War is the last resort, but when properly appealed to, its processes are due and reasonable processes, and, like the rest, must be allowed to work out results exclusively by its own rules.

"The body of a nation can not, then, abandon a province, a town, or even a single individual who is part of it, unless compelled to it by necessity, or indispensably obliged to it by the strongest reasons, founded on the public safety.

"Since, then, a nation is obliged to preserve itself, it has a right to every thing necessary for its preservation. For the law of nations gives us a right to every thing without which we can not fulfill our obligation; otherwise it would oblige us to do impossibilities, or rather, would contradict itself in prescribing us a duty, and, at the same time, debarring us of the only means of fulfilling it." . . .

"*A nation or State has a right to every thing that can help to ward off imminent danger, and keep at a distance whatever is capable of causing its ruin, and that from the very same reasons that establish its right to the things necessary to its preservation.*" (Vattel's Law of Nations, 5, 6.)

The right of nations here described has been fully preserved to the United States by their Constitution, so far as the question under debate is affected. The power to make war is given without limitations. So far as war may be a means of preservation, or for warding off imminent danger, and keeping at a distance whatever is capable of causing its ruin, the nation is safe. The rights of war are as sacredly guaranteed as trial by jury, or personal liberty, or any other right whatever. The President can not claim to have preserved, protected, and defended the Constitution, TO THE BEST OF HIS ABILITY, until he shall have used all the ability given him by the utmost rights of war. He who declares he is willing to support the war, provided it creates no disturbance, only declares he is willing to support it, provided it shall be so conducted as to be really something else, and not war.

The Constitution does not define the meaning of Habeas Corpus, or trial by jury, or liberty, or war. They were to be ascertained elsewhere. I have before shown a definition of civil liberty. One of its conditions is an abridgment of natural liberty. Liberty was not abridged of the right to call in war to her defense, but she could not be endowed with a capacity for impossibilities. She could not require of human nature that which would be impossible to God himself, repose and commotion, peace and war at the same time. War could do little for Liberty, if she should hang forever sobbing on his neck, pinioning his arms, and holding him back from being War indeed. No! in this solemn time of domestic sorrow and of public peril, it is little better than sacrilege thus to potter with the meaning of words. By liberty was intended such liberty as was possible to mankind. By war was intended not a hollow pretext of war, but a lifting high of the red right hand of avenging justice. A thorough, condign, effectual laying hold of enemies ; a summary breaking-up of their hiding places, and a terrifying, deathly pursuit, until they shall cease to exist, or cease to be enemies.

In Scott's Military Dictionary, a recent work, which, he says, was not prepared in view of existing disturbances, he states the following rule, p. 273 :

"With regard to the requisition of military aid by the civil magistrate, the rule seems to be that when once the magistrate has charged the military officer with the duty of suppressing a riot, the execution of that duty is wholly confided to the judgment and skill of the military officer, *who thenceforward acts independently of the magistrate until the service required is fully performed.* The magistrate can not dictate to the officer the mode of executing the duty; and an officer would desert his duty if he submitted to receive any such orders from the magistrate. Neither is it necessary for the magistrate to accompany the officer in the execution of his duty. The learning on these points may be gathered from the charge of Mr. Justice Littledale, to the jury, in the trial of the Mayor of Bristol for breach of duty in not suppressing the riots at that city in 1831."

I have spoken of military law, which is claimed, by learned counsel on the other side, to be a law for military men. This law is often mistaken for or confounded with martial law, but the terms are very far from convertible. Martial law is often defined as no law at all; but this definition is rather an objurgation against than a description of it. I venture to define martial law to be the rule of action adopted by all nations, and at all periods of the world, by which, in times of war, to guard against dangers that often arise, and by reason of the necessity of it, such discretion is given to the military commander, measured by the requirements of the situation, as shall insure to his force the best chances of success. It is that established practice, that common law of nations, by which, under the compulsion of right reason, when they have called an army into the field for war, and confided to it the safety of the commonwealth, they allow it, without hinderance or interruption, to perform its work.

Counsel for petitioner reads to us many authorities to show that military law applies only to military men. Beyond this his argument is comprised either in a broad denial that *martial law* means any thing more than is intended by *military law;* or, if it does, an equally broad denial that it does or can exist in Great Britain or the United States. His limitation of the *military law*, so called, appears to me rather more narrow than the authorities justify; but for the purposes of this argument, I have no controversy with him there. Let him take for granted all that I understand him to claim, as to the rule concerning *military law.* The questions remain whether martial law or the laws of war, or the rights of war — phrases interchangeably used by the Supreme Court of the United States, in discussing the theme, and by writers — mean more than military law; and if they mean more, whether they can exist in Great Britain or the United States. On both these questions counsel for petitioner takes the negative. If I can show him to be wrong here,

I shall have defeated his whole argument. For, although his argument is not confined to these inquiries, all other parts of it depend upon them.

I have already cited Vattel to show that the same rules or laws of war apply, or ought to apply, to civil as to foreign war. The only doubt is, whether persons in insurrection against their own government, can rightfully claim the same treatment applied in mitigation of the rigors of war to foreign enemies. The most merciful rule is the one to which Vattel inclines for reasons of expediency and humanity. It is the rule applied by our own government in this war. It is quite unnecessary to cite authorities to show that in foreign war the authority of a General is not limited to the military force under his command. During the Peninsular war, Wellington governed Spain and Portugal, and afterward a part of France, in the exercise of well-known and commonly-acknowledged rights of war. In our war with Mexico General Scott promulgated and enforced a plan for the government of Mexico. Some debate was raised at home whether the Constitution conferred so much power on a General. It was acquiesced in and approved. There could be no doubt of the authority to make war, and this was a necessary incident. Under the same rule Rosecrans controls civil administration in Tennessee, and Banks in Louisiana, and Curtis did in Missouri. Doubtless persons captured in flagrant acts of treason may be hung. As the greater includes the less, the right to hang implies the right to inflict lesser evil. They are, therefore, allowed to be treated as prisoners of war. I am now speaking of the existence of rights of war, laws of war, or martial law, and showing them not to be limited to military men, and to be much more comprehensive than *military law*—indeed, entirely distinct and different from it. I am not now making the application to Vallandigham. That is a question of circumstances. I am replying to the argument which denies the existence or application of such a law under any circumstances.

To maintain his denials counsel cites many English authorities—among them Sir Matthew Hale—and he claims, as the result of those authorities, that martial law has been definitively abandoned and prohibited in England. These authorities do, some of them, show that certain gross abuses, which were practiced by the Stuarts in England, under the pretext and name of martial law, but which found as little justification under martial law as under any other, have been prohibited. Perhaps he could show, with smaller research, that measures have been taken to prevent a repetition of the infamous and bloody assizes of Jefferies ; but this would not go very far to discredit trial by jury. Trial by jury yet exists in England; and martial law is applied there as often as occasion requires. If any thing may be fairly assailed by holding it responsible for abuses, the judiciary would be one of the first institutions of government to fall. Looking over the history of past ages, it is apparent that military men would have some difficulty in establishing a claim to a leadership in the abuses inflicted on mankind. Most of the historical struggles for liberty have resulted from a real and natural antagonism between peoples and their rulers; rulers claiming, by some heritable superiority, to govern, and people feeling the government mainly in its oppressions. Whether judges or military men are most responsible for the cruelties inflicted in such struggles may be doubted. From a somewhat patient reading of law-books, I am, however, prepared to admit that judges have felt much less alarm and indignation at stretches of power practiced by themselves, than they have felt at the assumption of undue power by military men. If there were no history except what we find in law-books, judges would have a decided advantage over Generals. There are, also, specimens of popular forensic eloquence, originally delivered as the voice of the people against despotic governments, (some of them quite out of hearing), which never lose their attractions. We rather like to hear them launched against our own government, that is to say, ourselves. The difficulty of playing both people and tyrant, at the same time, is scarcely appreciable in these popular amusements.

I am relieved from stating my own conclusions concerning the numerous English authorities cited, by finding an examination of them, and an opinion concerning them, by Mr. Attorney-General Cushing. (Opinions of Att'ys Gen'l U. S., vol. 8, p. 365.)

The Attorney-General, after remarking upon English authorities, sums up:

"*In fine, the common law authorities and commentators afford no clue to what martial law, as understood in England, really is; but much light is thrown upon the subject by debates in Parliament, and by facts in the executive action of government.*"

This is a report to his own government by one of the most learned and laborious Attorneys-General the United States ever had. He quotes Sir Matthew Hale, also:

"Martial law is not, in truth and reality, a law, but something indulged rather than allowed as a law: the necessity of government, order, discipline in the army, is that only which gives these laws a countenance." (Hist. Com. Law, p. 39.)

Mr. Attorney-General says:

"This proposition is a mere composite blunder, a total misapprehension of the matter. It confounds *martial law* and *law military:* it ascribes to the former the uses of the latter; it erroneously assumes that the government of a body of troops is a *necessity*, more than that of a body of civilians, or citizens. It confounds and confuses all the relations of the subject, and is an apt illustration of the incompleteness of the notions of the common-law jurists of England in regard to matters not comprehended in that limited branch of legal science."

"Even at a later day, in England, when some glimmerings of light on the subject began to appear, the nature of the martial law remained without accurate appreciation in Westminster Hall."

He cites the case of Grant *v.* Sir Charles Gould, (2 H. Blackstone, 98), decided by Lord Loughborough, who said: "The essence of martial law consists in its being a jurisdiction over all *military* persons, in all circumstances." And because military men are triable for many offenses, and have their personal rights, for the most part, regulated by law—"Therefore," he says, "it is totally inaccurate to state martial law as having any place whatever in the realm of Great Britain.'

Mr. Attorney-General says: "This is *totally inaccurate*," and explains why.

Mr. Attorney-General then quotes Stephens's commentaries, vol. 11, p. 602, note.

> "Martial law," says Stephens, "may be defined as the law, whatever it may be, which is imposed by military power; and has no place in the institutions of this country, (England), unless the Articles of War, established under the acts just mentioned, be considered as of that character."

The Attorney-General proceeds:

> "Here again is pitiable confusion; for the Articles of War are not a law 'imposed by the military power,' nor is martial law confined in its origin to the military power as the source of its existence."

The confusion among English lawyers, remarked by the Attorney-General, will account, probably, for some inconsistencies of *expression* among English statesmen on this subject, though the *action* of English statesmen is sufficiently clear and consistent. The question whether martial law has "a place in the realm of Great Britain," as denied by Lord Loughborough, or "a place in the institutions of England," as denied by Mr. Stephens, is purely a question of historical fact, and history is against them. Nor is the question open to doubt. Martial law, such as I claim, has been unquestionably adopted and enforced in Great Britain and her provinces as often as any occasion has been felt for it. I may here dismiss the English authorities.

Mr. Attorney-General Cushing, in his opinion, makes a most learned examination of the topic, and says:

> "Looking into the legislation of other countries, we shall find all the legal relations of this subject thoroughly explained, so as to furnish to us ideas at least, if not analogies, by means of which to appreciate some of its legal relations in the United States."

These legal relations appear to be better defined in France than elsewhere. Three conditions or states are there provided for. 1. Peace. In the state of peace, all military men are subject to the law military, *leaving the civil authority untouched*, in its own sphere, to govern all persons, whether civil or military, in class. 2. The state of war. When it exists, the military authority *may have to take precedence of the civil authority, which, nevertheless, is not deprived of its ordinary attributes, but, in order to exercise them, must, of necessity, enter into concert with the military commander*. 3. The state of siege. When it exists, all the local authority passes to the military commander, who exercises it in his own person, or delegates it, if he please, to the civil magistrates, to be exercised by them under his orders. The civil law is suspended for the time being, or, at least, made subordinate, and its place is taken by martial law, under the supreme, if not direct administration of the military power. "*The state of siege may exist in a city, or in a district of country, either by reason of the same being actually besieged or invested by a hostile force, or by reason of domestic insurrection.*"

Of these different stages, Mr. Cushing concludes, the state of siege is equivalent to the proclamation of martial law in England and the United States.

I remark upon this, that these distinctions, after all, between a state of war and a state of siege, are not very valuable. Martial law is a thing of necessity, and is limited by the necessity, so that the less urgent the necessity, the less extensive the power. It places in the hands of the General a discretion, as discretion is placed sometimes in the hands of judges and chancellors. It is said that martial law is no law; and it is said that equity is the length of the chancellor's foot. But the chancellor, like the General, is required to exercise a "sound discretion," a "reasonable discretion," a "wise discretion, in view of all the circumstances."

The New American Cyclopedia says:

"Martial law is often confounded with military law; but these terms are by no means convertible." Speaking of martial law, it says: "It proceeds directly from the military power which has now become supreme. Yet, remotely and indirectly, martial law expresses the will of the people."

"Martial law has often been confounded with military law, but the two are very different. Military law, with us, consists of the 'Rules and Articles of War,' and other statutory provisions for the government of military persons, to which may be added the unwritten or common law of the 'usage and custom of military service.' It exists equally in peace and in war, and is as fixed and definite in its provisions as the admiralty, ecclesiastical, or any other branch of law, and is equally, with them, a part of the general law of the land. But, in the words of Chancellor Kent, 'martial law is quite a distinct thing.' It exists only in the time of war, and originates in military necessity. It derives no authority from the civil law (using the term in its more general sense), nor assistance from the civil tribunals, for it overrules, suspends, and replaces both. It is, from its very nature, an arbitrary power, and 'extends to all the inhabitants (whether civil or military) of the district where it is in force.' It has been used in all countries, and by all governments, and it is as necessary to the sovereignty of a state as the power to declare and make war. The right to declare, apply, and enforce martial law, is one of the sovereign powers, and resides in the governing authority of the state, and it depends upon the constitution of the state whether restrictions and rules are to be adopted for its application, or whether it is to be exercised according to the exigencies which call it into existence. But even when left unrestricted by constitutional or statutory law, like the power of a civil court to punish contempts, it must be exercised with due moderation and justice; and, as 'paramount necessity' alone can call it into existence, so must its exercise be limited to such times and places as this necessity may require; and, moreover, it must be governed by the rules of general public law, as applied to a state of war. It, therefore, can not be despotically or arbitrarily exercised, any more than any other belligerent right can be so exercised." (Cushing, Opinions of U. S. Att'ys Gen'l, vol. 8, pp. 365, et. seq.; Wolfius, Jus Gentium, sec. 863; Grotius, De Jur. Bel. ac Pac., lib. 2, cap. 8; Kluber, Droit des Gens, sec. 255; O'Brien, American Military Law, p. 28.) (International Law and Laws of War. Halleck, 373.)

"Martial *law*, then, is that military rule and authority which exists in time of war, and is conferred by the laws of war, in relation to persons and things, under and within the scope of active military operations in carrying on the war, and which extinguishes or suspends civil rights, and the remedies founded upon them, for the time being, so far as it may appear to be necessary in order to the full accomplishment of the purpose of the war—the party who exercises it being liable in an action for any abuse of the authority thus conferred. It is the application of military government—the government of force—to persons and property within the scope of it, according to the laws and usages of war, to the exclusion of the municipal government, in all respects where the latter would impair the efficiency of military law or military action." (Benet's Military Law and Courts-martial, 14.)

"We remark, in conclusion, that the right to declare, apply, and exercise martial law is one of the rights of sovereignty, and is as essential to the existence of a state as is the right to declare or carry on war. It is one of the incidents of war; and, like the power to take human life in battle, results directly and immediately from the fact that war legally exists. It is a power inherent in every government, and must be regarded and recognized by all other governments; but the question of the authority of any particular functionary to exercise this power, is a matter to be determined by local and not by international law. Like a declaration of a siege or blockade, the power of the officer who makes it is to be presumed until disavowed, and neutrals who attempt to act in derogation of that authority, do so at their peril." (International Law and Laws of War. Halleck, 380.)

"The English common law authorities and commentators generally confound *martial* with *military* law, and, consequently, throw very little light upon the subject, considered as a domestic fact; and in parliamentary debates, it has usually been discussed as a *fact*, rather than as forming any part of their system of jurisprudence. Nevertheless, there are numerous instances in which martial law has been declared and enforced, in time of rebellion or insurrection, not only in India and British colonial possessions, but also in England and Ireland. It seems that no act of Parliament is required to precede such declaration, although it is usually followed by an act of indemnity, when the disturbances which called it forth are at an end, in order to give constitutional existence to the *fact* of martial law. (*Id.*, *Ib.* 374.)

I will now ask attention to two cases discussed in the Supreme Court of the United States, which give the sanction of that Court to the doctrine I am endeavoring to sustain.

The Constitution provides that private property shall not be taken for public use without due compensation. Yet a General, going to war, could not post his sentinels without committing what would be, in peace, a trespass. Every mile of his march, with ordinary military precautions, every encampment, would be a violation of law. In Mitchell *v.* Harmony, 13 How. 115, the plaintiff below had sued an officer of the army of the United States for taking his property during the war with Mexico. It was taken on error to the Supreme Court of the United States, on exceptions to the charge of the Circuit Judge to the jury. Chief-Justice Taney said, p. 133:

"Upon these two grounds of defense the Circuit Court instructed the jury that the defendant might lawfully take possession of the goods of the plaintiff to prevent them from falling into the hands of the public enemy; but in order to justify the seizure, the danger must be immediate and impending, and not remote or contingent. And that he might also take them for public uses and impress them into the public service, in case of an immediate and pressing danger or urgent necessity existing at the time, but not otherwise."

The charge, as thus stated, was sustained. Again, on page 134, the Chief-Justice said:

"There are, without doubt, occasions in which private property may lawfully be taken possession of or destroyed, to prevent it from falling into the hands of the public enemy; and also where a military officer, charged with a particular duty, may impress private property into the public service, or take it for public use. Unquestionably, in such cases, the government is bound to make full compensation to the owner; *but the officer is not a trespasser.*" . . . "It is the emergency that gives the right, and the emergency must be shown to exist before the taking can be justified. *In deciding upon this necessity, however, the state of the facts, as they appeared to the officer, at the time he acted, must govern the decision; for he must necessarily act upon the information of others, as well as his own observation.*"

Mr. Justice Daniel delivered a dissenting opinion on other points. But on this point he said, p. 139:

"The principle itself, if properly applied, of the right to take property to prevent it from falling into the hands of the enemy, is undisputed."

And again, same page:

"I have no doubt of the right of a military officer, in a case of extreme necessity, for the safety of the government or army, to take private property for the public service."

Again, p. 140:

"*The safety of the country is paramount, and the rights of the individual must yield in case of extreme necessity.*"

Observe that this is not placed on the ground that, in extreme necessity, the Constitution is suspended, and the laws properly broken; but it is held to be a lawful act. They do not look upon it as trespass, excusable from great urgency, but they declare it not to be a trespass. The officer is clothed with a lawful right to do it. But this property right is guarded by the same sanctions in the Constitution with the right of personal liberty. Inasmuch as a *person* may give the enemy more help, or expose our own army to greater dangers than *property* could, the reason is more cogent when applied to persons.

During the celebrated Dorr rebellion, the Legislature of Rhode Island passed an act declaring the State under martial law. One Martin Luther being charged with aiding and abetting the rebellion, his house was broken open and entered, and he was arrested, or, in the language of the petition in this case, he was "seized by overpowering numbers." He brought an action against the parties who made the arrest, in trespass *quare clansum fregit.* They justified under the statute declaring martial law. It appears that there was not, in that case, more than in this, "any warrant issued upon probable cause, supported by oath or affirmation." In that action martial law, as a topic, came under discussion in the Supreme Court of the United States. (Luther *v.* Borden *et al.*, 7 H. 1.) Chief-Justice Taney delivered the opinion of the Court, from which I shall presently read. But before doing so, I propose to read from the dissenting opinion of Mr. Justice Woodbury, and to invite the attention of learned counsel on the other side to his descriptions of martial law, and the distinction he makes between what is called military law and martial law. It will appear that Mr. Justice Woodbury entertained an antipathy to martial law, at least, as vehement as that of counsel on the other side. The kind of martial law then under discussion, and which was sanctioned by the Court, well appears in his opinion. I shall read some passages showing that, with all his antipathy for military power, he did admit the propriety of an occasional exercise of military authority, precisely such as I say is authorized by martial law, and under precisely such circumstances. The difference between his position and the one which I am endeavoring to maintain, is this: He considers the exercise of the power in question to be meritorious, and deserving the gratitude of the country, but a breach of the law. I am endeavoring to maintain that it is in accordance with law. His Honor quotes the language of the Rhode Island statute, declaring martial law to be in force over the entire State, and on page 59 says:

"Now the words martial law, as here used, can not be construed in any other than their legal sense, long known and recognized in legal precedents as well as political history. (See it in Hallam's Const. Hist. ch. —, p. 258. 1 MacArthur on Courts-martial, 33.) The legislature evidently meant to be understood in that sense by using words of such well-settled construction, without any limit or qualification, and covering the whole State with its influence, under a supposed exigency and justification for such an unusual course. I do not understand this to be directly combated in the opinion just delivered by the Chief-Justice."

He then declares it to be manifest that it meant the ancient martial law "often used before the Petition of Right, and sometimes since." He adverts to the fact that defendants do not aver the existence of any civil precept, which they were aiding civil officers to execute, but set up merely military orders under martial law. The dissenting opinion then argues that this did not mean merely a suspension of Habeas Corpus, nor the military code used in the armies of the United States and England:

> "For," said his Honor, "nothing is better settled than that military law applies only to the military, *but martial law is made here to apply to all.*"

Again, page 61:

> "So it is a settled principle, even in England, that under the British Constitution the military law does, in no respect, either supersede or interfere with the civil law of the realm; and that the former is, in general, subordinate to the latter, (Tytler on Military Law, 36, 51), *while martial law overrides them all.*"

On page 62 his Honor gives us a lively description of martial law, such as was declared by the statute in Rhode Island, and such as "described in judicial as well as political history." The rhetoric of learned counsel on the other side has often excited my admiration; never more than in his opening argument, when he denounced martial law. But here is a passage from Judge Woodbury, written, probably, with more care, and, perhaps, with greater experience, which I hope to be pardoned for saying, is rather superior to any thing we had the pleasure of listening to this morning. It lacked only the fine voice and elocution of the advocate of Mr. Vallandigham to make it even more effective than any thing he uttered:

> "It exposed," says Mr. Justice Woodbury, "the whole population, not only to be seized without warrant or oath, and their houses broken open and rifled, and this where the municipal law and its officers and courts remained undisturbed and able to punish all offenses, but to send prisoners, thus summarily arrested in a civil strife, to all the harsh pains and penalties of courts-martial, or extraordinary commission, and for all kinds of supposed offenses. By it every citizen, instead of reposing under the shield of known and fixed laws as to liberty, property, and life, exists with a rope round his neck, subject to be hung up by a military despot at the next lamp-post, under the sentence of some drum-head court-martial."

After reading these animated and highly-wrought judicial statements of impressions of a military court, one feels an inclination, from motives of literary curiosity, to read some description, by an imaginative military man, of a Court of Chancery. The effect of subordinate and accidental circumstances on the imagination is notable. His Honor had been obviously affected by thoughts of a drum-head as one of the articles sometimes made use of at a military trial. They do not use drum-heads in the Supreme Court of the United States, having conveniences for writing of a more fixed and satisfactory nature. One would wish to see an equally vivid account, by some General, how his imagination was affected by sight of his Honor's long black gown, without hoops or tournure. The drum-head excited in his Honor's mind thoughts of a whole population, and especially peaceful citizens, each with a rope round his neck, waiting to be hung—hung to a lamp-post, and not only a lamp-post, but the nearest lamp-post. It is to be presumed that the thoughts suggested to a General by his Honor's wig and gown, might have been more maternal and far less suffocating. But it may be reckoned as certain that a military commander would have felt some shock or revulsion at hearing from that august tribunal, issuing solemnly forth from the blackness of an aged and collapsed gown, a judicial representation of martial law: not invoked as a shelter from imminent peril to the State, and used because nothing less summary could be availing, nor used in the interest of civil order, but as inexcusably obtruded upon a people enjoying the beatitudes of undisturbed peace, and who but for it would be "reposing under the shield of known and fixed laws as to liberty, property, and life." Such being the product of judicial reason in the highest civil tribunal, a General might turn back to his drum-head without a very deep conviction of its inferiority.

His Honor says, p. 64:

"It appears, also, that nobody has dared to exercise it, in war or peace, on the community at large, in England, for the last century and a half, unless specially enacted by Parliament in some great exigency, and under various restrictions, and then under the theory not that it is consistent with bills of rights and constitutions, but that Parliament is omnipotent, and, for sufficient cause, may override and trample on them all temporarily."

"After the civil authorities have become prostrated in particular places, and the din of arms has reached the most advanced stages of intestine commotions, a Parliament, which alone furnishes the means of war—a Parliament unlimited in its powers—has, *in extremis*, on two or three occasions, ventured on martial law beyond the military," etc.

The question now under debate is, not who may declare martial law, but whether, in any emergency, it may be declared. Nevertheless, his Honor is under a mistake as to the fact. (See Hansard's Parl. His. 1801, vol. 35, pp. 1013, 1018, 1024.) In a debate in the House of Commons, in 1801, Lord Castlereagh said:

"I perfectly understand that the prerogative of the Crown authorizes those acting under its authority to exercise martial law. I maintain that it is a constitutional mode for the executive government to exercise martial law in the first instance, and to come to Parliament for indemnity afterward, and is preferable to applying to Parliament first. . . . . *The rebellion in Ireland broke out in May, 1798: the executive government published a proclamation of martial law wherever the rebellion existed, without any express law for that purpose.* They did it on the principle that they were authorized by the king's prerogative, provided they did not transgress the necessity of the case, and sure I am that nothing could have induced them to have departed from the strict constitutional system, but that they felt they must deny to a great part of the country the advantages of the civil law, unless it were incorporated with the martial law. The two systems, existing at the same time, led to such a conflict of jurisdiction it was impossible to give effect to others."

It was denied by others that the proclamation of martial law could rightfully be made by virtue of the king's prerogative. The fact, however, is beyond question: *it was made, and not by Parliament.*

His Honor, Judge Woodbury, p. 69, says:

"All our social usages and political education, as well as our constitutional checks, are the other way. It would be alarming enough here to sanction an unlimited power, exercised by legislators, or the executive, or courts, when all our governments are themselves governments of limitations and checks, and of fixed and known laws; and the people a race above all others jealous of encroachments by those in power."

He nowhere drops the fallacy of regarding martial law as a substitute for civil law in time of peace and safety. He keeps up the illusion of constitutional checks and limitations standing unassailed, free from threatened overthrow, and needing no military support. On this halcyon scene he imagines to be thrust the sudden, unnecessary march of armies; he is startled at the vision of bayonets and the sound of military command. With equally cogent logic might he demonstrate the inappropriateness of snow in harvest. Through all this elaboration, there breaks upon him, at last, a dim consciousness of not having met the question. He rids himself of it by one dogmatic stroke, and hurries forward to lose himself again in a thicket of evasions. During this moment of consciousness, he says, p. 69:

"And it is far better that those persons should be without the protection of the ordinary laws of the land, who disregard them in an emergency, and should look to a grateful country for indemnity and pardon, than to allow, beforehand, the whole frame of jurisprudence to be overturned, and every thing placed at the mercy of the bayonet."

Here, at last, is all the argument against martial law that is produced, either in this dissenting opinion, or elsewhere. *Multum in parvo.* The occasional necessity for extraordinary remedies is admitted. That it is a rule of action among men to resort to these remedies, when needed, is not denied. That those who, in cases of peril, perform these services are entitled to the gratitude of their country, and may properly look to it for indemnity, is not only conceded, but is urged as part of the argument. If we may be grateful to those who, in an emergency, overturn the whole frame of jurisprudence, might we not be still more grateful to those who made a frame of jurisprudence which does not require, in an emergency, to be overturned? It is conceded that, in times of peril, the public safety is the supreme law. But it is argued that because this law might be perverted and abused, it should itself be considered a perversion and abuse; one which entitles the performer to the gratitude of his country. It is customary to erect monuments to those who are entitled to public gratitude. On the theory I am combating, the inscription should be, "*Sacred to the memory of a patriot, who earned the gratitude of his country by perverting and abusing its laws, and by overturning the whole frame of its jurisprudence.*" The argument presupposes that persons intrusted with government functions are so bad that, if allowed by law to do the act when necessary, they would be likely to do it when not necessary. To avoid this danger, they are to be considered so good as to be relied upon to overturn the government, if need be, in order to save it. There is so much danger that public men will violate the law under false pretexts, they are to be encouraged to violate it without any pretext. And such violation is to be considered a legitimate means of becoming public benefactors. Is it possible for absurdity to go further?

In the next paragraph, we find his Honor no more face to face with the question, but retired behind a screen:

> "No tribunal or department in our system of governments ever can be lawfully authorized to dispense with the laws, like some of the tyrannical Stuarts, or to repeal, or abolish, or suspend the whole body of them; or, in other words, appoint an unrestrained military dictator at the head of armed men."

Again and again, the question is not whether the laws may be dispensed with. It is whether the laws authorize, in certain situations, the performance of acts which, if performed, even against the law, would be titles to public gratitude. Why should we be always answered only by an absurd jingle of words—

about being "*lawfully authorized to dispense with the laws, like some of the tyrannical Stuarts.*" Is it claimed that the tyrannical Stuarts were lawfully authorized to dispense with the laws? Or, if they were, did his Honor imagine that the fair administration and enforcement of a law is the same sort of thing, the same kind of tyranny, as dispensing with it? On his own theory, the Stuarts might have been entitled to public gratitude, if they had happened to overturn the law at the right time. The question is, whether, in great emergencies, the commander of the military force may be considered as lawfully intrusted with a discretion, limited and restrained strictly within the necessity of the occasion? In reply to this question, his Honor denies that there ought to be "an unrestrained military dictator at the head of armed men." He denies that authority exists to repeal, abolish, or suspend, the whole body of the laws. But if no tribunal or department in our government is authorized to overthrow or suspend the laws, are they authorized to allow others to overturn them? The question is, what may be done to save the laws from overthrow? The army and navy and militia are at the President's command, and his oath binds him "to the best of my ability."

On pages 75 and 82, his Honor refers to the different steps toward war powers, which precede the shock of war and the laws of war. And, on page 83, he says:

"The necessities of foreign war, it is conceded, sometimes impart great powers as to both things and persons. But they are modified by those necessities, and subjected to numerous regulations of national law and justice and humanity. . . . . *So may it be in some extreme stages of civil war. Among these, my impression is that a state of war, whether foreign or domestic, may exist, in the great perils of which it is competent,* UNDER ITS RIGHTS, AND ON PRINCIPLES OF NATIONAL LAW, for a commanding officer of troops, under the controlling government, to extend certain rights of war, not only over his camp, but its environs and the near field of his military operations. But no further nor wider. On this rested the justification of one of the great commanders of this country, and of the age, in a transaction so well known at New Orleans." . . . . "If matters in this case had reached such a crisis, and had been so recognized by the government, or if such a state of things could and did exist as to warrant such a measure, independent of that government, and it was properly pleaded, *the defendants might, perhaps, be justified within those limits, and under such orders, in making search for an offender, or an opposing combatant, and, under some circumstances, in breaking into houses for his arrest.*"

I will restore the passage omitted at the place of the asterisks above: "But in civil strife, they (the rights of war) are not to extend beyond the place where insurrection exists. Nor to portions of the State remote from the scene of military operations. Nor after the resistance is over. Nor to persons not connected with it. Nor even within the same, can they extend to the person or property of citizens against whom no probable cause exists which may justify it. Nor to the property of any person without necessity or civil precept."

His Honor, at last, after all his reluctance, comes to a full admission of the legality of such arrests. The only condition is, time, place, circumstance. His Honor, however, substitutes a phrase. I have called it martial law. He calls it the rights of war. It is of no importance to my argument which phrase is used. The thing which he has been denouncing as an overthrow of all law, he at last admits to be lawful. He also places these personal arrests in the same category with military seizures of property, which that Court holds to be lawful.

I may now turn to the opinion of the Court as delivered by Chief-Justice Taney, p. 45:

"The remaining question," says the Chief-Justice, "is whether the defendants, acting under military orders, issued under the authority of the government, were justified in breaking and entering the plaintiff's house. In relation to the act of the Legislature declaring martial law, it is not necessary, in the case before us, to inquire to what extent, or under what circumstances, that power may be exercised by a State. Unquestionably a military government, established as the permanent government of a State, would not be a republican government, and it would be the duty of Congress to overthrow it. But the law of Rhode Island evidently contemplated no such government.

It was intended merely for the crisis, and to meet the peril in which the existing government was placed by the armed resistance to its authority. It was so understood and construed by the State authorities, and, unquestionably, a State may use its military power to put down an armed insurrection too strong to be controlled by the civil authority. *The power is essential to the existence of every government, essential to the preservation of order and free institutions, and is as necessary to the States of this Union as to any other government.* The State itself must determine what degree of force the crisis demands. And if the government of Rhode Island deemed the armed opposition so formidable, and so ramified throughout the State, as to require the use of its military force, and the declaration of martial law, we see no ground upon which this Court can question its authority. *It was a state of war; and the established government resorted to the rights and usages of war to maintain itself, and to overcome the unlawful opposition.* And, in that state of things, the officers engaged in its military service might lawfully arrest any one who, from the information before them, they had reasonable grounds to believe was engaged in the insurrection, and might order a house to be forcibly entered and searched, when there were reasonable grounus for supposing he might be there concealed. *Without power to do this, martial law and the military array of the government would be mere parade, and rather encourage attack than repel it.* No more force, however, can be used than is necessary to accomplish the object. And if the power is used for purposes of oppression, or any injury willfully done to person or property, the party by whom, or by whose order, it is committed, would undoubtedly be answerable."

"We forbear to remark upon the cases referred to in the argument, in relation to the commissions anciently issued by the kings of England to commissioners to proceed against certain descriptions of persons, in certain places, by the law martial. These commissions were issued by the king at his pleasure, without the concurrence or authority of Parliament, and were often abused for the most despotic and oppressive purposes. They were used before the regal power of England was well defined, and were finally abolished and prohibited by the Petition of Right, in the reign of Charles the First. But they bear no analogy in any respect to the declaration of martial law by the legislative authority of the State, made for the purposes of self-defense, when assailed by an armed force; and the cases and commentaries concerning these commissions can not, therefore, influence the construction of the Rhode

Island law, nor furnish any test of the lawfulness of the authority exercised by the government."

This decision does not determine in what branch of the government resides authority to declare martial law. But it recognizes martial law as a legitimate means of preserving the government in emergencies calling for it. It shows that the ground taken by counsel on the other side, that no such authority is lodged in any branch of the government, is untenable. On page 44, the Court replies to the same kind of argument we have heard here, of the danger of intrusting so much power to the President.

"It is said that this power of the President is dangerous to liberty, and may be abused. All power may be abused if placed in unworthy hands. But it would be difficult, we think, to point out any other hands in which this power would be more safe, and, at the same time, equally effectual. When citizens of the same State are in arms against each other, and the constituted authorities unable to execute the laws, the interposition must be prompt or it is of little value. The ordinary course of proceedings in courts of justice would be utterly unfit for the crisis. And the elevated office of the President, chosen as he is by the people of the United States, and the high responsibility he could not fail to feel when acting in a case of so much moment, appear to furnish as strong safeguards against willful abuse of power as human prudence and foresight could well provide. At all events, it is conferred upon him by the Constitution and laws of the United States, and must, therefore, be respected and enforced in its judicial tribunals." (7 H. 44.)

"Moreover, when a military force is called out to repel invasion or suppress a rebellion, it is not placed under the direction of the judiciary, but under that of the executive. Suppose the military force, legally and constitutionally called into service for the purposes indicated, should find it necessary, in the course of its military operations, to occupy a field or garden, or destroy trees, or houses, belonging to some private person, can a court, by injunction, restrain them from committing such waste? It can do so in time of peace, and if its powers are to continue in time of war, the judiciary, and not the executive, will command the army and navy. The taking or destroying of private property, in such cases, is a military act, an act of war, and must be governed by the laws of war; it is not provided for by the laws of peace. In the same way, a person taken and held by the military forces, whether before, or in, or after a battle, or without any battle at all, is virtually a *prisoner of war.* No matter what his alleged offense, whether he is a rebel, a traitor, a spy, or an enemy in arms, he is to be held and punished according to the *laws of war*, for these have been substituted for the laws of peace. And for a person so taken and held by the military authority, a writ of Habeas Corpus can have no effect, because, in the words of the United States Supreme Court, 'the ordinary course of justice would be utterly unfit for such a crisis.'" (International Law and Laws of War. Halleck, 378.)

The same writer states circumstances in the history of this country, which your Honor will find it easy to verify. From this statement it appears that the practice, now complained of as strange and unprecedented, was commenced under the administration of Washington. Jefferson and Jackson are also implicated. When Vallandigham shoots his poisoned arrows at President Lincoln, if there should prove to be strength enough in the bow, the same aim will pierce a succession of illustrious defenders of liberty. Here is the statement:

"During the administration of President Washington, in the Pennsylvania 'Whisky Insurrection' of 1794 and 1795, the military authorities engaged in suppressing it disregarded the writs which were issued by the courts for the release of the prisoners who had been captured as insurgents. General Wilkinson, under the authority of President Jefferson, during the Burr Conspiracy of 1806, suspended the privilege of this writ, as against the Superior Court of New Orleans. General Jackson assumed the right to refuse obedience to the writ of Habeas Corpus, first in New Orleans, in 1814, as against the authority of Judge Hall, when the British army was approaching that city; and afterward, in Florida, as against the authority of Judge Fromentin."

May it please your Honor! I have spoken some words of praise of the character and services of General Burnside. I can now be silent. The patriot who, in these times, can get himself abused for following in the footsteps of Washington, Jefferson, and Jackson, has triumphed over all need of my poor commendation. The wrath of his country's enemies has been made to praise him.

The authorities relied upon to show that the laws of war, or martial law, are not any more allowed in Great Britain, I have shown to be in error. The statements, though made by parties whom we might expect to be informed, and which have probably misled counsel on the other side, are shown by Mr. Cushing, Attorney-General under the late President Pierce, to have resulted from misapprehension and confusion of ideas. But this showing depends not on the authority alone of his name, strong as it may be. The errors referred to are so demonstrable to reason, and so utterly at variance with history, it is quite unnecessary to go into a further exposition concerning them. In the dissenting opinion of Judge Woodbury, which I have freely adverted to, he was misled into a similar statement; but he let into it a sufficient number of exceptions to correspond with all the occasions there have been in Great Britain for martial law within the last hundred years. He insisted, however, that they had no constitution, and such acts were only done by Parliament in virtue of its unlimited power. I must again say, that the question is not, who may do it, but can it be done? For the purpose of my argument it is sufficient if done by Parliament, but the fact is otherwise. The quotation from Hansard's Debates shows that once, at least, it has been done by the executive. I have no doubt the same is true in other instances. The important matter is, however, it has been done, both in Great Britain and this country, every time there has been occasion for it. It is a rule of action in both countries.

The misconception of terms and confusion of ideas among common lawyers, on this topic, are not confined to England. A much clearer perception is shown by American writers on the main question involved; but even Mr. Cushing and Mr. Halleck fall into error in some particulars. The relations of suspension of Habeas Corpus to martial law are less well defined. They explain these to us in a jumble of words, which need more explanation than the facts sought to be explained. It has been the good fortune of Great Britain and the United States to experience so few occasions for the laws of war within their own borders, and those occasions have been of duration so brief, that a prompt and unflinching recognition and use of martial law, when the occasions have happened, are all that I need show. Peace turns attention to thoughts of peace. The judges, then, take *their* turn; and danger being over, they sometimes bite their thumbs at the Generals in a very affecting manner. We are told that acts of indemnity are passed in order to cover the illegality of the laws of war, as if a law could be illegal!

When lawyers and judges fall to using rigmarole, it is not common for politicians and pamphleteers to allow themselves to be outdone. In the passage quoted from Hansard, Lord Castlereagh is made to say:

> "I maintain that it is a *constitutional mode* for the executive government to exercise martial law in the first instance, and to come to Parliament for indemnity afterward. . . . *They did it on the principle that they were authorized by the king's prerogative, provided they did not transgress the necessity of the case.*"

This call for indemnity is often said to signify that the act was unlawful. What indemnity could be needed for a lawful act? So, then, it would appear to be a constitutional mode to do the unconstitutional thing, intending presently to apologize for it. Mr. Grey (afterward Earl Grey) was not impressed with the clearness of this explanation. He says:

> "It was better that the executive government should resort to what had been called (he thought not legally) its prerogative of proclaming martial law. That was no prerogative of the Crown, but, rather, an act of power sanctioned by necessity, martial law being a suspension of the king's peace."

Here, then, is a blaze of light. It was better to resort to that which did not exist, to-wit: the prerogative. It was an act of power "*sanctioned*" by necessity, "martial law being a suspension of the king's peace." This luminous expounder had arrived at the conclusion that in war peace must be considered as suspended. It did not, however, occur to him that it is war itself which suspends peace, and not the laws of war, which of necessity exist when war exists.

Our own writers follow in the same train. Mr. Attorney-General Cushing, in the opinion before quoted, says:

"*We have in Great Britain several recent examples of acts to give constitutional existence to the fact of martial law.*"

Mr. Halleck says:

"*It seems that no act of Parliament is required to precede such declaration, although it is usually followed by an act of indemnity, when the disturbances which called it forth are at an end, in order to give constitutional existence to the fact of martial law.*"

They are explaining the laws of England, and on this part of the topic relax their vigilance, repeating merely the incongruous failures which they find. Passing over the idea that Parliament can make a thing constitutional which is not—an absurdity—they are not boggled at the declaration that an act already gone by and ended, can be made *to have been* constitutional, which was at the time not so. On the theory thus furnished by Englishmen, and incautiously followed by some of our best writers, indemnity acts, if truly expressing their meaning, would read as follows: "*Whereas, certain acts have been done which are known to have been unconstitutional and illegal, therefore they were and are constitutional, legal acts.*" This is carrying the power of Parliament to a pitch compared with which Omnipotence is feeble.

If I may venture to suggest the explanation they were manifestly groping for, it is in the fact alluded to by Earl Grey: the king's peace is suspended. This suspension of peace being usually accompanied by more or fewer proclamatory documents, and these documents being the only part taken in war by judges and legislators, they have mistaken the documents for the war. They have omitted to remember that a failure of documents would not change the fact of war. The war, and not the documents, suspends peace. Of this the writers are sufficiently aware in other parts of their discussion. Mr. Attorney-General Cushing says:

> " *When martial law is proclaimed under circumstances of assumed necessity, the proclamation must be regarded as the statement of an existing fact, rather than the legal creation of that fact.*"

In this statement Mr. Halleck concurs. Indeed, nothing can be more obvious. Yet most of the antipathy and all the arguments I have met with, directed against martial law, are arguments against enforcing it during peace. In other words, they are arguments against inflicting the rigors of war under false pretexts. A part of the confusion is occasioned by speaking of martial law as if it were distinct and different from the laws of war, or rights of war. No one doubts that, when war exists, it is a thing of such a paramount and supreme nature that its laws must prevail. The existence of war is not a suspension of Habeas Corpus; but, for all arrests authorized by the laws of war, the answer that war exists, and that the arrest was made in accordance with its rules, is a lawful and sufficient answer to a Habeas Corpus. General Burnside has expressed it very well: "We are in a state of civil war, and an emergency is upon us which requires the operations of some power that moves more quickly than the civil. *There never was a war carried on successfully without the exercise of that power.*"

Indemnity acts are sufficiently accounted for without supposing them to be necessary as a legal justification for acts of war. They are commonly enacted in civil wars, in which the application of the rigors of war is startling to people long accustomed to peace and civil administration. A concurrence of all branches of government in any public acknowledgment of its necessity, either before or after the fact, can not fail to produce a valuable effect on the public mind. Such acts may, also, in England answer a good legal purpose. They may close the courts to vicious and experimental litigation, by which persons engaged in the public service in time of war, might, on the return of peace, be ruined or compelled to flee their country. Counsel on the other side, I understood him to say, by instruction of his client, has, at some length, called our attention to the number and variety of civil actions, to which, on his theory, General Burnside has exposed himself, as well as all who acted under his orders. On his theory, no act of indemnity can shield our soldiers. The right he claims is a constitutional right, which legislation can not affect. On his theory, every act of war by our soldiers is a trespass, and no act of indemnity can reach them. Hard as the fortunes of soldiers may be in war, on his theory, peace will bring them no repose. Our poor country, defended by their valor, enriched by their blood, however grateful it may be, can only welcome them home to the embrace of bailiffs. We may ring bells, kindle bonfires, and pour out our hearts in thankfulness to God for returning peace, but the noble boys who won it for us must skulk in hiding-places, to dream only of writs and constables and the law's delays; certain that their danger in peace is in proportion to their valor in war, and that he only can be hopeful who can prove himself to have been useless. This is not an exaggeration, but a necessary, logical result of the doctrine advanced here on behalf of Mr. Vallandigham.

The proposition is that the right to personal liberty, freedom of speech, etc., are absolute, inalienable rights, guaranteed inflexibly by the Constitution, and not to be suspended in any emergency, nor made to yield to any public necessity. I repeat that the question argued by counsel on the other side is not a question under what circumstances these rights may be abridged, but he denies the legal possibility of such abridgment. These rights extend to all citizens—to persons subject to military duty as well as the rest. Yet the same Constitution which guarantees these inalienable rights, authorizes the making of war and the calling out of the militia. Pressed by this fact, counsel do not seek to deny that the liberty of the soldier is, for the time of his service, abridged. This is too palpable for denial. He seeks, therefore, to get round it by reading from an English decision, to the effect that the soldier gives up his liberty by contract. This poor evasion does not apply to persons who are drafted against their will; but it is itself a denial that these rights are inalienable, for it speaks of alienating, by contract, an inalienable right.

The conclusion is inevitable. These rights, so carefully enumerated in the Constitution, and so often referred to by learned counsel, are liable to be abridged under particular circumstances. The Constitution contemplates and provides for such abridgment. This abridgment is especially provided for in time of war. And since no limits are fixed to the means to be used in war, every thing may be done which the necessities of war require. The laws of war are, for the time, as much a part of the Constitution as the laws of civil procedure are in time of peace.

My argument is founded on the idea that the laws of war are a necessary incident of a state of war, and, therefore, depend for existence only on the fact of war. It is quite unnecessary to refer to proclamations or advertisements of the fact. Order No. 38 is a proclamation, if it were a question of proclamations. Every branch of government, State and Federal, has made numerous annunciations of this war. Counsel calls our attention to certain proclamations of the President relating to emancipation of slaves, which define, for that purpose, the insurrectionary districts; and counsel insists that these must be held as limiting martial law to those districts. Those proclamations do not include Missouri, Kentucky, Tennessee, Western Virginia, or portions of Eastern Virginia, or Norfolk or Portsmouth. If the laws of war depend on these proclamations, they are excluded from the places where the war has been most active. They did not purport to define the limits of war, but the limits of emancipation. If my argument is sound, neither the presence nor absence of proclamations can, materially, affect the question. It is a question of the existence of war.

It may be said that this argument, if correct, reduces us to a state of dependence on military power. Far otherwise. It is not a state to be argued into, or argued out of. If, when threatened by Generals and armies who are traitors and enemies, we are obliged to depend upon Generals and armies who are patriots and friends, nothing can be gained by denying the fact, or by keeping up a false pretext of being in some other condition. The danger, whatever it may be, is not very much diminished by going into hysterics; nor is it greatly changed in its character by the names applied. It is sometimes called "*no law*"—"*an abrogation of law*"—"*a supension of law*," because for a time the ordinary civil administration is suspended or subordinated to a great public necessity. But the law provided for such occasions is in force. It is appealed to, to protect us when other laws fail.

The laws of war have their appropriate checks and limitations. The General in command of an army, in the field of his operations, for purposes of war, is expected to act with promptness, and sometimes with secrecy. He is not expected to write out and deliver his opinions, or to wait for briefs. This may be his misfortune; it certainly is not his fault. His action in this sense may be called "arbitrary," and his administration "despotic." But, after all, he is limited and restrained. If he push beyond the rights of war, the laws of war do not protect him. In applying those laws, he is further restrained by a sense of propriety and duty. He acts in peril of the disapprobation of higher authority, who may displace, or, in some cases, impeach, him; in peril of the disapprobation of the Supreme Being and of his countrymen; in peril of that sure infamy which awaits all who unnecessarily aggravate the evils of war. It is not easy to conceive a situation appealing to higher sanctions than that of a General commanding in war. "*At all events*," says General Burnside, "*I will have the consciousness before God of having done my duty to my country.*"

May it please your Honor! I have pursued this branch of the argument at some length. If the view of the Constitution here presented be, as it appears to me, well grounded in reason, and sustained by authority, the main proposition on which the petitioner rests his application is overthrown, and, with it, the claim to a writ of Habeas Corpus.

I did not understand counsel to argue that, in the case of Vallandigham, there were circumstances to render this arrest illegal or unnecessary, provided such arrests can in any case be justified. I did distinctly understand him to disclaim the idea that the Constitution permits a military arrest to be made, under any circumstances, of a person not engaged in the military or naval service of the United States, nor in the militia of any State called into actual service; and to rest his case on that broad denial. The whole petition is framed on this idea, for none of the charges are denied.

Upon first impression, your Honor may have inclined to the belief that petitioner had assumed an unnecessary burden, and might have more easily made a case by putting General Burnside to show the propriety of this arrest; admitting the general right to make such arrests as were indicated by the necessities of the service, but denying any ground for this arrest. But your Honor will find that no mistake has been made by learned counsel on the other side, in this particular. The circumstances shown justify the arrest, if any arrest of the kind can be justified. If General Burnside might have arrested him for making the speech face to face with his soldiers, the distance from them at which it was uttered can make little difference. He might make it in camp; and unless he could be arrested, there would be no way to prevent it. The right of publication, of sending by mail and telegraph, are of the same grade with freedom of speech. If utterance of the speech could not be checked, its transmission by mail and telegraph could not be. And I so understand the argument of the counsel of Vallandigham. It appears to claim, and go the whole length of claiming that it can do the army no harm to read such addresses; nor, of course, to hear them. It is necessary the argument should not stop short of that in order to meet the question, and it does not. Yet this is not the whole extent to which it must go to avail the petitioner. It must go to the extent of showing that this Court is authorized to determine that such addresses may be heard by the army, the opinion of the commanding General to the contrary notwithstanding. It goes and must go the extent of transferring all responsibility for what is called the *morale* and discipline of the army from its commanding General to this Court.

Is it not certain that if these addresses shall persuade nobody, their authors will be disappointed? Is it not certain that any soldier persuaded to believe that his government is striving to overthrow liberty, and for that purpose is waging a wicked and cruel war, can no longer, in good conscience, remain in the service? The argument leads to one of two conclusions. We are to be persuaded by the men who make the speeches, that the speeches will not produce the effect they intend—a persuasion in which their acts contradict their words—or we are to consent to the demoralization of the army. The Constitution authorizes and even requires the army to be formed, but at that stage of the transaction interposes an imperative prohibition against the usual means of making it effective.

It is said, however, that the charges against Vallandigham are triable in the civil tribunals. So are a large proportion of all the charges which can be brought against any one engaged in an insurrection. No rebel soldier has been captured in this war, no guerrilla, who was not triable in the civil tribunals. The argument in this, as in other particulars, necessarily denies the applicability of the laws of war to a state of war.

Learned counsel on the other side has cited to us and read passages from decisions and text-books, on two points, the relevancy of which to the question now before us I am not able to perceive. One series of these citations reminds us of arrests which were not made in accordance with any laws, either of peace or war, which were declared illegal and punished. I can, if he shall think them useful, furnish him many more of the same kind. But I am under an impression that when an arrest has been shown to be illegal, no further authority will be necessary to show that the person making it is liable to punishment. He has read to us an account of the execution of Governor Wall. *After peace had been restored*, and *after a pretended but illegal trial by court-martial, he caused a punishment to be inflicted which resulted in the death of the soldier punished!* He was himself punished for the act. What has that to do here?

He cites to us a case where a justice of the peace, *not liable to military duty*, had been fined by a militia court-martial, *which had no jurisdiction over him*, for omitting to do what he was not bound to do; and the whole proceeding was declared illegal. What has that to do here? He cites to us a case, growing out of the celebrated John Wilkes controversy, where arrests were made, and houses and papers searched, *under a pretended warrant, issued by a person having no right to issue a warrant*. It was a trespass, and the jury put on, as they ought, heavy damages. What has that to do here?

I need not follow these citations. None of them have any other bearing that I am able to perceive, than to show that illegal arrests are not to be justified. Who claims that they are? None of these citations show, or tend to show, that the arrest here is not in accordance with the laws of war. It comes back to the original question. In time of war, do the rules of war prevail? If they do, arrests made in accordance with them are legal. If they do not, every rebel who has been captured has his action of trespass and false imprisonment against the soldiers who captured him. If they do not, every soldier who has killed his enemy in battle is liable to be prosecuted for it as a crime. This is the only alternative. Need I pursue the argument?

Another class of authorities cited by counsel bears upon the old and familiar doctrine of constructive treason. Its bearing on the question before the Court I am not able to discover. But since there may be some connecting link, not visible to the naked eye, let me say that, on the strength of his own citations, I should expect your Honor to feel compelled to instruct the jury, if Vallandigham were now on trial before a jury, charged with treason, that the case was a serious one, and deserved their most solemn deliberation. His citation from Blackstone gives us a clue, if one were needed, to the whole labyrinth. "How far mere words, spoken by an individual, and NOT RELATIVE TO ANY TREASONABLE ACT OR DESIGN THEN IN AGITATION, shall amount to treason, has been formerly matter of doubt." So in his citation from 1 Hale's Pleas of the Crown, 146, a bare detainer, or shutting the gates, against the government, might not amount to treason. "*But if this be done* IN CONFEDERACY WITH *enemies, or rebels, that circumstance will make it treason.*" Again, his citation from 4 Cranch, 127: "It is not the intention of the Court to say, that no individual can be guilty of this crime who has not appeared in arms against his country. *On the contrary, if war be actually levied, that is, if a body of men be actually assembled*, for the purpose of effecting, by force, a treasonable purpose, ALL THOSE WHO PERFORM ANY PART, HOWEVER MINUTE, or HOWEVER REMOTE from the scene of action, and who are actually leagued in the general conspiracy, *are to be considered as traitors.*"

Admitting that words, or a mere conspiracy to levy war, no war being yet levied; or enlisting of men for war, no war being yet levied, do not amount to actual levying of war, the whole doctrine claimed by counsel, yet the case of Vallandigham has not been reached. *War is levied. A body of men is assembled for the purpose of effecting, by force, a treasonable purpose.* This body of men has military occupation of a large part of the country. There is no doubt of the establishment of this part of the case. What follows? The Court would tell the jury that "all those who perform *any* part, however *minute*, or however *remote* from the scene of action, and who are actually leagued in the general conspiracy, are guilty of treason." The Court would tell the jury, that the acts of Vallandigham were not too minute nor too remote for guilt. The question for them would be, whether he was actually leagued in the general conspiracy? And this they would be able to form their opinion upon from all the circumstances. They must impute to him a design to accomplish just what his actions had a tendency to accomplish; this is the only legal way of ascertaining motives. Were the acts of Vallandigham apparently aimed at the same result with the acts of those unequivocally engaged in open treason? His determination to resist Order No. 38, which forbade lending assistance to the rebellion, was a circumstance. His former and present relations with the leading traitors might be considered. His pretended knowledge of terms offered by those engaged in the rebellion, to the government, not known to the loyal part of the people, and his hearty indorsement of their side of the negotiation, might be considered. The jury must remember that many things besides bearing arms were necessary to the success of the general purpose, and so on. If the charges against Vallandigham, which stand here without denial, are true, his conviction of treason, before an impartial jury, would be almost certain. But on an application for a Habeas Corpus, the Court does not determine the question of guilt or innocence. I can not, therefore, see the relevancy of this part of the argument.

Learned counsel has read to us certain resolutions of the Ohio Legislature, said to have been adopted during the Mexican war, strongly pronouncing against that war, and advising its discontinuance. Does he claim that there was then on foot any military force levying a *treasonable* war against the United States? What, then, has that to do here? What, in any event, has it to do here? Does he claim that those resolutions were justifiable?

Among the numerous instances cited of constructive treason, is one quite touching. A man, whose deer had been killed by the king, wished it, horns and all, in the king's belly. The judge is reported to have held this to be a treasonable saying, and the man was executed. The horns might have been troublesome, but one would think the horns part might have been pardoned or condoned, considering the manifest benevolence of wishing all the rest of the deer there, also. Why, counsel is seeking to impress us with a sense of the danger of allowing any kind of cases to be withdrawn from the courts; and he reads us instances showing that whatever abuses may have been committed by military men, they fall short of the abuses committed by courts and juries! What has all that to do here?

May it please your Honor! I must bring this argument to a close. Are we in a state of war or not? Did the Constitution, when it authorized war to be made, without limitations, mean war, or something else? The judicial tribunals provided for in the Constitution, throughout twelve States of the Union, have been utterly overthrown. In several other States they are maintaining a feeble and uncertain hold of their jurisdiction. None of them can now secure to parties on trial the testimony from large portions of the country, to which they are entitled by the Constitution and laws. The records of none of them can be used in the districts dominated by the insurrection. They are all struck at by this insurrection. Counsel tells us that, except the Union provided for in the Constitution, there is no legal Union. Yet that Union is, temporarily I hope, but for the present, suspended and annulled. This Court can have no existence except under that Union, and that Union now, in the judgment of those who have been intrusted by the Constitution with the duty of preserving it, depends upon the success of its armies. The civil administration can no longer preserve it.

The courts which yet hold their places, with or without military support, may perform most useful functions. Their jurisdiction and labors were never more wanted than now. But they were not intended to command armies. When Generals and armies were sent here, they were sent to make war according to the laws of war. I have no authority from General Burnside to inquire, and I have hesitated to inquire, but, after all, will venture to inquire, whether an interference by this Court with the duties of military command must not tend to disturb that harmony between different branches of government, which, at this time, is most especially to be desired?

Counsel expresses much fear of the loss of liberty, through the influence of military ascendency. Are we, on that account, to so tie the hands of our Generals, as to assure the overthrow of the Constitution by its enemies? I do not share that fear. It has been the fashion of society in many countries to be divided into grades, and topped out with a single ruling family. In such societies the laws and habits of the people correspond with its social organization. The two elements of power—intelligence and wealth—are carefully secured in the same hands with political power. It has happened in a number of instances, that a successful General gained power enough to push the monarch from his throne and seat himself there. In such instances the change was chiefly personal. Little change was necessary in the social organization, laws or habits. It has also happened that democracies or republics, which have, by a long course of corruption, lost the love and practice of virtue, have been held in order by a strong military hand. But in this country no man can gain by military success a dangerous ascendency, because the change would require to be preceded by a change in the whole body of laws, in the habits, opinions, and social organization. History furnishes no example of a successful usurpation under similar circumstances, and reason assures me it would prove impossible. Our society has no element on which usurpation could be founded. My sleep is undisturbed, and my heart quite fearless in that direction. I do not fear that we shall lose our respect for the laws of peace by respecting the laws of war; nor our love for the Constitution by the sacrifices we make to uphold it. I do not fear any loss of democratic sympathies by the brotherhood of camps. I do not fear any loss of the love of peace by the sufferings of war. I am not zealous to preserve, to the utmost punctilio, any civil right at the risk of losing all, when all civil rights are in danger of overthrow. The question of civil liberty is no longer within the arbitrament of our civil tribunals. It has been taken up to a higher court, and is now pending before the God of Battles. May he not turn away from the sons whose fathers he favored! As he filled and strengthened the hearts of the founders of our liberty, so may he fill and strengthen ours with great constancy! Now, while awaiting the call of that terrible docket, while drum-beats roll from the Atlantic Ocean to the Rocky Mountains, while the clear sound of bugles reaches far over our once peaceful hills and valleys; now, when the hour of doom is about to strike, let us lose all sense of individual danger; let us lay upon a common altar all private griefs, all personal ambitions; let us unite in upholding the army, that it may have strength to rescue from unlawful violence, and restore to us the body of the American Union—*E Pluribus Unum!* Above all, O Almighty God! if it shall please thee to subject us to still more and harder trials; if it be thy will that we pass further down into the darkness of disorder, yet may some little memory of our fathers move thee to a touch of pity! Spare us from that last human degradation! Save! O save us from the littleness to be jealous of our defenders!

ARGUMENT

OF

HON. FLAMEN BALL.

May it Please the Court:

In rising to address your Honor on behalf of General Burnside, I can not refrain from expressing the feeling which I entertain in regard to the great importance of this application; for the result of your decision, whatever it may be, must be looked upon with the greatest interest, not only by the applicant, in whose behalf it has been invoked, but by the people of our country, whose national rights are, nay, whose very existence as a great nationality is imperiled by a gigantic rebellion against the Constitution and the laws of the United States—a rebellion, I take leave to say, originating in a deeply-laid and maturely-planned conspiracy for the overthrow of the Constitution, fostered and encouraged by official perjury and official plunder, and prosecuted, without just cause, with cruel and relentless hate, and with remorseless energy, against a government whose sway over the people for more than seventy years has been exercised with the utmost benignity; carefully guarding the rights of all, and jealously protecting the liberties of all. The darkest pages of the history of the world furnish no parallel to the scene now presented in the United States.

The quiet paths of domestic peace, which, until lately, were trodden by the industrious pursuits of honest labor, have been suddenly invaded by an armed rebellion, whose sole object is the overthrow of the institutions of the republic, established by the valor, the patriotism, and the wisdom of our ancestors, and the erection, upon their ruins, of an absolute despotism.

I yield to no man in reverence for the sacredness and inviolability of that great guarantee of personal liberty, the writ of HABEAS CORPUS, which has been applied for in this case; for, next to the principles and precepts of religion, the value and importance of that writ, as the safeguard of the humblest citizen, were inculcated in my mind in youth, and have become, as it were, a part of my very existence; but while I fully recognize the right of every citizen, who may be restrained of his personal liberty, to have the cause of that restraint judicially inquired into, I must also recognize the great fact that, by reason of this rebellion, the very existence of our whole country, as a nation, is in jeopardy; and that, while on the one hand the personal rights of the citizen are to be protected, (unless by reason of crime he may have forfeited those rights), we must all remember that our country has rights, and that, in this great crisis in her history, those rights must be asserted and maintained. Among those rights the right of self-preservation is paramount.

If, by reason of the continuance of the civil war now so wickedly waged against the government, the abstract rights of the citizen should be brought into question, I think it may not be regarded as claiming too much for me to insist that the private and personal rights of the individual, when their exercise by him conflict with, and tend to overthrow, the great national right of self-existence, must give way to the rights of the nation.

It has been well remarked by De Lolme, in in his treatise on the Constitution of England, that,

"There have been times of public disturbance when the Habeas Corpus Act was indeed suspended, which may serve as a proof that, in proportion as a government is in danger, it becomes necessary to abridge the liberty of the subject; but the executive power did not thus of itself stretch its own authority; the precaution was deliberated upon and taken by the representatives of the people; and the detaining of individuals, in consequence of the suspension of the act, was limited to a certain fixed time."

It is evident that the power of suspending the writ was vested solely in Parliament, because the people of England, taught by the severe lessons of experience, in the invasions and encroachments upon their liberties by the executive tyranny of ancient times, were jealous of the kingly prerogative, and were determined to limit and restrain it, in all cases where the right of the subject to the enjoyment of personal freedom might be drawn in question. Hence it became a received and well-settled principle of constitutional law, that the sovereignty of the British Constitution is lodged in Parliament, in whose collective capacity of the Crown, the Lords, and the Commons, the "omnipotence" of Parliament resides; therefore, the power to suspend this great writ is conceded to rest solely within the discretion of Parliament. The right to the writ exists at common law. It is not conferred by statute; for the several statutes of Charles I, Charles II, William and Mary, George III, and other enactments on that subject, do not confer the right, but are simply declaratory of that which had existed beyond the memory of man, or are directory to the courts and judges, in respect of the practice to be pursued by them, in cases where the writ is demandable. The suspension of this writ may become necessary when the State is in real danger; and when such an emergency shall arise, Parliament may authorize the Crown to suspend the writ for a limited time, and to imprison suspected persons, without giving any reasons for so doing. "An experiment," says Blackstone, "which ought only to be tried, and which we believe has never been tried, but in cases of extreme emergency; and in these the nation parts with a portion of its liberty for awhile, in order to preserve the whole forever."

With us the case is different. The written Constitution is the supreme law of the land; and, if governmental omnipotence resides anywhere, it resides there. No act of either the executive, the legislative, or the judicial branches of the government, conflicting with the provisions of that instrument, is valid. But that instrument nowhere, in express terms, confers upon the citizen the right to the writ of Habeas Corpus. It guarantees to him many civil rights, which are specifically enumerated; but the right to this writ is not one of them. It impliedly concedes that the privilege of the writ exists as a common-law right, when it provides that, "The privilege of the writ of Habeas Corpus shall not be suspended unless, when in cases of rebellion or invasion, the public safety may require it." But it does not prohibit the President from suspending it: it merely provides that it shall not be suspended unless, when in cases of rebellion or invasion, the public safety may require it. For aught that appears in the Constitution, the right to exercise the discretionary power of suspension is vested in the President; and this inference is much strengthened by the fact, that the great lawyers who framed that instrument were all of them learned in the common law, and in all the statutes of the British Parliament. Themselves born and educated as British subjects, and familiar with every struggle ever made for freedom, and every triumph for liberty ever achieved by the people of England over kingly usurpation, they inherited the natural jealousy of Englishmen of executive encroachments; and, had they intended to deprive the President of the power of suspending this writ, in cases of great public emergency, as they well knew was the case with respect to the power of the Crown, and to vest the power of suspension solely with the Congress, they would have so provided in the Constitution. It is fair, then, to conclude that the power vests in the President; and, in the exercise of that power, as the chief civil magistrate, he may, in his discretion, when the safety of the republic requires it, suspend the writ generally over the whole country, or in a particular department, or in respect of a particular person. This view is strengthened by the late act of Congress, (March 3, 1863,) which expressly provides that the President may, during this rebellion, "whenever, in his judgment, the public safety may require it, suspend the privilege of the writ of Habeas Corpus, *in any case*, throughout the United States, or any part thereof." And thus the question as to which branch of the government is intrusted with the power of suspension seems to be settled by Congress in favor of the President. If, then, the power of suspension is vested in the President, he may exercise that power, in a great crisis like the present, by any appropriate agent he may select for that purpose; and if, as is now the case, the civil authority vested in the marshals, as conservators of the public peace, is insufficient to sustain the Government, and enforce the execution of the laws, he may, as he has done, command the aid of the military arm of the nation.

The able argument of my learned colleague has relieved me from the necessity of discussing at great length the various questions which arise in this case, and I shall, therefore, confine myself to the discussion of such points as, in my judgment, most intimately relate to the subject.

Upon the original application, the learned counsel for the relator claimed that the case came within the purview of the act of Congress relating to the writ of Habeas Corpus, approved March 3, 1863; that the allowance of the writ was a matter of strict right on the part of the applicant; and that on the return of the writ, with the production of the body of the applicant, the cause of caption and detention could then be inquired into.

But such is not the practice of this Court. At the October term, 1862, the Court held, on the application for a writ of Habeas Corpus, made on behalf of one Bethuel W. Rupert, then held as a prisoner under an order of the Secretary of War, that the writ was not allowable as of course, but that the Court would decide upon the hearing of the application, and grant or withhold the writ in its discretion. That practice is still unchanged, and it must be regarded as the law of this Court. It is not a new rule of practice, but has been the rule of practice of other courts, and I will briefly refer to some of the cases.

In 1759, a motion, based upon affidavit, was made before the Court of King's Bench, for a Habeas Corpus, to be directed to one Rigby, keeper of the town jail of Liverpool, to bring up the body of one Barnard Schiever, a subject of a neutral power, who had been taken on board of an enemy's ship, but forced, as it was alleged, into the enemy's service. His counsel urged that it would be very hard upon this man to be kept in prison until exchanged by cartel, and then sent back to France, where he would be forced into their service again. But the Court,

Lord Mansfield presiding, thought this man, upon his own showing, clearly a prisoner of war, and lawfully detained as such, and denied the motion. (1 Burr. R. 765.)

Again: In the case of Hobhouse (3 B. & Ald. 420), the Court, Abbott, C. J., and Bayley, Holroyd, and Best, Justices, were unanimous in establishing the rule of practice that the writ of Habeas Corpus, at common law, although a writ of right, is not grantable of course, but only on motion in term time, stating a probable cause for the application, and verified by affidavit.

I also refer to 2 Black. R. 1324; and to 2 Chitty R. 207.

In the case of Husted, before the Supreme Court of New York, an application was made for a Habeas Corpus, on the ground that he was detained in custody by a captain in the army of the United States, who claimed him as a soldier, enlisted under the authority of the United States. But the Court denied the application on the ground that if the facts stated were returned on the Habeas Corpus, it would be conclusive against his discharge. (1 John. Ca. 136.) So, in the matter of Yates, who had been committed by the Court of Chancery for a contempt, a motion, grounded on sundry affidavits, was made for the allowance of a Habeas Corpus as of course. But Mr. Chief-Justice Kent said, that, as this was a matter of importance, the Court would take until the next day to consider whether it was proper to grant the motion, and another motion to let the applicant to bail was refused. (4 John. R. 318.)

In the recent case of Sims, the fugitive slave, which came up before the Supreme Court of Massachusetts, Chief-Justice Shaw held, that before a writ of Habeas Corpus is granted, sufficient probable cause must be shown; but when it appears, upon the party's own showing, that there is no sufficient ground, *prima facie*, for his discharge, the Court will not issue the writ. (7 Cush. R. 285.)

In the Supreme Court of the United States, it is the settled practice to hear argument, either on the motion for the allowance of the writ, or upon the return of a rule to show cause why the writ should not issue. In the case of Kearney (7

Wheat. Rep. 38), who sought release from a commitment for a contempt, the Court heard the parties on the motion, and Mr. Justice Story, delivering the opinion, denied the writ.

In the case of Watkins (3 Peters R. 193), who was imprisoned by the condemnation of the Circuit Court of the United States for the District of Columbia, the Court, Mr. Chief-Justice Marshall presiding, on the motion of the applicant for the allowance of a writ, and counsel not agreeing as to the time of hearing the motion, awarded a rule to show cause why the writ should not issue, and assigned the next motion day as the time for hearing the argument. It was accordingly heard, on the return of the rule, and the motion for the writ was denied. A similar practice has been pursued in other cases. (*Ex parte* Robinson, 1 Serg. & R. 353; *Ex parte* Campbell, 20 Ala. R. 89; Hurd on Hab. Corp. 222; *Ex parte* Bushnell, 8 Ohio St. R. 599.) The practice pursued by the Court in this case, in requiring notice of the motion to be served on General Burnside, is substantially the same as that pursued by Mr. Chief-Justice Marshall, in Watkins's case.

The allowance of the writ rests within the discretion of the Court or judge before whom the application is made. It does not address itself to the whim or caprice of the Court or judge, nor does it involve the exercise of an arbitrary discretion; but it is addressed to the sound judicial discretion of the Court—a discretion illuminated by the lights of judicial precedents and authority, of judicial wisdom, experience, and observation, and by a judicial review of all the facts and circumstances of the particular case. Discretion (says Lord Coke, 2 Inst. 56) is to discern between right and wrong; and, therefore, whoever hath power to act at discretion, is bound by the rule of reason and law. It is the right, then, nay, it is the duty of the Court to hear argument upon the motion, so that the whole merits of the application may be ascertained, and a wise discretion exercised.

The first legislation of Congress upon the subject of Habeas Corpus was the act of September 24, 1789, which conferred upon the Courts of the United States, and the respective justices and judges of those courts, the power to grant the writ, agreeably to the principles and usages of law; but the power to award the writ *ad subjiciendum*, and to inquire into the cause of commitment, did not extend to prisoners in jail, unless where they were in custody under or by color of the authority of the United States. Afterward, and when, by reason of the State legislation of South Carolina, officers of the United States, charged with executing the laws of the United States, were imprisoned, by State authority, for the alleged offense against State sovereignty, of obeying the laws of the United States in preference to the laws of the State of South Carolina, the act of March 2, 1833, commonly called the Force Bill, was enacted, whereby the jurisdiction of the Federal Courts and judges was extended, to grant writs of Habeas Corpus in all cases of prisoners in jail, who had been committed for any act done, or omitted to be done, in pursuance of a law of the United States, or any order, process, or decree of any judge or Court thereof.

Thus the legislation stood until 1842, when an apprehended difficulty with England superinduced the passage of the act of August 29, 1842. The Court well remembers the case of Alexander McLeod. In 1837, he, a British subject, was one of a military expedition sent by the Canadian provincial authorities to destroy an American vessel, the steamboat Caroline, then lying at the port of Schlosser, in American waters, and laden with stores and supplies for the rebels congregated at Navy Island. The boat was destroyed, and an American citizen, standing on the shore, was killed. Afterward, McLeod came to New York and boasted that he participated in that outrage. He was arrested and indicted for murder. A writ of Habeas Corpus was applied for and obtained in his behalf, from the Supreme Court; but the Court, Cowen, J., presiding, refused his discharge on the ground that such a case as his was not provided for by law. The Queen of Great Britain avowed the act of McLeod, and demanded his release, which demand, after much controversy, was acquiesced in by Mr. Webster, then Secretary of State.

That act extended the jurisdiction of the justices and judges of the United States to the granting of writs of Habeas Corpus in all cases of a prisoner or prisoners in jail or confinement, when he or they, being subjects of a foreign State and domiciled therein, shall be in custody under any authority or law of the United States, or any one of them, on account of any act done or omitted under any alleged right, title, authority, privilege, protection, or exemption, set up or claimed, under the commission, or order, or sanction, of any foreign State or sovereignty, the validity and effect whereof depend upon the law of nations, or under color thereof.

The only remaining legislation on this subject is the act of March 3, 1863. This act had its birth in consequence of the present rebellion, and its provisions will become inoperative when the insurrection shall have been suppressed. It is evidently intended, so far as may be consistent with the public safety, to provide for a speedy trial of all persons who may be summarily arrested by or under the authority of the President, and to prescribe a limit to the imprisonment consequent upon snch arrests. Its object is twofold:

By sections one, two, and three, it authorizes the President, whenever, in his judgment, the public safety may require it, to suspend the privilege of the writ of Habeas Corpus during the present rebellion; and it exempts all officers, civil and military, from liability, in answer to any writ of Habeas Corpus, to return with it the body of any person retained by the authority of the President, and suspends all proceedings under the writ before the Court or judge issuing it, so long as said suspension shall remain in force and said rebellion continue. It also provides that persons held as State prisoners by order or authority of the President or of the Secretaries of State and of War, may, in certain cases, be discharged or let to bail upon the terms provided by the act.

By sections four, five, six, and seven, it provides that any order of the President, or under his authority, made at any time during the existence of said rebellion, shall be a defense in all courts in any action, civil or criminal, pending or to be commenced, "for any search, seizure, arrest, or imprisonment made, done, or committed, or acts omitted to be done, under and by virtue of such order, or under color of any law of Congress;" and it further provides for the removal from the State Courts to the Federal Courts of all suits and prosecutions which have been or shall be commenced against any officer, civil or military, or against any person for any arrest or imprisonment made, or other trespasses or wrongs done, or any act omitted to be done at any time during the present rebellion, by virtue or under color of any authority derived from, or exercised by or under the President of the United States, or any act of Congress.

If the first three sections of the act referred to are prospective in their operation, then it is clear that inasmuch as no proclamation suspending the writ of Habeas Corpus has been issued by the President since the passage of the act, the application of Mr. Vallandigham does not come within any of its provisions. On the other hand, if those sections be retrospective as well as prospective in their operation, and his case falls within the act, then he is expressly excluded from the privilege of the writ, and if it should issue to Major-General Burnside, he will be bound to make the return provided for by the act, and this proceeding would be suspended so long as the rebellion shall continue.

It is evident that the last four sections of the act are intended to embrace all cases of arrest under the authority of the President, past as well as future; but as these are solely remedial in their nature, and have no bearing on the motion now before the Court, it is unnecessary to discuss them further than to suggest that, if it shall become the duty of the Secretary of War to report to the Judge of this Court the name of Mr. Vallandigham as a State prisoner, held under his authority, and the next grand jury should terminate its session without finding an indictment against him, it would then become his right to apply to the judge for an order that he may be brought before him, that his case may be examined into, and that he may be discharged or let to bail, according to the circumstances of the case.

In my judgment, however, the application now presented falls solely within the provisions of the act of September 24, 1789.

He is in custody "under or by color of the authority of the United States," and if he be entitled to any relief, it must be under the act last named.

By the creation of the Department of the Ohio, the President invested Major-General Burnside, the commander thereof, with all the powers necessary to perform his whole duty. That Department comprises the States of Kentucky, Ohio, Indiana, Illinois, and Michigan, of which, as stated by General Burnside, one State is at this moment invaded, and three others have been threatened by the enemy. It is a period of domestic war, and all the energies, powers, and resources of the nation are necessarily called into exercise for the maintenance of the Constitution and laws of the country, for the restoration of peace, and for the preservation of the liberties of the whole people. The civil arm of the Government has proved powerless to effect this object, and it has been necessary for the President to call forth the army and the navy in order that he may, as his official oath requires him to do, "preserve, protect, and defend the Constitution of the United States." To that end, it became necessary to subdivide the country into military departments, in order that his great duty of preserving, protecting, and defending the Constitution might be faithfully and effectively performed. Of no other officer under the Constitution is such an oath required, and it is manifest that in requiring that oath of the chief executive authority, and thus reposing in his hands alone that great and solemn trust, it was intended, by the framers of the Constitution, that he should possess, and in his discretion exercise, all the powers necessary to enable him to execute the trust, and to transmit to his successors, through all coming time, a great NATIONAL UNITY, to all intents and purposes the same, unabridged and unimpaired, as it had been transmitted to him by his predecessors. All the wealth and all the military and naval power of the nation were at his service to enable him to perform that duty, and it was expressly provided by Congress, by the act of February 28, 1795, that, "Whenever the laws of the United States shall be opposed, or the execution thereof obstructed, in any State, by combinations too powerful to be suppressed by the ordinary course of judicial proceedings, or by the powers vested in the marshals by this act, it shall be lawful for the President of the United States to call forth the militia of such State, or of any other State or States, as may be necessary to suppress such combinations, and to cause the laws to be duly executed." The President is the sole and exclusive and final judge whether the exigency contemplated by the Constitution and by the act of Congress has arisen, and this has been the construction put upon this act by the Supreme Court of the United States in the case of Martin *v.* Mott, (12 Wheat. R. 19.)

In this case Mott, a private militiaman, was called into service in the war of 1812, by the Governor of New York, upon a requisition of the President of the United States, but did not go out. In 1814, Mott was summoned before a court-martial and tried for the offense of neglecting the call of the Governor, was convicted and sentenced to pay a fine, or, in case of non-payment, to imprisonment for twelve months. The sentence of the Court was approved by the President, and Martin, a deputy marshal, collected the fine. Mott sued Martin for so doing, and the case, having passed through the State Courts of New York, was finally decided by the Court of Errors in favor of Mott, and Martin then obtained his writ of error to the Supreme Court of the United States, where the judgment of the Court of Errors was reversed. Mr. Chief-Justice Marshall, who delivered the opinion of the Court, after affirming the constitutionality of that act of Congress, expressly says of the President:

"He is, necessarily, constituted the judge of the existence of the exigency in the first instance, and is bound to act according to his belief of the facts."

On the breaking out of this rebellion he did so act. In his proclamation of April 15, 1861, he says:

"Whereas, the laws of the United States have been, for some time past, and now are opposed, and the execution thereof obstructed, in the States of South Carolina, Georgia, Alabama, Florida, Mississippi,

Louisiana, and Texas, by combinations too powerful to be suppressed by the ordinary course of judicial proceedings, or by the powers vested in the marshals by law; now, therefore, I, ABRAHAM LINCOLN, President of the United States, in virtue of the power in me vested by the Constitution and the laws, have thought fit to call forth, and hereby do call forth, the militia of the several States of the Union, to the aggregate number of seventy-five thousand, in order to suppress said combinations, and to cause the laws to be duly executed. The details for this object will be immediately communicated to the State authorities through the War Department.

"I appeal to all loyal citizens to favor, facilitate, and aid this effort to maintain the honor, the integrity, and the existence of our National Union, and the perpetuity of popular government; and to redress wrongs already long enough endured.

"I deem it proper to say that the first service assigned to the forces hereby called forth will, probably, be to repossess the forts, places, and property which have been seized from the Union; and, in every event, the utmost care will be observed, consistently with the objects aforesaid, to avoid any devastation, any destruction of, or interference with, property, or any disturbance of peaceful citizens in any part of the country."

The proclamation closes with a command to the persons so combining to disperse within twenty days, and with an order to convene the Congress on the fourth day of the following July. The Congress convened accordingly, and, in order to sustain the President in the performance of his great duty, provided for an increase of the regular army and of the navy, and also placed at his disposal an additional force of five hundred thousand volunteers. Thus the war for the preservation of the National Union was fully inaugurated, and the President, as the civil executive, and as commander-in-chief of the army and navy, was fully clothed with all the necessary, legal, and physical power to accomplish the object of his proclamation.

The creation of the Department of the Ohio, and the appointment of a Major-General to command it, were part of the necessary means employed, in the discretion of the President, to accomplish the end in view; and the official acts of the Major-General, performed under the direct authority of the President, must be regarded as the acts of the President himself. In the case of Martin *v.* Mott, just referred to, the Chief-Justice says:

"If he does so act, and decides to call forth the militia, his orders for this purpose are in strict conformity with the provision of the law; and it would seem to follow, as a necessary consequence, that every act done by a subordinate officer, in obedience to such orders, is equally justifiable. The law contemplates that, under such circumstances, orders shall be given to carry the power into effect; and it can not, therefore, be a correct inference that any other person has a just right to disobey them. The law does not provide for any appeal from the judgment of the President, or for any right in subordinate officers to review his decision, and, in effect, defeat it. Whenever a statute gives a discretionary power to any person, to be exercised by him upon his own opinion of certain facts, it is a sound rule of construction that the statute constitutes him the sole and exclusive judge of those facts; and, in the present case, we are all of opinion that such is the true construction of the act of 1795."

This doctrine of the Chief-Justice is the same recognized in the law of nature as applied to the law of nations. Vattel says, (Bk. 3, ch. 2, sec. 19):

"Every military officer, from the ensign to the general, enjoys the rights and authority assigned him by the sovereign; and the will of the sovereign, in this respect, is known by his express declarations, contained either in the commissions he confers, or in the military code, or is, by fair deduction, inferred from the nature of the functions assigned to each officer: for every man who is intrusted with an employment is presumed to be invested with all the powers necessary to enable him to fill his station with propriety, and successfully discharge the functions of his office."

It would be a very difficult task, if, indeed, I could succeed in doing it, to enumerate all the duties which General Burnside is called upon to perform by reason of the command thus conferred upon him. Charged with the care of an extensive Department, comprising five States, one of which is already invaded by the enemy, and three others have been threatened; controlling a large army now in the field; obliged to issue requisitions for food, clothing, medicines, and all other munitions and habiliments of war; liable to have his plans made known and thwarted by spies communicating with the enemy, and the power of his army weakened by the falsehoods published and circulated within his lines by rebel emissaries and rebel sympathizers seeking to sow seeds of distrust and disaffection in the minds of his soldiers, it became necessary to establish a rigorous police system throughout his Department, and in so doing he promulgated "GENERAL ORDER No. 38."

This Order is intended to embrace as well those in civil life who may offend against its provisions by declaring sympathy for the enemy in words or speeches, and discouraging the soldiers now on duty, and those who may be hereafter called upon to perform military service, as those who, by carrying secret mails, and recruiting soldiers for the enemy, commit overt acts of treason by giving aid and comfort to the rebels. It was not necessary to issue such an order to his soldiers, for they are all honestly engaged in performing their high duties in the field; and the Rules and Articles of War, with which they are familiar, provide for the punishment of all persons in the military service for all offenses committed by them. But the civilian, not being strictly under military control, need not, unless he chooses, subject himself to any of the penalties provided for by the Order. In the case of Mr. Vallandigham, he saw proper, at a public meeting held in Ohio, and in a public speech, to express his sympathies with the rebels in arms against their country, to declare disloyal sentiments and opinions, and, so far as he could, to weaken the power of the government in its efforts to suppress the rebellion. For this offense, in open violation of that General Order which he then referred to and denounced, he was arrested, brought before a military commission, tried and convicted. He now seeks relief from that sentence, whatever it may be, and asserting, by his counsel, the great privilege of the writ of Habeas Corpus, demands of this Court his discharge. The violation of this Order by him was not the result of accident; it was deliberately, and, for aught I can see, purposely violated, in order either to defy the military power of the President, or to bring about a conflict between the military and the civil power of the government. It may be that he desired to show to the people that liberty of speech meant a license to say whatsoever he pleased, without regard to times, persons, or circumstances. It is claimed for him, by his learned counsel, that he is guilty of nothing but the use of words; that the utterance of words is not treason; and that an overt act must be shown to have been committed to constitute the crime of treason.

But may not words be actionable? Is not the utterance of words often held to be a misdemeanor? Words of slander are actionable; words which provoke a breach of the peace are punishable; words used to entice a soldier to desert are indictable; so are words used in resisting an officer attempting to serve legal process.

General Burnside saw that, to a considerable degree, his earnest efforts to perform the trust reposed in him in his Department were seriously impeded, not only by the presence of spies, recruiting officers, and writers of letters, and the carrying of secret mails to the rebels, but by the promulgation of disloyal sentiments and opinions, and the expression of sympathy for the rebels within his lines. He saw that the expression of such sentiments and opinions had a tendency to bring the constitutional government of the country into contempt, and consequently to weaken his authority and abridge his usefulness, and to that extent sustain and encourage the enemy and protract the war. He had no alternative but either to act as he did, or to abandon his Department. He needed no written law to direct him in his course, for the law of self-preservation, which is the law of nature, is higher than any written law, or written constition. Clothed as he was with power commensurate with the great duties he was called upon to perform in this extraordinary exigency of the nation, whatsoever in the conduct of any person seriously impeded him in the performance of that duty, it was his right, nay, it was his high duty, to remove. The nature and extent of his power, as a military commander, is very forcibly stated by Mr. Adams, in his speech in Congress, delivered in 1842. He says:

"I lay this down as the law of nations. I say that military authority takes, for the time, the place of all municipal institutions, and slavery among the rest; and that, under that state of things, so far from its being true that the States where slavery exists have the exclusive management of the subject, not only the President of the United States, but the commander of the army, has power to order the universal emancipation of the slaves."

This being true in regard to the institution of slavery, which exists by force of positive law, it must be held to be the law in respect of all other institutions which, during the great public emergency which has been forced upon the country, conflict with or impair the power of the government in its military operations. A similar principle was afterward promulgated by that distinguished political leader and sincere patriot, Senator Dickinson. He said:

"There is a power upon which the Constitution stands, that lies beneath the Constitution and rises above the Constitution, and is in and under the Constitution: it is the great law of self-preservation—for communities, nations, and States, as well as individuals. It is older than this government. It is as old as civilization. It had no rise in the Constitution. It arises in the very necessity of the existence of civil government."

The natural right to acquire and possess property, to pursue or not to pursue a particular vocation, to bear or not to bear arms, to speak and write freely our sentiments and opinions upon all subjects, must give way whenever the exercise of those rights by the individual endangers the public safety, and conflicts with the paramount right of national self-preservation.

The nation can well afford to suspend the enjoyment by the individual of these rights, for a season, in order that, by preserving its own existence, it may secure them unabridged to the whole people forever.

It has been asserted, in argument, that there is no war in Ohio; that the law martial does not exist here, and that martial law is no law at all. But is not Ohio at war? If our State, with its two and a half millions of freemen, is not one of the United

States, then Ohio is not at war; but, if otherwise, and the silver light of Ohio's star still radiates from the azure field of the national flag, then Ohio is at war, and has contributed, and will ever contribute her full proportion of men, money, and munitions of war toward sustaining the existence of the nation of which it forms a part. It is true that the foot of no hostile foe in arms has ever trodden our soil, or invaded our peaceful homes; but thousands of those homes have already yielded their fathers and sons to the service of their country, many of whom are gone never to return; and it will be but a poor solace to the bereaved wives and mothers of the slain to say to them, "Your husbands and sons have fallen in battle, while fighting to uphold the Constitution and laws of their country; but Ohio is not at war." Ohio is at war because the United States are at war; and, as a part of a military department of the United States, the citizens of the State of Ohio are liable to the operation of the laws of war, as administered *ex necessitate rei*, by courts-martial or military commissions. These courts, and the rules by which they are governed, had their origin in high antiquity. The ancient Court of Chivalry was the fountain of martial law, and, in some form or other, courts-martial have always been recognized in England. Formerly, martial law was exercised at the discretion of the Crown, and too frequently it was made subservient to bad purposes, and hence it very justly became obnoxious to the people; and not only the propriety, but the legality of its being executed in times of peace, has been absolutely denied. Hence it is laid down by Lord Coke, (3 Inst. 52), "that if a lieutenant or other, that hath commission of martial law, doth, *in time of peace*, hang or otherwise execute any man by color of martial law, this is murder, for it is against *Magna Charta*." Hence, also, Lord Hale, in his History of the Common Law, declares martial law to be, in reality, no law, "but something indulged rather than allowed as law: that the necessity of order and discipline is the only thing which can give it countenance, and therefore it ought not to be permitted *in time of peace*, when the king's courts are open for all persons to receive justice according to the laws of the land; and if a court martial put a man to death, *in time of peace*, the officers are guilty of murder." But it is now well settled in England, that courts-martial are courts of special and limited jurisdiction, and are bound by the same rules and principles of evidence as the courts of common law, and their decisions have often been examined and reviewed on Habeas Corpus by the courts of the common law. (Rex *v.* Suddis, 1 East R. 306; Crosby's case, 3 Wils. 199; Barnes's case, 2 Roll. R. 157.)

So, also, in the United States, proceedings of courts-martial have frequently been reviewed by the civil courts, as well, collaterally, upon writs of Habeas Corpus, as directly upon writs of error. I refer to a few of the cases. (Vanderheyden *v.* Young, 11 John. R. 150; Houston *v.* Moore, 1 Wheat. R. 1; Martin *v.* Mott, 12 Wheat. R. 19.)

It is true that martial law has not been proclaimed in Ohio; but the formal proclamation of martial law is not necessary in order to give efficiency to the public official orders of the Major-General commanding the Department, or to confer jurisdiction upon the military courts and commissions organized by him for the purpose of trying offenders against said orders. The power of the Major-General to exercise the functions of his office, and the duty of the citizen to refrain from interfering with the exercise of those functions *in time of war*, exist without any proclamation of martial law. The power of the one, and the duty of the other, arise from the situation in which the country is placed by the civil war now waged against the Constitution; and the power of the President, and of the officers whom he has selected to execute that power, is a power which, to use the language of Senator Dickinson, is a power upon which the Constitution stands, that lies beneath the Constitution, and rises above the Constitution, and is in and under the Constitution. It is the supreme law of national self-preservation. It is the exercise of that right conferred by the Creator upon man, the assertion of which, in an individual, no one will dispute, but which exists with more potency with many men, united in a political society, and constituting a great nation.

"Since, then," says Vattel, "a nation is obliged to preserve itself, it has a right to every thing necessary for its preservation. For the law of nature gives us a right to every thing without which we can not fulfill our obligation; otherwise it would oblige us to do impossibilities, or, rather, would contradict itself in prescribing us a duty and at the same time debarring us of the only means of fulfilling it."

This is the right which has been denominated by Grotius as the internal law of nations, and it applies to nations as well as to individuals. Vattel also says:

"As men are subject to the laws of nature—and as their union in civil society can not have exempted them from the obligation to observe those laws, since by that union they do not cease to be men—the entire nation, whose common will is but the result of the united wills of the citizens, remains subject to the laws of nature, and is bound to respect them in all her proceedings. And since right arises from obligation, as we have just observed, the nation possesses also the same right which nature has conferred upon men in order to enable them to perform their duties."

The eloquent advocate of Mr. Vallandigham, controverting the assertion of General Burnside, that "there is no fear of the people losing their liberties," has expressed the fear that our liberties can not survive a patient submission to arbitrary power. Certainly not, when, in a time of profound peace, when all the civil machinery of the government is everywhere in perfect and harmonious operation, unchecked and undisturbed by the discordant action of armed rebellion and of civil war, then a tame and continued submission to the encroachments of any arbitrary power must inevitably lead to the overthrow of the liberties of the people, and to the establishment of a despotism. But the case is entirely different in a time of war, and of such a war, the like of which neither this nor any other country has ever witnessed. Now, no temporary sacrifice ought to be too great, in order to preserve the unity of the nation; but, when the blessings of peace shall return, and the national life shall be no longer threatened, all the power of the country will be devoted to the suppression of every attempt, let it come from whatsoever quarter it may, to invade the liberty of any, even the meanest citizen.

I now leave this important question with the Court, feeling confident that the discretionary power which has been vested in your Honor will be wisely exercised. In the investigation of the questions which have arisen in this case, this Court will consider, not only the allegations of the relator as set forth in his application, but will take judicial notice of the state of the country, torn and distracted by this wicked rebellion. And the Court will also notice judicially all the efforts of the executive, and of those acting under his authority, which are made for the suppression of the rebellion, and the preservation and perpetuation of constitutional liberty; and I doubt not your Honor will endeavor not only not to derogate from executive authority by bringing about a conflict between one branch of the government and another, but, by co-operating as far as possible with the other departments, seek to secure unity of action in all the departments, and a speedy restoration of our country to its former dignity, grandeur, and power, as a great and a united nation. I feel sure, also, that there is no judge now on the bench of the Courts of the United States whose patriotic heart does not fill with indignation at the wrongs inflicted on our country by the armed traitors now levying war upon the Constitution and laws, and by those unarmed, but quite as dangerous enemies, who sympathize with and encourage domestic treason. I therefore commit this case to the Court, with the firm belief that, by your decision, the hands of the Federal executive and of the army and navy will be sustained and strengthened in this great struggle; that the hopes of the patriot in the perpetuity of Union will be encouraged; that the attempts of rebel sympathizers to stimulate the rebellion and dishearten our army will be discouraged and frustrated; and that all disloyal citizens, as well those who indirectly, as those who directly furnish aid, comfort, and encouragement to the enemy, will find that a sure and speedy punishment awaits them at the hands of the military authorities, from whose action they can hope to find no shelter in the technical forms and rule of the courts of the civil law.

I trust that the time may soon arrive when the din of arms shall cease, and when our beloved country, purified by the severe trial through which she is passing, shall be once more restored to the delightful avocations of peace, and again stand forth among the nations of the earth, a great, united, and free people, purged of every element of despotism, opening wide her portals for the reception of the oppressed of every nation and of every clime, and exhibiting to the admiration of civilization throughout the world, through all coming time, the example of a pure, a just, a free and UNITED REPUBLIC.

CLOSING ARGUMENT

OF

HON. GEORGE E. PUGH.

May it Please your Honor:

To much that has been said by the counsel for the defendant, I shall make no particular reply; nor, if I can well avoid it, indulge in repetition of my former argument.

Mr. Perry complains that the petition is not verified by the oath of the petitioner, but by that of his attorney; and, also, because the verification is upon belief merely, and not from personal knowledge. As to the first objection, it has the merit of novelty, and no other; the rule being well established that any person may make the affidavit on which a writ of Habeas Corpus is demanded. If this were not so, a prisoner could easily be deprived of all means of redress. It would only require that the person holding him in custody should prevent the access of any officer competent to administer an oath.

There is nothing in the case of Dorr (3 Howard, 103) to support such an objection. He was in jail, as a convict, under the sentence of a State Court; and for that reason (as the act of 1789 declares) no Federal Court could bring him before it, by writ of Habeas Corpus, except as a witness. It is true that the Supreme Court did not allow Mr. Treadwell to assign errors upon the record of conviction, with a view to the prosecution of a writ of error; but only because he admitted, in advance, that he had no authority to act as such attorney, and could not even assure the Court that Dorr wished him to interpose. (Pp. 105,

106.) If he had assigned the errors, at once, without any statement in regard to his authority, the Court never would have questioned it. (Osborne *v.* Bank of the United States, 9 Wheaton, 830.)

As to the other objection, I confess it well taken. The affidavit should have been positive, and from personal knowledge. I adopted, inconsiderately, the form of verification required by the Code of Civil Procedure in Ohio, and to which we are most accustomed. But that defect can be supplied, if necessary, in a few minutes; and there is a precedent for such amendment in the case of Bruce, *ex parte*, 8 East, 27. I know the fact that Mr. Vallandigham is in the custody of a guard of soldiers, in this city, under the command of General Burnside, and the fact, also, that he has been arraigned before a military commission, at the St. Charles Exchange, upon the charge and specification of which a copy is annexed to his petition. As to the circumstances of his arrest, in the city of Dayton, they are within the knowledge of several gentlemen present. I will offer this testimony if the Court require it; but how can it be necessary in view of the written statement of General Burnside? He admits every material fact alleged by the petitioner; and he assumes to justify, in the boldest manner, all the proceedings of which the petitioner complains.

The District Attorney has referred to the case of Sims, (7 Cushing, 285,) in support of his proposition that notice should be given to the defendant, in applications like the present, before granting a writ of Habeas Corpus. If he means only, as that case imports, that a rule absolute will not be granted, in the first instance, when it appears, by the petitioner's own statement, or by the affidavit submitted in lieu of a petition, that his right to be discharged from imprisonment is doubtful, I have nothing to say in opposition. The authorities mentioned by Mr. Chief-Justice Shaw (page 292) decide that, and nothing more.

Blake's case (2 M. & Selwyn, 428) was an application by a military officer who had been arrested for misconduct, and was based upon an affidavit that he had not been brought to trial as soon as a court-martial might have been conveniently assembled.

In Marsh's case, (3 Bulstrode, 27,) the applicant was confined in the prison of the admiralty as a pirate; and the ground of his application was that several indictments had been preferred against him, and all of them had been ignored. His counsel proceeded, however, to state all the circumstances from which any crime could be inferred.

COKE, C. J.—"If you had not opened the matter as you have done, then, peradventure, upon the *ignoramus* found, we would have granted a Habeas Corpus; but as you have now opened the verity of the matter (in which you have done well) we will not grant you a Habeas Corpus—*for, upon your own showing, we have very great cause now to suspect him for piracy.*"

And so the prisoner was left for another opportunity of indictment.

In the case of the Hottentot Venus, (13 East, 195,) a rule *nisi* was granted in the first instance. But that was an application by strangers, and without the knowledge of the person supposed to be imprisoned; the affidavit alleging that she was a foreigner, and ignorant of her rights, and, as the affiant surmised from her demeanor at a public exhibition, detained against her wishes. The Court hereupon directed certain of its officers to inquire of her, distinctly, in the absence of the persons having her in charge, whether she was contented with her situation; and it appearing that she was, and that no restraint or improper influence had been practiced, the application was dismissed.

These were cases in the Court of King's Bench where (first) a rule *nisi* is customary in all cases, and (second) the rule operates to prevent any change in the situation of the parties until it has been decided.

How is it possible, then, from *these* instances (and these are all) to infer a practice — a "settled" practice — of giving notice to the defendant, in advance of a writ of Habeas Corpus, where the application is made at the express direction of the prisoner, and where it manifestly appears that he has been arrested and confined without any warrant — that he has been subjected to a mode of trial forbidden by the Constitution of his country, and upon a charge which describes no crime or offense whatsoever—and that he is in imminent peril, it may be of his life, by a course of proceedings at once illegal, violent, and unprecedented? Ah, sir, no!—it is not without precedent; but the sequel of that precedent has not been imitated on this occasion. I refer to the case of Theobald Wolfe Tone, a British subject, who accompanied and voluntarily served with a French fleet designed for the invasion of Ireland, and who was taken prisoner, in arms, upon the dispersion of the fleet and the capture of the principal vessel, October 10, 1792. That he was guilty of high treason, and would have been convicted by a jury, admits of no doubt; but the military commander, Lord Cornwallis, subjected him to trial by a court-martial, at Dublin, on the 10th of November, 1792, and he was sentenced to be hanged on the second day thereafter. On the day appointed for execution, Mr. Curran applied to the Court of King's Bench, in which Lord Kilwarden, a supporter of the ministry then in power, presided as Chief-Justice, for a writ of Habeas Corpus. I will read the story as Mr. Charles Phillips narrates it:

"'I do not pretend,' began Curran, 'that Mr. Tone is not guilty of the charge of which he is accused. I presume the officers were honorable men. But it is stated in this affidavit, as a solemn fact, that Mr. Tone had no commission under his majesty; and, therefore, no court-martial could have cognizance of any crime imputed to him while the Court of King's Bench sat in the capacity of the great Criminal Court of the land. In times when war was raging, when man was opposed to man in the field, courts-martial might be endured; but every law authority is with me while I stand upon the sacred and immutable principle of the Constitution that martial law and civil law are incompatible, and that the former must cease with the existence of the latter. This is not, however, the time for arguing this momentous question. *My client must appear in this Court.* He is cast for death this very day. He may be ordered for execution while I address you. *I call on the Court to support the law, and move for a writ of Habeas Corpus, to be directed to the provost marshal of the barracks and Major Sandys, to bring up the body of Tone.*'

"CHIEF-JUSTICE—'*Have a writ* INSTANTLY *prepared.*'

"CURRAN—'My client may die while the writ is preparing.'

"CHIEF-JUSTICE—'Mr. Sheriff! proceed to the barracks, and acquaint the provost marshal that a writ is preparing to suspend Mr. Tone's execution—*and see that he be not executed.*'

"In a short time the sheriff, having returned, thus addressed the Court:

"'My lord! I have been to the barracks in pursuance of your order. The provost marshal says he must obey Major Sandys. Major Sandys says he must obey Lord Cornwallis.'

"At this time Mr. Curran announced the return of Tone's father with a message that General Craig refused to obey the writ of Habeas Corpus.

"CHIEF-JUSTICE—'MR. SHERIFF! TAKE THE BODY OF TONE INTO CUSTODY; TAKE THE PROVOST MARSHAL AND MAJOR SANDYS INTO CUSTODY; AND SHOW THE ORDER OF THE COURT TO GENERAL CRAIG.'"

Tone was not executed; but, while this scene was being enacted, and in ignorance of it, he inflicted a wound upon himself, of which he died, in prison, shortly afterward.

Less tragical in the circumstances, but no less decisive in principle, was the conduct of Mr. Chief-Justice Kent and his illustrious associates, composing the Supreme Court of New York, in August, 1813. (Matter of Stacy, 10 Johnson, 328.)

That was a case in which a Commissioner of the Court had allowed a writ of Habeas Corpus, in vacation, addressed to "Isaac Chauncey, commandant of the Navy of the United States on Lake Ontario, and to Morgan Lewis, commanding the troops of the United States at the station of Sackett's Harbor, and to each and every subordinate officer under said commandants, or either of them," requiring them to produce, immediately, the body of Samuel Stacy, junior, together with the cause of his caption and detention. The writ was not defied, but merely evaded; General Lewis returning that Stacy was not in his custody, and the provost marshal (Torrey) objecting that it was not directed to him, "either by name or description," and that no copy of the warrant of commitment had ever been demanded of him. The facts were that Stacy had been arrested by the order of Commodore Chauncey, upon a charge of "*carrying provisions and giving information to the enemy*" in Canada, and was thereupon delivered into the custody of the provost marshal of General Lewis's command. The Commissioner submitted the papers to the Supreme Court for its aid and advice.

KENT, C. J.—"The only question that can be made is whether the motion for an attachment shall be granted, or whether there shall be only a rule upon the party offending to show cause, by the first day of the next term, why an attachment should not issue. After giving the case the best consideration which the pressure of the occasion admits, I am of opinion that the attachment ought to be *immediately* awarded.

"The attachment is but process to bring in the party to answer for the alleged contempt; and, upon the present motion, we must act—as the Courts have always, of necessity, acted in like cases—upon the return itself, and the accompanying affidavits of the complainant.

"This is a case which concerns the personal liberty of the citizen. Stacy is now suffering the rigor of confinement in close custody, at this unhealthy season of the year, at a military camp, and under military power. He is a natural-born citizen, residing in this State. He has a numerous family dependent upon him for their support. He is in bad health, and the danger of a protracted confinement to his health, if not to his life, must be serious. *The pretended charge of treason* (for, upon the facts now before us, we must consider it as a pretext) *without being founded upon oath, and without any specification of the matters of which it might consist, and without any color of authority in any military tribunal to try a citizen for that crime, is only aggravation of the oppression of the confinement.* It is the indispensable duty of this Court, and one to which every inferior consideration must be sacrificed, to act as a faithful guardian of the personal liberty of the citizen, and to give ready and effectual aid to the means provided by law for its security. One of the most valuable of those means is this writ of Habeas Corpus, which has justly been deemed the glory of the English law; and the Parliament of England, as well as their Courts of justice, have, on several occasions, and for the period at least of the last two centuries, shown the utmost solicitude, not only that the writ, when called for, should be issued without delay, but that it should be punctually obeyed. Nor can we hesitate in promptly enforcing a due return to the writ when we recollect that, in this country, the law knows no superior, and that, in England, their Courts have taught us, by a series of instructive examples, to exact the strictest obedience, to whatever extent the persons to whom the writ is directed may be clothed with power or exalted in rank. . . . IF EVER A CASE CALLED FOR THE MOST PROMPT INTERPOSITION OF THE COURT, TO ENFORCE OBEDIENCE TO ITS PROCESS, THIS IS ONE. A MILITARY COMMANDER IS HERE ASSUMING CRIMINAL JURISDICTION OVER A PRIVATE CITIZEN; IS HOLDING HIM IN THE CLOSEST CONFINEMENT, AND CONTEMNING THE CIVIL AUTHORITY OF THE STATE."

I have said that I agree with the Supreme Court of Massachusetts in Sims's case: "The Court will not grant the writ of Habeas Corpus when they see that, *in the result*, they must *remand* the party." (7 Cush. 292.) To that effect is the case of Hobhouse, (3 B. and Ald. 420,) and its doctrine is perfectly just and reasonable.

Unless, therefore, upon the statement of his petition, *as confessed by the answer of General Burnside*, it now appears that Clement L. Vallandigham is unlawfully imprisoned, and ought to be discharged, or, at least, admitted to the privilege of bail, he is not entitled to a writ of Habeas Corpus.

This leads me to the criticism in which Mr. Perry has indulged respecting the petition. Its rhetoric is mine, and that I leave with no apology but this: I did intend, by narrating the arrest of Mr. Vallandigham as accurately as possible, to demonstrate how many of his rights had been violated, and with what circumstances of aggravation. If, in so doing, I have employed such words, or nearly such, as KENT employed in a judicial opinion, describing the case of Samuel Stacy, in August, 1813, that may suffice to comfort me under the new dispensation of rhetoric, as well as of constitutional law and of military privilege, which the defendant and his learned counsel have proclaimed.

The petition recites that Mr. Vallandigham is a citizen of Ohio by birth, as distinguished from naturalization, because it is usual in pleading, whenever a party alleges his own title, to allege, also, the derivation of that title, and because the fact of his citizenship draws after it three important conclusions:

1. Being a citizen of Ohio, he is *thereby* a citizen of the United States, and entitled to the protection of their Constitution and laws.

2. Inasmuch as Ohio is not one of the States in which a rebellion or insurrection exists, no military officer has, or can have, any *civil* authority or jurisdiction within it.

3. Citizenship in Ohio, added to the fact (also alleged) of residence in Montgomery County, one of the counties composing the Southern judicial district, entitles the petitioner to call upon this Court for a writ of Habeas Corpus, to prevent his being removed, except by legal process, into any *other* State or district.

The petition next recites that Mr. Vallandigham is not enlisted or commissioned in the land or the naval service of the United States, and that, although liable to be called into their service, as one of the militia of the State of Ohio, he has not been so called: from which premises it follows that he is not subject to the Rules and Articles of War, and, also, that he can not be tried, or even arrested, for a military offense.

The petition then states particularly (and, if my learned opponents will so have it, rhetorically,) the fact of Mr. Vallandigham's arrest, and the fact of his having been brought to this city, and here detained, as a prisoner. The arrest, the removal hither, and the imprisonment are alleged to have been by persons armed and in uniform as soldiers, and obeying the orders of the defendant as a Major-General in the army of the United States. From all which, as I understand the law, a conclusion results that these were acts done "by color of authority" from the United States, and that they are cognizable, therefore, as well in this Court as in the Courts of the State of Ohio.

But the Habeas Corpus Act of 31 Charles II requires (and the statute of Ohio is to the same effect) that every person applying for a writ of Habeas Corpus shall exhibit with his application a copy of the warrant on which he has been arrested, or else allege that there is no warrant in existence, or that he can not obtain a copy of it. Therefore, the petition next alleges that there is not, and never was, any such paper as, by the Constitution of the United States, could be a warrant—or, in other words, no paper in which a "probable cause" of arrest is specified, and "supported by oath or affirmation." Nevertheless, a paper having been delivered to the petitioner while imprisoned, he exhibits that; and it proves to be a charge and a specification signed by Captain Cutts, Judge-Advocate, with a view to the trial of the petitioner by some military tribunal. The fact that the petitioner has been so arraigned for trial is next alleged; and this to demonstrate the urgency of his case, and the necessity for this Court to interpose and to deliver him at once.

Then follows the prayer of the petition—part of it being in the words of Mr. Chief-Justice Kent, already quoted, and part of it taken from the old form of the writ of Habeas Corpus ad subjiciendum.

The point of Mr. Perry's criticism is very notable; it is a category of the most categorical description. Either, he argues, this arrest was made by "authority" of the United States, or it was not: if it was, the Court must deny a writ of Habeas Corpus for lack of merits; if it was not, the Court must deny a writ for lack of jurisdiction. Add to this Mr. Attorney's wonderful deduction from the Wisconsin case, (Ableman *v.* Booth, 21 Howard, 506,) to-wit: that no STATE Court has jurisdiction of the controversy, and we are brought to the conclusion that, although Mr. Vallandigham has been illegally arrested, is illegally imprisoned, and is now in peril of his life (it may be) from an illegal sentence, there is no Court of civil judicature anywhere to which he can apply for redress!

These dissertations of the learned counsel would be amusing, and, on that account, perhaps, worthy of additional notice, but for the solemn issue on which they are wasted. I have no doubt of the jurisdiction of the Courts of Ohio; but I apply here because my client has so instructed me, and because the jurisdiction of this Court is equally indisputable.

The act of September 24, 1789, declares that writs of Habeas

Corpus allowed by the Federal Courts or Judges "shall in no case extend to prisoners *in gaol* unless where they" (the prisoners) "are in custody under or by color of authority of the United States, or are committed for trial before some Court of the same, or are necessary to be brought into Court to testify." (U. S. Statutes at Large, vol. 1, p. 82.) Now, sir, although he is imprisoned, and that closely, Mr. Vallandigham is not "in gaol" at all—and never has been. But suppose this were otherwise: what did Congress intend by "color of authority" as distinguished from authority itself? I answer that it is a distinction between appearance and reality: the two are outwardly alike; but one is unlawful, and the other is lawful. But, objects Mr. Perry, you deny that this arrest was made by "authority" of the United States. Yes, sir, I do. The United States have no such *real* authority, and, therefore, can impart none to General Burnside or any other man, soldier or civilian, officer or plain individual. If so, argues Mr. Perry, you must observe the rule of pleading in confession and avoidance; you must assign to General Burnside a colorable title, although a fictitious one, and then avoid his proceedings by an allegation of some fact consistent with the title so assigned. Well, sir, I have done that. I assign him the title of a Major-General commanding this Department; in virtue of which title, he may arrest and imprison, without warrant, any soldier or enlisted officer. But that title gives him no authority to arrest, imprison, or even command, a citizen who is not in the military service: as to such persons, and all of them, his title is fictitious—and for the reason that his assumption of authority over them is unlawful. Thus, while imputing color to his proceedings, as those of a Major-General in the army of the United States, I avoid them (I mean, sir, in a *legal* sense) by the allegation that Mr. Vallandigham is not a soldier, nor a military officer, and that he has not been called into the service of the United States as a militiaman.

Approaching the principal themes of Mr. Perry's argument, I find it rather difficult to persuade myself that all we have heard in fact proceeded from the lips of one man; since, if I rightly comprehend the various propositions, half of them completely demolish the rest, and yet without securing themselves any better foundation.

For example: the learned counsel deprecates, "in the interests of mercy," a subjection of my client to the ordeal of a trial by jury, in "such moments of overwhelming excitement" as the present, because "no good man," as we are told, "could be impartial," and every man "who claims to be impartial" thereby "impeaches himself." The merciful deduction from which, one might suppose, would be that the trial of accused or suspected persons ought to be postponed until more quiet times, or guarded, at least, against every incentive to hatred and prejudice. Instead of that, I had scarcely thanked the learned counsel for so humane a suggestion, and concluded that he would certainly offer to release my client on bail, or advise that he should be retained in civil custody as a prisoner awaiting trial, than I heard his utter and irrevocable condemnation pronounced, his guilt taken for granted, his character maligned, his courage and his talents alike depreciated, even his eloquence degraded to the office of eking out a sneer. And, all the while, pleading to save my client—mark you!—from the partiality of jurors so immaculate in patriotism that they would not observe their oath lest they should impeach themselves, the learned counsel seemed innocently unconscious of the fact, proclaimed in General Burnside's statement, that my client has been tried already (if trial you call it) and sentenced, perhaps to death, perhaps to some degree of suffering compared with which death is preferable. The learned counsel must pardon me; but, as to my choice, the utmost risk of unfairness in a jury would little incline me to a contest with General Burnside before judges, and *military* judges, of his own appointment. I have the certificate of Juvenal on that subject:

> "Justissima centurionum
> Cognitio est igitur de milite; nec mihi deerit
> Ultio, si justæ defertur causa querelæ."

Again: the learned counsel informs us that "the liberty of the citizen is touched when he is compelled, either by a sense of duty or by conscription, to enter the army." I was not aware of that: I had supposed—traitorously, no doubt, and in pursuance of some suggestion from Jefferson Davis—that when a citizen enlisted himself as a soldier, by his own volition, induced thereto "by a sense of duty" as distinguished from the persuasions of the conscription act, he was exercising as much liberty as a man could well enjoy. I had supposed, also, and probably with an equal degree of treason, that one of the rights of an American citizen, being thus an essential part of his liberty, was to serve in the militia when regularly called, and assist in defending the republic. I imagined that I had read something of the kind in the Constitution of the United States.* But now, sir, inasmuch as I have heard "a solemn accord of voices rising from the graves" of its founders, and likewise heard, through Mr. Perry, "the response of the loyal and true friends of liberty everywhere," I shall correct my erroneous impressions, and probably console myself with the virtues of a commutation. To pause here would be ingratitude to the learned counsel: he has told me of injuries which I never suspected. "The liberty of the citizen is touched when he is forbidden to pass the lines of any encampment." I supposed, inasmuch as General Burnside has no right to enter my house without my consent, or by special authority of law, that so, without his consent, or some such authority, I had no right to intrude into the precincts of his encampment; but we learn more as we live longer. Listen, therefore, to something else: "The liberty of the citizen is touched when he is forbidden to sell arms and munitions of war, or to carry information, to the enemy." I thought these were crimes—overt acts of treason as defined in the Constitution of the United States: if they form any part of my liberty, as the learned counsel pretends, I will surrender that part to General Burnside without the slightest compunction. Mr. Perry then adds an expression of surprise that we should

---

* Second Amendment.—"A well-regulated militia being necessary to the security of a free State, the right of the people to keep and bear arms shall not be infringed."

"ever" have "felt justified in thinking so meanly of the people of any section of the country as to suppose they could be persuaded their liberties were attacked, and yet not make an appropriate resistance." Sir, is that a strain from the "solemn accord of voices" to which our attention has been called, or a part of the supposed speech of Jefferson Davis? I almost fear to repeat it: I fear that is treason implied, if not expressed, and strongly implied too, without satisfactory obedience to General Order No. 38.

Well, having been thus newly instructed with regard to my liberty, and to divers infractions thereof which I had never imagined, and being thus taunted, also, by Mr. Perry, for want of "appropriate resistance" on that account, I listened with unusual interest and astonishment. And then followed questions of this character:

> "Have not these baleful experiments of an unbridled license of tongue been carried far enough? May we not, at length, cease to trifle, and do what is possible to check these rivers of blood by obstructing the head-waters from which they flow? All other experiments having failed, may we not, as a last resort, listen to the dictates of common sense?"

And so, instead of enjoying my new liberty, as Mr. Perry warranted it, I am not only to lose that, but with it, and forever, the liberty of which I have been always conscious, and which my fathers enjoyed before me! There must be a bridle in some man's mouth—not to curb his tongue merely, as he will soon discover, but to enable another man, booted and spurred, to mount upon his back and ride him. The words of our Constitution are too tame: these must be expunged, or turned to naught, in order that the learned counsel, transformed into a Pythia of bravest ecstacy, and self-inspired, may deliver us the oracles of "common sense" for admonition and government.

Once more. Mr. Perry argues, upon detached sentences from Vattel's treatise, that the rights of public war, as between two nations, apply to the present controversy between the Federal Government and the people of the States in rebellion; and thence adopts the conclusion that General Burnside, as the commander of an army, "in the field of military operations, for the purposes of war, and in the presence of the enemy," can seize and hold, as prisoners, not only those in arms, their assistants and abettors, but persons totally indifferent, non-combatants, and even women and children. Thus, having clothed the General with a right of arrest and imprisonment purely belligerent in its character, he transfers that right from the presence of the enemy, and from the field of military operations, to the peaceful cities of Dayton and Cincinnati, in the State of Ohio, and would exercise it here for no purpose of war, but only for the detection and punishment of a supposed crime. Could any process of reduction to absurdity be more complete? And yet, sir, that is the pith of the gentleman's whole argumentation; take that away, and nothing but words remain. It is a right which, as expounded, hath more changes, and in briefer time, than the cloud respecting which Hamlet and Polonius compared their observations.

But, granting it all, and as the counsel has claimed it, what then results? I answer: It results, inevitably, that all persons so seized, anywhere, in the exercise of a belligerent right, are prisoners of war. And, if so, how is it that my distinguished client, arrested as a prisoner of war, has been arraigned for trial, as if he were a criminal, before a commission of officers, upon such a charge and such a specification as are here exhibited? Why is he not, at least, allowed the privilege of parole, or of being exchanged, as perfectly as if he had been captured in arms and upon a field of battle?

Hardly, sir, in any place, does the learned counsel build a nest of excuses for his client—patiently, anxiously, and most lovingly, with a twig chosen here, and a little gum found there, and with leaves from all the trees of the forest—than the client himself, with soldierlike impatience, and somewhat of disdain, kicks it into a thousand fragments.

And now, that I may not be under the necessity of pursuing the devious path of Mr. Perry's wandering, I will demonstrate a proposition which, if I can establish it, destroys the whole foundation of his defense, and restores the case immediately to the dominion of those principles in regard to which I have already addressed the Court at length.

I affirm, then, distinctly, that the government of the United States can not exercise, and can not claim, the rights of public war as against the people of a State in rebellion; in other words, sir, it has, at present, no *belligerent* right whatsoever.

I state my proposition in the plainest as well as the largest possible terms; and I intend to urge it, by reason and by authority, to the full scope of its legitimate consequences. All that I ask of candid or honorable men is to give me their patient attention; they will not, I think, be dissatisfied with my conclusions.

Observe, once more, the language of the proposition: I say that the government can not exercise the RIGHTS of public war. I do not say that it can not exercise the *amenities* of public war; nor that it is not, in view of the usages of civilized nations, under a high moral obligation so to do. That is what M. Vattel argues, and what he enforces, ably, and, as I think, conclusively, in the chapter from which Mr. Perry has given us a mutilated excerpt. Let any one read the chapter—the eighteenth chapter of book third—and compare it with the tenor of Mr. Perry's speech. No two things could be more discordant. But to the particular section (294th) of which so little has been quoted, and that in a sense totally variant from the author's intention. After urging that although, in a civil war, "one of the parties may have been to blame in breaking the unity of the State, and resisting the lawful authority, they," the two parties, "are not the less divided in fact," and urging, also, that "they have no common superior" on earth, M. Vattel proceeds:

"This being the case, it is very evident that the common LAWS of war—*those maxims of humanity, moderation, and honor which we have already detailed in the course of this work*—ought to be observed, by both parties, in every civil war. For the same reasons which render the observance of *these* maxims a matter of obligation between State and State, it becomes equally and even more necessary in the unhappy circumstance of two incensed parties lacerating their common country. Should the sovereign conceive he has a right to hang up his prisoners as rebels, the opposite party will make reprisals. If he does not religiously observe the capitulations, and all other conventions made with his enemies, they will no longer rely on his word. Should he burn and ravage, they will follow his example. The war will become cruel, horrible, and every day more destructive to the nation."

M. Vattel then takes notice of the atrocities practiced by both parties, Catholics and Protestants, during the religious wars of France, and thus concludes:

"At length it became necessary to relinquish those pretensions to judicial authority over men who proved themselves capable of supporting their cause by force of arms, and to treat them not as criminals, but as enemies. Even the troops have often refused to serve in a war wherein the prince exposed them to cruel reprisals. Officers who had the highest sense of honor, though ready to shed their blood in the field of battle for his service, have not thought it any part of their duty to run the hazard of an ignominious death. Whenever, therefore, a numerous body of men think they have a right to resist the sovereign, and feel themselves in a condition to appeal to the sword, the war ought to be carried on by the contending parties in the same manner as by two different nations; and they ought to leave open the same means for preventing its being carried to outrageous extremities, and for the restoration of peace."

M. Vattel then says that a sovereign, if at length completely victorious, can punish the rebels, as such, or as many of them as he sees fit; adding, however, that an amnesty is usual, and fully explaining that subject.

But in this, obviously, the rights of war, except as to the combatants in arms, are not at all considered: it is merely a discourse as to the *manner* in which hostilities ought to be conducted, and whether humanely or otherwise. In order to ascertain the rights of public, just, or solemn war—for it has all these titles of description—we must ascertain what such a war is. It commonly begins by a declaration of defiance; as in the Constitution of the United States, article first, section eighth, power is conferred on Congress "to *declare* war." And Grotius saith:

"But, that this war be called just, it is not enough that it is made between sovereigns, but, as we have heard before, it must be *publicly* denounced, and that so publicly that both parties may have equal knowledge of it." (Treatise on the Rights of War and Peace, Book III, ch. 3, sec. 5.)

Again:

"By the law of nations, a public denunciation is required in all cases, *as to those peculiar effects of a just war*, if not on both sides, yet on one." (Sec. 6.)

Vattel speaks in the same manner, book third, chapter fourth. Why such a declaration, and what are the "peculiar effects" of a "just" or "solemn" war? Grotius will answer:

"War denounced against a sovereign is presumed, also, to be denounced *against* ALL *his subjects, allies, and adherents.* And this our modern lawyers mean when they say: A prince being defied, all his adherents are defied. For, to denounce war they call diffidare, to bid defiance, which is to be understood of that very war which is made upon him against whom it was to be proclaimed." (Book III, ch. 3, sec. 9.)

Or, as more distinctly expressed by the Supreme Court of the United States, in the case of the Rapid, (8 Cranch, 155):

"In the state of war, nation is known to nation only by their avowed exterior, each threatening the other with conquest or annihilation. The individuals who compose the belligerent States exist, as to each other, in a state of utter occlusion. *If they meet, it is only in combat.*' (Pp. 160, 161.)

Again:

"The whole nation are embarked in one common bottom, and must be reconciled to submit to one common fate. *Every individual of the one nation must acknowledge every individual of the other nation as his own enemy, because the enemy of his country.*" (P. 161.)

The case of Touteng *v.* Hubbard, (3 Bos. & Puller, 291,) affords a clear illustration. That was an action by the owners of a Swedish vessel against a British subject for not employing it as stipulated in a written agreement. The defendant had chartered the vessel to proceed from London to Ponte del Gada, in the island of St. Michael's, and there receive a cargo of fruit, and bring the same to London. The vessel started on her voyage, and was driven back to Ramsgate by contrary winds: while there, on the 15th of January, 1801, an embargo was laid, by the British Government, on all Swedish vessels in British ports. This vessel was detained, by the embargo, until the 19th of June, 1801, and was then released: whereupon the master tendered to make the voyage to St. Michael's; but, as the fruit-season there was over, the defendant declined his offer.

The Court of Common Pleas gave judgment against the plaintiffs:

1. Because the embargo was a hostile act.

2. Because, being an act of the British Government, the Courts of Great Britain were under obligation to maintain the justice of it, and to hold that Sweden had committed some aggression of which retaliation, by laying an embargo, was the necessary consequence.

3. Because the fault of the government of Sweden was, in such circumstances, the fault of the plaintiffs, *personally*, as Swedish subjects.

Lord Alvanley, C. J., delivered the opinion of the Court after advisement:

"There may be no great reason why one British subject should not insure another against the effects of an embargo laid on by the British Government; the policy of the State is not concerned in preventing such an insurance. But the case is very different where the embargo is laid on by way of hostility and reprisal against foreign subjects. All the cases admit that where a party has been disabled from performing his contract by his own default, it is not competent to him to allege the circumstances by which he was prevented as an excuse for his omission. May not the loss which the present plaintiff has sustained be considered, in a political point of view, as arising from his own default? He undertook to proceed with all convenient speed; and, if he had loitered, it would have been an answer to this action. Then, must not every subject of the Swedish State be answerable for what we must consider as an act of aggression on the part of his sovereign? Perhaps, if the embargo had been laid on by a third State, it might only have produced a suspension of the contract, upon the principle that the impossibility of proceeding had not arisen from the default of the Swedish captain. *But here the impossibility has arisen from an act of the British State, to which all his majesty's subjects are parties, occasioned by an act of the Swedish Court, to which all the subjects of Sweden are parties.*" (P. 302.)

To the same effect, in principle, are the cases reported under the title of Conway *v.* Gray, (10 East, 536.*)

Now, sir, is it contended that such enmity prevails, and rightly prevails, *as an obligation of law*, between every man, woman, and child, white and black, in the eleven States which have seceded, upon one side, and every man, woman, and child, upon the other side, in the States which have not seceded? If so, then, whether secession was constitutional or unconstitutional, it has at length attained the dignity of an acknowledged fact. There is no escaping this conclusion: it ensues, immediately, as soon as the government of the United States, by exercising the rights of a belligerent, assumes the existence of WAR between the Confederate States, so called, and itself. Belligerent rights attend war; and war presupposes two hostile sovereigns or nations. Is the government of the Confederate States entitled to the attributes of sovereignty? Does it represent a nation? If so, why talk, any longer, of rebellion or of rebels?

I bid the learned counsel to beware. They are treading on most perilous ground. In their undue haste to discover some pretext for the oppression of Mr. Vallandigham, they have abandoned—utterly abandoned—the sole argument by which the cause of our Federal Government stands this day supported in arms.

And what of those "Union men" described by one of the

---

* See, also, Usparicha *v.* Noble, 13 East, 332. Mennett *v.* Bonham, 15 East, 477.

learned counsel (Mr. Perry) as appealing to us, and uttering "weak prayers" for our success, even in the darkest corners of Confederate dominion? Does he mean to say that, in addition to their sufferings at home, in addition to the enmity of the rebels in martial array, he and I are also their enemies, and under the highest obligation of duty, as patriots, to intensify their afflictions? If so, how can the gentleman speak kindly of them, as he has done, without committing that very offense with which, in all the sentences of his speech, Mr. Vallandigham is falsely charged? On the other hand, if they are not our enemies, but legally, as in fact, our friends, how can it be said that every citizen of South Carolina, or of Georgia, for example, is at war with every citizen of Ohio and of Indiana?

Recollect, sir, that I am speaking of this question from *our* point of observation, and not from the point assumed and, at present, occupied by the authorities of the eleven States which have seceded. They claim to be no longer citizens of the United States, or subject to the government acknowledged by us; they claim to have established a new sovereignty, or aggregation of sovereignties, by the title of the Confederate States of America; they claim to be of a different nation, altogether, from the nation of which the State of Ohio is an integer. They do not deny, or even question, the sovereignty of the United States—intending by that title, however, only the States which have not seceded. They profess to regard our Federal Government as the government of a foreign and a hostile nation. They have declared war against us—just, solemn, public war—by a formal act of their Congress, at Montgomery, Alabama, in April, 1861. As they view the question, consequently, and according to the terms of their argument, each citizen of the United States is at enmity with each citizen of the Confederate States; and it is in virtue of the existence of a public war, as they claim this to be, that they claim and exercise belligerent rights. I shall not insist on the lawfulness of their proceedings; but I affirm that they are consistent, and that such proceedings conform, logically, to the premises which they assume, and which we controvert as well in argument as by the force of arms.

Nor am I speaking of the question as other nations—England, France, and Denmark, for example—have chosen to view it. They accord to the government of the Confederate States all the rights of a belligerent power; and this they can do, by the law of nations, without a formal acknowledgment of its sovereignty or national independence. We behaved in like manner while Spain was endeavoring to subdue her rebellious provinces in South America; and our Supreme Court maintained, on several occasions, the rightfulness of such behavior. (U. S. *v.* Palmer, 3 Wheaton, 610; Divina Pastora, 4 Wheaton, 52; Santissima Trinidad, 7 Wheaton, 283, 284.) But foreign nations are not, like ourselves, constrained to the necessity of a preordained position: foreign nations may acknowledge the independence of the Confederate States at any time, or, as a lower degree of the same authority, acknowledge their belligerent character. It is a question of inexorable logic with us; but it is a question of mere discretion, or even caprice, with others.

In my opinion, therefore, no government can be at war with its own subjects. To allege that, is to allege a self-contradiction. Subjects may rebel against their government, and the government may, if it can, suppress their rebellion. No matter how fierce the controversy, or how nearly soever it may assume the lineaments or dimensions of war, it is rebellion—armed insurrection—and nothing else. We often speak of it as a "civil" war; but that title has no legal signification, and involves no belligerent right. M. Vattel admits this, distinctly, except in cases where the "STATE" is dissolved. (Book III, ch. 18, sec. 295.) We can not acknowledge that to be our case, at present, unless we acknowledge the death of that Union for the sake of which we have taken up arms, and in the very name of which we are now contending with secessionists and rebels.

War, as I have said, means war publicly declared. It begins with formal defiance. But how can a government defy its own subjects? It would thereby, and at once, discharge them of allegiance.

The learned counsel for the defendant, therefore, must abandon their whole argument—every material proposition in it—or else they must declare that the Confederate States have achieved independence, attained sovereignty, and are entitled to recognition as a separate nation.

I may be asked, however, if I mean to affirm that belligerent rights pertain exclusively to war, or a state of hostility, between two sovereigns. I do, sir; I mean precisely that. Belligerent rights are the correlatives of belligerent duties; and both depend on the premises already established—on the fact that, in time of war, every subject of one nation is at personal enmity with every subject of the hostile nation. Let us hear what Chancellor Kent has to say:

"When war is duly declared, it is not merely a war between this and the adverse government in their *political* characters. Every man is, in judgment of law, a party to the acts of his own government; and a war between the governments of two nations is a war between all the individuals of the one, and all the individuals of which the other nation is composed. Government is the representative of the will of all the people, and acts for the whole society. This is the theory in all governments; and the best writers on the law of nations concur in the doctrine that when the sovereign of a State declares war against another sovereign, it implies that the whole nation declares war, and that all the subjects of the one are enemies to all the subjects of the other. *Very important consequences, concerning the obligations of subjects, are deducible from* THIS *principle.*" (1 Kent's Com. 55.)

What the "consequences" are, I shall by and by demonstrate: my purpose, at present, is to direct your Honor's attention to the fact that they result entirely, and exclusively, from the state of enmity, *as individuals*, between all the subjects of one nation and all the subjects of another. Until THAT foundation be laid, by reason of the existence of just, solemn, or public war, no superstructure of "consequences" can possibly arise. (Grotius: Book III, ch. 4, sec. 1.)

The "consequences" are, as Chancellor Kent proceeds to enumerate, those rights and those duties which are known as belligerent rights and belligerent duties. I will reverse the order in which he has considered them. As to belligerent duties:

1. The subjects of one hostile nation can not "adhere" to the cause of the opposing nation by giving "aid and comfort" to its government or its armed forces. What is meant by those words, "*aid and comfort*," I have defined already, in defining overt acts of treason. Suffice it, as I then proved, that mere words are not sufficient.

2. The subjects of one belligerent can not trade, or have any commercial intercourse, with the subjects of the other belligerent, except in virtue of a license from their own government.

They can not, without such license, bring into their own country, even by means of a neutral ship, goods purchased in the country of the enemy after a declaration of war. (Potts *v.* Bell, 8 Term Rep. 548.)

They can not, without license, send a vessel to the enemy's country for the purpose of bringing away such of their property as happened to be there at the time when war was declared. (The Rapid, 8 Cranch, 155.)

"The interdiction," says Chancellor Kent, "flows NECESSARILY from the principle already stated—*that a state of war puts all the members of the two nations, respectively, in hostility to each other.*" (1 Com. 66.)

But, obviously, the principle leads much further than this. "It is lawful," says Grotius, "for one enemy to hurt another, both in person and goods; not only for him that makes war on a just account, and does it within those bounds which are prescribed by the law of nature, as we have said in the beginning of this book, but on both sides, and without distinction; so that he can not be punished as a murderer, or a thief, though he be taken in another prince's dominions; neither can any make war upon him barely upon this account. And in this sense we are to take Sallust: *By the right of war, all things are lawful to the conqueror.*" (Book III, chap. 4, sec. 3.)

"This right of license," he adds, "is of a large extent; for it reaches not only those who are actually in arms, and the subjects of the prince engaged in war; but, also, all those who reside within his territories—as may appear from that form in Livy: *Let him, and all that live within his country, be our enemies.* And no wonder, since we may apprehend damage from them, which, in a war long and general, is enough to justify the right here spoken of; otherwise than in reprisals, which, as I have said, were first introduced after the manner of taxes laid for the payment of public debts. Wherefore, no marvel if, as Baldus observes, this license in war be much greater than that in reprisals. And, without doubt, strangers that come into an enemy's country, after a war is proclaimed and begun, are liable to be treated as enemies." (Sec. 6.)

"Such as are natural subjects of the enemy, if we respect only their persons, may, in all places, be assaulted; because, as we have shew'd already, when war is proclaimed, it is done against a prince and his people in the form of denunciation. So, in the decree against King Philip, *They did will and command that war should be denounced against him, and the Macedonians under his dominion.* And he that is an enemy may, by the law of nations, be assaulted everywhere. . . . They may, then, lawfully be killed in their own country, in the enemy's country, in a desert that belongs to nobody, or on the sea. But, that we may not kill or plunder them in a peaceable country, proceeds not from their own persons, but from the right of that prince in whose dominions they are." (Sec. 8.)

He admits that such license also extends, in strictness of authority, to the cases of women and children (as my learned opponents claim) and of captives, of suppliants in battle, of those who surrender without condition, and of hostages. In modern times, however, these are generally regarded as cases of exception.

Other belligerent rights are of the same nature, and depend on the same principle:

1. The right of confiscating the property of alien enemies.
2. The right to blockade the ports of a hostile country.
3. And the right to detain, as a prisoner of war, without specific accusation, or intention of trial, any subject of the enemy, whether captured in battle or otherwise.

These, I say, are belligerent rights; they are defined by the law of nations, and, except confiscation, require no statute.

Our act of Congress approved July 17, 1862, is not a law of confiscation, but of penal forfeiture.

And so, a vessel seized by authority of the act approved July 13, 1861, can not be prize of war. It is only seized in the exercise of a municipal, and not of a belligerent right. (Rose *v.* Himely, 4 Cranch, 241; St. Jago de Cuba, 9 Wheaton, 409.)

In truth, as demonstrated by Chief-Justice Marshall, in the case of the Antelope, (10 Wheaton, 66, 67,) no nation can add to, or subtract from, the general law of nations. "Each legislates for itself; but its legislation can operate on itself alone." (P. 122.)

Does it follow, from what I have said, that the government of the United States can not subdue a rebellion by the force of arms? No, sir; it does not follow. The government has ample authority in such cases. The government needs, for that purpose, no belligerent right, nor any assistance from the law of nations. The government needs only to pursue the path of the Constitution—a path so plain that statesmen of ordinary experience and tolerable ability have no excuse for supposing that war and rebellion are equivalents, or attended by consequences of the same legal importance.

I put aside, as wholly inapplicable, the power of Congress "to declare war." Instead of that, I take (first) its power "to provide for calling forth the militia to execute the laws of the Union, suppress insurrections, and repel invasions." Under this authority, on the 28th of February, 1795, Congress enacted a law of which I will read the second and third sections:

SEC. 2. "That whenever the laws of the United States shall be opposed, or the execution thereof obstructed, in any State, by combinations too powerful to be suppressed by the ordinary course of judicial proceedings, or by the powers vested in the marshals by this act, it shall be lawful for the President of the United States to call forth the militia of such State, or of any other State or States, as may be necessary, to suppress such combinations, and to cause the laws to be duly executed; and the use of the militia so to be called forth may be continued, if necessary, until the expiration of thirty days after the commencement of the then next session of Congress."

SEC. 3. "*Provided, always, and be it further enacted*, That whenever it may be necessary, in the judgment of the President, to use the military force hereby directed to be called forth, the President shall forthwith, by proclamation, command such insurgents to disperse, and retire peaceably to their respective abodes, within a limited time."

The clause of the Constitution which I have quoted was necessary in order that Congress might authorize the militia of the several States to be called into the Federal service; but presupposed, evidently, that the government of the United States could employ for the same purposes, and at discretion, the officers and men, whether of the land or the naval forces, whom it had appointed or enlisted by their voluntary engagement. For the Constitution had empowered Congress, in the same article and section, to raise and support armies, to provide and maintain a navy, and to make rules for the government and regulation of the land and naval forces. And in article fourth, section fourth, we find this obligation:

"The United States shall guarantee to every State in this Union a republican form of government; and shall protect each of them against invasion, and, on application of the legislature, or of the executive (when the legislature can not be convened,) against domestic violence."

And this, finally, in article sixth:

"This Constitution and the laws of the United States which shall be made in pursuance thereof, and all treaties made, or which shall be made, under the authority of the United States, shall be the supreme law of the land; and the judges in every State shall be bound thereby, any thing in the constitution or laws of any State to the contrary notwithstanding.

"The senators and representatives before mentioned [in Congress] and the members of the several State legislatures, and all executive and judicial officers, both of the United States and of the several States, shall be bound by oath or affirmation to support this Constitution."

Accordingly, on the 3d of March, 1807, Congress enacted:

"That, in all cases of insurrection, or obstruction to the laws, either of the United States, or of any individual State or territory, where it is lawful for the President of the United States to call forth the militia for the purpose of suppressing such insurrection, or of causing the laws to be duly executed, it shall be lawful for him to employ, for the same purposes, such part of the land or naval forces of the United States as shall be judged necessary, having first observed all the prerequisites of the law in that respect."

These were the acts of Congress in existence at the time when Fort Sumter was besieged, assaulted, and captured. On the 15th of April, 1861, President Lincoln made proclamation commencing thus:

"Whereas the laws of the United States have been for some time past, and now are, opposed, and the execution thereof obstructed, in the States of South Carolina, Georgia, Alabama, Florida, Mississippi, Louisiana, and Texas, by combinations too powerful to be suppressed by the ordinary course of judicial proceedings, or by the powers vested in the marshals by law:

"Now, therefore, I, Abraham Lincoln, President of the United States, in virtue of the power vested in me by the Constitution and the laws, have thought fit to call forth, and hereby do call forth, the militia of the several States of the Union, to the aggregate number of seventy-five thousand, in order to suppress said combinations, and to cause the laws to be duly executed."

I will not read the entire proclamation; but these two paragraphs are very important:

"I deem it proper to say that the first service assigned to the forces hereby called forth will probably be to repossess the forts, places, and property which have been seized from the Union; and, in every event, the utmost care will be observed, consistently with the objects aforesaid, to avoid any devastation, any destruction of or interference with property, or any disturbance of peaceful citizens, in any part of the country

"And I hereby command the persons composing the combinations aforesaid to disperse, and retire peaceably to their respective abodes, within twenty days from this date."

Evidently, at that time, President Lincoln did not imagine that he was declaring war. He had not found it necessary to consult Vattel's treatise, nor to concern himself, in any degree, with the law of nations. He was proceeding in strict conformity with the Constitution of the United States and with the several acts of Congress which I have read. And, so far from claiming any right to confiscate the property of a citizen—even of a rebel in arms—or any right (as Mr. Perry now claims) to arrest, detain, and imprison at will non-combatants, the aged, the sick, the women, the children, Mr. Lincoln promised that, "*in every event*," there should be no "interference with property" and no "disturbance of peaceful citizens" anywhere.

Half a million of men arose, with one accord, upon hearing that proclamation; and millions more, if necessary, would have followed them. The voice of controversy was no longer heard; past differences of opinion were laid aside as if by unanimous agreement. It ceased to be a question how the terrible exigency had come upon us, or what man, or body of men, ought chiefly to be censured. The President was speaking in the very words of the Constitution and the law; and all the people made affectionate obeisance.

I need not pursue the comparison of that time with the present; suffice it that no misfortune, how grievous soever, can cause the hearts of a patriotic people to despond. It is the extravagance of your "war power" which wrought this appalling calamity, and has reduced you to the necessity of conscription—your pretended exercise of belligerent rights, not only in the States where rebellion exists, but throughout the land—your confiscations by executive will, and without even the form of a statute—your arbitrary arrests, imprisonments, searches, and seizures—your mock-trials by military commissions—your assumption of despotic power called martial law.

But, exclaims Mr. Perry, can not General Burnside command

the soldiers under him to fire upon the rebels, and kill them? Undoubtedly; such killing is not murder, or even manslaughter, but justifiable homicide. So, if rioters do not disperse after proclamation, or, as it is sometimes called, reading of the riot act, the sheriff may order his assistants, whether those assistants be soldiers or mere citizens, to fire and to kill. And even if a bystander should be slain, although innocent of any participation in the riot, it is excusable homicide as to him; for he ought to have gone away, at once, when commanded.

Well, inquires Mr. Perry, if, instead of killing a rebel in battle, or while otherwise promoting the rebellion, General Burnside should take him prisoner, and bring him into the State of Ohio, would that rebel be entitled to a discharge by writ of Habeas Corpus? No, sir, certainly not. But, quoth Mr. Perry, he was arrested without a warrant. Yes; but he was arrested on view, and in the act of committing treason. I have explained that, fully, in my former speech.

A prisoner charged with treason, or any other capital offense, under the laws of the United States, can not be admitted to bail except by the Circuit or District Court, or some judge thereof; and only in cases where the proof is not evident, nor the presumption great. Such a prisoner, consequently, would not be entitled to bail. There is another reason. The fact that an insurrection exists, sufficient to require the assistance of the army or the militia to suppress it, indicates that the ordinary course of judicial proceeding is interrupted; otherwise, there would have been no occasion for the use of military power, or for the President's proclamation. Undoubtedly, therefore, until "the ordinary course of judicial proceedings" can be resumed, a prisoner taken in arms, or engaged in assisting the rebels, may be detained in custody; but as soon as he can be brought to trial, in the "ordinary" manner, he must be. That will depend on the time at which the usual authority of the Circuit Court is restored in the particular district where the crime of treason was committed. Or, even if exchanged, or discharged on parole, by the President's order, that will not prevent an arrest and trial of the prisoner, in due course of law, after the rebellion has been suppressed. Such cases, however, are seldom prosecuted; an amnesty becomes indispensable.

But, argues Mr. Perry, it may be advisable to arrest a non-combatant in some State where insurrection and rebellion exist. Well, possibly that is so; it is an act to be avoided, but it may be necessary, or at least advisable, in particular circumstances. Of course, the judicial authority having been overthrown, and the military power called into action for that reason, and that alone, it is idle to speak of arresting with warrant; for there would be no authority in the district from which a warrant could proceed. The officer must act at his peril; just as a naval officer would act with regard to the search or seizure of a vessel on the high seas. This subject has been discussed frequently in our negotiations with the British Government; and the rule, as we understand it, and as we have always maintained it, in America, depends on very plain principles. The officer who arrests, or searches, or seizes, at his own discretion, acts, as I have said, at his peril; that is to say, he will be amenable for all the consequences. The act is a trespass; of that, I suppose, there can be no doubt. If it should prove to be a justifiable arrest, or search, or seizure, on account of crime really committed, or about to be committed, the trespass would be of little consequence. But if the party arresting, or searching, or seizing, acted wantonly, or without probable cause, a jury must award compensation, and even exemplary damages.

These considerations, however, can not apply to districts in which no insurrection or rebellion prevails, and where no such combinations ever existed as alone would authorize the President of the United States to intervene.

And here I must call your Honor's attention, particularly, to the language of the act approved February 28, 1795,* as well as to the language of the President's proclamation, April 15, 1861. Observe, then, that the President is authorized to call forth the militia (or, by the act of March 3, 1807, employ the land and

* The act of July 29, 1861, employs the same language, and, therefore, does not require any special notice.

naval forces) only in case the laws of the United States are opposed, or their execution obstructed, in a State, "by combinations too powerful to be suppressed *by the ordinary course of* JUDICIAL *proceedings*, or by the powers vested in the marshals." And the military power is to be used only "to suppress *such* combinations, *and to cause the laws to be duly executed*." President Lincoln's proclamation follows this language closely, and in some places literally.

The power of a marshal is to summon the bystanders to his assistance in executing a writ; so that, really, the two alternatives are equivalent.

It must follow, unquestionably, from this language, and from the whole tenor of the statute, that whenever, in any State, "the ordinary course of *judicial* proceedings," together with the power of the marshal to summon bystanders to his assistance, is quite sufficient to put down all opposition, and to execute the laws of the United States, the President has no authority to call forth the militia, or to use the land or the naval forces. Then how can he employ the one or the other, I would ask, in a State where the laws of the United States never have been opposed at all, nor their execution obstructed or resisted in any, even the slightest, degree? Sir, it is too plain a thing to be argued. The President has no such authority; and, certainly, his subordinates, civil or military, have none.

The District Attorney seems to suppose that creating the "Department of the Ohio" has some legal significance. Speaking of the President, he says that "it became necessary to subdivide the country into military departments in order that *his* great duty of preserving, protecting, and defending the Constitution might be faithfully and effectively performed." Well, sir, the President has no right even to preserve, protect, or defend the Constitution in any other manner than as prescribed by the Constitution and by the acts of Congress made in pursuance of it; and neither the Constitution nor any act of Congress provides for such military departments. Nor did the President create them: they were created by the General commanding the army, and for his own official convenience. He can alter them, and he does alter them, as often as he may choose. Such departments have existed ever since we had an army, and have extended over the whole territory of the United States. Ohio was in the Department of the East, commanded by General Wool, before the beginning of this rebellion; she has been attached first to one department, and then to another, since that event. The subdivision has no civil importance: its military effect is to give the command of certain troops, within certain limits, to a particular officer. Appointing a colonel to a regiment, or a captain to a company, has the very same effect.

I agree with Mr. Attorney that the President is the exclusive judge of the exigency contemplated by the act of 1795: that is the intention of the statute, and that was decided, exactly, in the case of Martin *v.* Mott, (12 Wheaton, 19.) It is an authority conferred by law; and it must be exercised according to law. And what does the law require? It requires the President to issue a proclamation; and that proclamation must specify the State in which an insurrection or rebellion exists, and must command the insurgents to disperse and retire peaceably to their abodes. The President has complied with the law in this respect: he has specified by proclamation, from time to time, the several States in rebellion; but he has never specified Ohio, nor authorized the employment of military power in substitution for "the ordinary course of judicial proceedings" within her limits. And now I turn upon Mr. Attorney with the proposition to which he and I have agreed, and with the decision of the Supreme Court to which we have both referred. If, as we agree, the President is the exclusive judge of the exigency contemplated by the act of February 28, 1795, how happens it, when HE has decided that the militia shall not be called forth, nor the land or the naval forces employed, to suppress an insurrection in Ohio, that General Burnside undertakes at pleasure, by promulgating General Order No. 38, to reverse the President's decision?

Perhaps it is upon the marvelous suggestion of that "Military Dictionary" which Mr. Perry commended to us. Your Honor will observe that while Mr. Perry has little respect for the opinions of judges, English or American, ancient or modern, although delivered on solemn argument, and after a deliberate examination of precedents and principles; while he cares nothing, absolutely nothing, for such venerable authors as Coke, and Hale, and Foster, and Blackstone, he has dealt largely, and with implicit faith, in dictionaries, cyclopedias, and, probably, in almanacs—at all events, sir, in books of the newest coinage, published yesterday, or the day before, by God knows whom, or to serve what especial purpose. Halleck and Benet may come to be great names in the law, or in constitutional history—as they will be, doubtless, when General Order No. 38, "Head-quarters Department of the Ohio," has at length, and completely, effaced the words of the Convention at Philadelphia, in September, 1787—but Mr. Perry must pardon us for a little while, and, at least, until—

> "Those rugged names to our like mouths grow sleek,
> That would have made Quintilian stare and gasp."

But to the "Dictionary" in question. Here is a paragraph containing two sentences, or thereabout, which, if they declare the law, or any thing like the law, may enable Mr. Attorney to answer me:

> "With regard to the requisition of military aid by the civil magistrate, the rule seems to be that when once the magistrate has charged the military officer with the duty of suppressing a riot, the execution of that duty is wholly confided to the judgment and skill of the military officer, who thenceforward acts independently of the magistrate until the service required is fully performed. The magistrate can not dictate to the officer the mode of executing the duty; and an officer would desert his duty if he submitted to receive any such orders from the magistrate. Neither is it necessary for the magistrate to accompany the officer in the execution of his duty. The learning on these points may be gathered from the charge of Mr. Justice Littledale to the jury, in the trial of the Mayor of Bristol for breach of duty in not suppressing the riots at that city in 1831."

All which, translated into plain English, means that when a civil magistrate has called upon a military officer to *assist* him in executing his duty, the military officer at once becomes the principal instead of an assistant, and may even treat the commands of the magistrate with contempt. I need not say, in the hearing of so many of my brethren, that such is not, and never was, the law. As for the instruction of Mr. Justice Littledale, in the case of the Mayor of Bristol, the author, if he ever read that instruction, has grossly misconceived it. One complaint against the Mayor was that, "upon being requested to ride along with Major Beckwith," who commanded the dragoons, and was ordered to charge the mob, "he did not do so." And Mr. Justice Littledale told the jury that the Mayor, being a civilian, and, for aught that appeared, an unskillful horseman, was under no obligation to ride with cavalry in a charge. That is the only point of his instruction which the "Dictionary" has correctly stated.

It has been claimed, also, that inasmuch as General Burnside is responsible to the President of the United States, as his military superior, and inasmuch as the President has charged him with the fulfillment of very important duties connected with the suppression of the rebellion, he is not amenable to the process of this Court. Indeed, sir, it has been plainly said—although with a disclaimer of authority from General Burnside on the subject—that the writ of Habeas Corpus, if issued, will not be obeyed.

As to the first point, luckily, the Supreme Court has given it a decisive and most comprehensive answer. I read from the opinion pronounced in the case of Kendall *v.* The United States, (12 Peters, 612, 613):

> "It was urged, at the bar, that the Postmaster-General was alone subject to the discretion and control of the President with respect to the execution of the duty imposed upon him by this law; and this right of the President is claimed as growing out of the obligation imposed upon him by the Constitution to take care that the laws be faithfully executed. This is a doctrine that can not receive the sanction of this Court. It would be vesting in the President a dispensing power which has no countenance for its support in any part of the Constitution, and is asserting a principle which, if carried out, in its results, to all cases falling within it, would be clothing the President

with a power entirely to control the legislation of Congress, and paralyze the administration of justice.

"To contend that the obligation imposed on the President to see the laws faithfully executed, implies a power to forbid their execution, is a novel construction of the Constitution, and entirely inadmissible."

As to the rest, I can not believe that General Burnside will adopt any such course as his counsel seem disposed to recommend. So gallant an officer as he has been represented should only wish to be told, by competent judicial authority, what the laws of his country demand. He can not excuse himself, any more than could the vilest felon dragged to the bar of this Court for sentence, by asseverating a private sense of duty toward God or his own conscience. How will General Burnside go forth to attack and slay rebels in arms for the purpose of opposing and obstructing the execution of the laws, and that by means of combinations too powerful to be suppressed by the ordinary course of judicial proceedings, after he shall have set an example, in his own person, and by the assistance of the troops under his command, of recklessly and forcibly contemning, opposing, and obstructing the ordinary course of judicial proceedings in the Southern District of Ohio, and, thereby, of trampling the Constitution and the laws of the United States under his feet!

May it please your Honor! I have spoken more fully than I intended on several subjects, and must, therefore, omit the consideration of others suggested by the counsel for the defendant. I will at once proceed to the alleged authority of General Burnside to enforce, with or without a proclamation, what is usually described as martial law. "LUCUS A NON LUCENDO." For, as we are told by Lord Chief-Justice Hale, and, after him, by Mr. Justice Blackstone, martial law is, "in truth and reality," no law. (1 Black. Com. 413, 414.) Mr. Perry carps at their declaration, but I do not see that he has attained any other result. A military commander who presumes to govern by martial law, so called, thereby ordains, *in the place of law*, the mere dictates of his own will. It is an assumption at once autocratic, arbitrary, and irresponsible. He threatens with a sword in his hand; and thus he governs by the sword, and according to his pleasure. You can make nothing else of it; no, sir, not if a thousand volumes had been written to explain it, or excuse it, or (if that be possible) to justify it.

Mr. Perry would fain argue that a commander, in the exercise of such authority, is, nevertheless, "limited and restrained." And by what? You shall hear: "If he push beyond the rights of war, the laws of war do not *protect* him." Ah! I can understand that in the case of a commander enforcing martial law (as, by the usages of war, he may) in another country than his own. He is then a conqueror, and, *ex vi termini*, a lord and master absolute. But Mr. Perry's claim is that General Burnside has conquered us, his own countrymen, and that for no fault which we have committed, but because others, in other States, and far distant, have chosen to rebel. If this be constitutional, as Mr. Perry asserts, what need has General Burnside of protection against us? Of what could we complain—or to whom? Mr. Perry tells us that we are not only prostrate, but helpless, and helpless forever; that we have no right of resistance, not even the poor privilege of criticism. Restraint, forsooth! To say that, is to add the shame of insult to the pain of injury. But, "in applying those laws, he," the conqueror, "is further restrained by a sense of propriety and duty." Indeed! And was there ever a tyrant, in all the tide of time, as to whom such restraint did not likewise exist? "He acts in peril of the disapprobation of higher authority, who may displace him, or, in some cases, impeach him." But suppose the higher authority—as, for example, the President of the United States—will not displace him, and does not disapprove his conduct. Suppose he is acting in the interest of the President, and for the promotion of the President's own scheme. Impeach the President! O yes, sir, undoubtedly—if he will be kind enough to allow that. "In peril of the disapprobation of the Supreme Being." All men, in all possible circumstances, encounter that peril; but I never heard it suggested as a substitute for the security of a written constitution, or of well-defined laws. "And of his countrymen." What chance have his countrymen—what chance can they have—for calling him to an account? Their lives, their liberty, their property—so Mr. Perry insists—are at his absolute disposition; and he can, if he will, keep them in that degraded estate forever. I do not marvel that the very name of PEACE should be distasteful to men possessed of such authority, and able to exercise it, constitutionally, so long as WAR continues. Can we hope for peace, on any terms, while such authority is admitted? No, sir, never—never! What man, of his own accord, will abdicate power so cheaply attained, and, withal, so vast and irresistible? Power which can perpetuate itself without any effort! Power which may even be transmitted, like an imperial diadem, to son from sire! Power from the dominion of which there is no peaceful deliverance on earth!

I intend no personal disrespect to Mr. Perry, nor to his associate, the District Attorney, when I express my utter abhorrence of the doctrines to which they have, on this occasion, lent the aid of their names and their abilities. But, sir, I can not say less—I can not—than that the advocacy of such doctrines, as I understand them, is a crime against the character of our profession, a crime against the justice of mankind, a crime against the rights of all ages. My learned opponents now have the distinction of being the first lawyers, in America, by whom those doctrines ever were maintained in a court of civil judicature. And General Halleck—who, as I understand, is also a lawyer—has written the first book, and, so far as I am advised, the only book, in the English language, affirming the right of any government, except an absolute monarchy, to put its own subjects under the dominion of martial law.

Such was not the opinion of the military profession in the United States until the time of this rebellion. Major O'Brien, a gallant officer and distinguished in the battle of Buena Vista, where he was wounded, in his Treatise on American Military Laws and the Practice of Courts-martial, observes:

"Many erroneous notions and much unfounded prejudice, in regard to military institutions, have arisen from confounding *military* with *martial* law. The popular opinion seems to be that these are but two names for the same code. Nothing can be further from the truth. Military law is a digested system of enactments, carefully made and deliberately confirmed by the supreme legislative authority of the commonwealth, and published for the observance of a body known to the Constitution, and created and sustained like any other executive organ of the country. Martial law is something very different from this. As Blackstone very truly remarks, it is, in fact, no law. It is an expedient resorted to in times of public danger, similar, in its effects, to the appointment of a dictator. The General or other authority charged with the defense of a country, proclaims martial law. By so doing, he places himself above all law. He abrogates or suspends, at his pleasure, the operation of the law of the land. He resorts to all measures, however repugnant to ordinary law, which he deems best calculated to secure the safety of the State in the imminent peril to which it is exposed. Martial law, being thus vague and uncertain, and measured only by the danger to be guarded against, exists only in the breast of him who proclaims and executes it. It is contained in no written code. It bears, therefore, no analogy whatever to military law, and should ever be carefully distinguished from it. Despotic in its character, and tyrannical in its application, it is only suited to those moments of extreme peril when the safety and even existence of a nation depend on the prompt adoption and unhesitating execution of measures of the most energetic character. That such cases do arise, all history attests; and that popular governments are illy calculated to meet them, it would be vain to deny. At such periods, republics especially require some prompt mode of suddenly drawing out, and instantaneously applying, the whole energies of the people. From this principle of self-preservation, the Constitution of the United States has wisely, and indeed necessarily, permitted the proclamation of martial law in certain specified cases of public danger, when no other alternative is left to preserve the State from foreign invasion or domestic insurrection." (P. 26.)

The martial law of which he speaks, as "permitted" by the Constitution, is only the suspension of the privilege of the writ of Habeas Corpus. We have an act of Congress on that subject, approved March 3, 1863; by means of which, whenever the public safety requires it, in his opinion, the President of the United States can *constitutionally* abridge the liberty of a citizen. He is not of opinion that the public safety so requires at present, or he would have exercised the power thus conferred on him by law.

Captain De Hart, another distinguished officer in the Mexican war, and aid to General Scott for seven years, in his Observations on Military Law and the Constitution and Practice of Courts-martial, says:

"Military law is that branch of the laws which respect military discipline, and the government of persons employed in military service. It is not exclusive of the common law, for a soldier does not cease to be a citizen; on the contrary, he is a citizen still, capable of performing the duties of such, and amenable to the jurisdiction of the civil courts for his acts or conduct in that capacity. It is, in fact, a rule superadded to the ordinary law, for regulating the citizen in his character of soldier.

"It will be perceived that the leading characteristic of this definition is that military law can not be applied for the regulation of the conduct of persons in private or civil life. Nor does it exclude the operation of the common law; for although the civil courts can not take cognizance of military offenses as such, strictly speaking, yet the principle of the superiority of the civil over the military authorities is clearly set forth by the 33d Article of War, and all officers are required thereby to deliver over offenders or accused persons to the civil magistrate, and to be aiding and assisting the officers of justice in apprehending and securing the person of the accused in order to bring him to trial." (Pp. 16, 17.)

"*It must be understood, however, that the term martial law has a different interpretation from that of military law. Military law, as has been stated above, is a rule for the government of military persons only; but martial law is understood to be that state of things when, from the force of circumstances, the military law is indiscriminately applied to all persons whatsoever.*" (P. 17.)

"How and where, under particular conjunctures of the time, martial law may be declared, and by whom, is not here considered; but the proclamation of such a rule, within the limits of the United States, is a very questionable proceeding, and thought to be an 'excrescence' not warranted or sanctioned by any distemper of the State. The substitution of this power for the civil courts subjects all persons to the arbitrary will of an individual, and to imprisonment for an indefinite period, or trial by a military body. Of such high importance to the public is the preservation of personal liberty, that it has been thought that unjust attacks even upon life or property, at the arbitrary will of the magistrate, are less dangerous to the commonwealth than such as are made upon the personal liberty of the citizen.

"Now, to guard against such abuse, the Constitution guarantees the privilege of the writ of Habeas Corpus, which it declares shall not be suspended unless when, in cases of rebellion or invasion, the public safety may require it. *And the intervention of* CONGRESS *is necessary before such suspension can be made lawful.* Such, too, is the doctrine of the British Constitution, where the Crown, invested with high prerogatives, is yet most scrupulously restricted in all that relates to the liberty of the person of the subject." (Pp. 17, 18.)

"As the promulgation and operation of martial law, within the limits of the Union, would necessarily be a virtual suspension of the Habeas Corpus writ, for the time being, it would consequently appear to stand in opposition to, or be in conflict with, that provision of the Constitution above cited." (Pp. 18, 19.)

He might have assigned a reason much more extensive; but, for the present, this will answer.

I have mentioned the doctrine of Hale and of Blackstone respecting martial law. Sir Edward Coke is even more explicit and decisive:

"If a lieutenant, or other that hath commission of marshall authority, in time of peace, hang or otherwise execute any man by colour of marshall law, this is murder; for this is against Magna Charta, cap. 29, and is done with such power and strength as the party can not defend himself; and here the law implieth malice." (3 Inst. 52, 53.)

By that phrase, "*in time of peace*," Coke means except in presence of the enemy, and while engaged in public or actual war. For he adds, immediately, that Thomas, Earl of Lancaster, "*being taken in an open insurrection*," was, "by judgment of marshall law," put to death in the 14th year of Edward the Second—"THIS WAS ADJUDGED TO BE UNLAWFUL."

The famous statute of 30 Charles I, commonly called the Petition of Rights and Liberties (English Statutes at Large, vol 7,

p. 317,) to which that monarch agreed, and for the violation of which, afterward, he was beheaded, speaks directly to this subject. The preamble recites that "divers commissions" had been issued, "of late time," under the great seal, appointing certain persons "with power and authority to proceed within the land, according to the justice of martial law, against such soldiers or mariners, or other dissolute persons joining with them, as should commit any murder, robbery, felony, mutiny, or other outrage or misdemeanor whatsoever, and by such summary course and order as is agreeable to martial law, and as is used in armies in time of war, to proceed to the trial and condemnation of such offenders, and them to cause to be executed and put to death according to the law martial."

"By pretext whereof," it is added, "some of your Majesty's subjects have been, by some of the said commissioners, put to death, when and where, if by the laws and statutes of the land they had deserved death, by the same laws and statutes also they might, and by no other ought to, have been judged and executed."

Whereupon the Petition demands:

"That the aforesaid commissions, for proceeding by martial law, may be revoked and annulled; and that, hereafter, no commissions of like nature may issue forth, to any person or persons whatsoever, to be executed as aforesaid; lest, by colour of them, any of your Majesty's subjects be destroyed, or put to death, contrary to the laws and franchise of the land." (Pp. 319, 320.)

This, together with the testimony of Blackstone (1 Com. 413, 414,) and of Lord Loughborough, as hereafter mentioned, ought to be a sufficient answer to the assertion of General Halleck, adopted by Mr. Perry, that "there are numerous instances in which martial law has been declared and enforced, in time of rebellion and insurrection, not only in India and British colonial possessions, but, also, in England and Ireland." Neither the Petition of Rights, nor the subsequent Bill of Rights, 1st William and Mary, session second, chapter second, (English Statutes at Large, vol. 9, p. 67,) extends to Ireland. In fact, Ireland had a separate Parliament at the time (1798) of the only instance specified. As to India and the colonial possessions, they have always been regarded as conquered countries, and not within the benefit of either of the two great statutes I have mentioned. It is true that the Parliament of England has on several occasions—not many—suspended the privilege of the writ of Habeas Corpus, within that kingdom, for a limited time; but it is not true, so far as I have been able to ascertain, that martial law has ever been proclaimed there, or even attempted, since Charles I laid his head on the block.

The opinion delivered by Lord Loughborough, Chief-Justice, in Grant *v.* Gould, (2 H. Bla. 69,) is very clear and decisive. He said:

"In the preliminary observations upon the case, my brother Marshall went at length into the history of those abuses of martial law which prevailed in ancient times. *This leads me to an observation that martial law, such as it is described by Hale, and such, also, as it is marked by Mr. Justice Blackstone, does not exist in England at all.* Where martial law is established and prevails, in any country, it is of a totally different nature from that which is inaccurately called martial law merely because the decision is by a court-martial, but which bears no affinity to that which was formerly attempted to be exercised in this kingdom; *which was contrary to the Constitution, and which has been for a century totally exploded.* Where martial law prevails, the authority under which it is exercised claims a jurisdiction over all military persons in all circumstances. Even their debts are subject to inquiry by a military authority; every species of offense, committed by any person who appertains to the army, is tried, not by a civil judicature, but by the judicature of the regiment or corps to which he belongs. It extends, also, to a great variety of cases, not relating to the discipline of the army, in those States which subsist by military power. Plots against the sovereign, intelligence to the enemy, and the like, are all considered as cases within the cognizance of military authority."

Mr. Perry objects that the Chief-Justice confounded military and martial law; but, most clearly, he did not. He used the term "martial law" to include both—as did all writers, English and American, until within a brief period—but he distinguishes the two systems with great accuracy and distinctness. And the example which he proceeded to give demonstrates this:

"In the reign of King William there was a conspiracy against his person in Holland, and the persons guilty of that conspiracy were tried by a council of officers. There was, also, a conspiracy against him in England; but the conspirators were tried by the common law. And, within a very recent period, the incendiaries who attempted to set fire to the docks at Portsmouth were tried by the common law. In this country, all the delinquencies of soldiers are not triable, as in most countries in Europe, by martial law; but, where they are ordinary offenses against the civil peace, they are tried by the common-law courts. *Therefore, it is totally inaccurate to state martial law as having any place whatever within the realm of Great Britain.*"

The case of Mostyn *v.* Fabrigas (Cowper, 161), arose in one of the colonial possessions, and yet it amply vindicates what I have said.

Anthony Fabrigas brought an action of trespass against John Mostyn for an assault and false imprisonment, and for compelling him (the plaintiff) to depart from the island of Minorca to Carthagena, in Spain, etc. The defendant pleaded, in justification, that he was Governor of the island, and invested, by the King's letters patent, with "all the powers, privileges, and authorities, *civil and military*, belonging to the government of the said island," etc. That the plaintiff was guilty of a riot, and was endeavoring to raise a mutiny among the inhabitants; whereupon, as Governor of Minorca, "in order to preserve the peace and government of the said island," the defendant caused him to be arrested, imprisoned six days, and then banished for twelve months. The cause was tried by Mr. Justice Gould and a jury, and the plaintiff obtained a verdict for £3,000 damages and £90 costs.

The defendant was unable to establish, by testimony, his allegation that the plaintiff had endeavored to raise a mutiny, or had instigated a riot. But he proved:

"That the plaintiff was a native of Minorca, and, at the time of seizing, imprisoning, and banishing him, as aforesaid, was an inhabitant of and residing in the Arraval of St. Phillip's, in the said island: that Minorca was ceded to the crown of Great Britain, by the treaty of Utrecht, in 1713: that the Minorquins are, in general, governed by the Spanish laws, but, when it serves their purpose, plead the English laws: that there are certain magistrates, called the chief-justice criminal and the chief-justice civil, in the said island: that the said island is divided into four districts exclusive of the Arraval of St. Phillip's, which the witness always understood to be separate and distinct from the others, and under the immediate order of the Governor; so that no magistrate of Mahon could go there to exercise any function without leave first had from the Governor: that the Arraval of St. Phillip's is surrounded by a line-wall on one side, and on the other by the sea, and is called the Royalty, where the Governor has greater power than anywhere else in the island, and where the judges can not interfere but by the Governor's consent: that nothing can be executed in the Arraval but by the Governor's leave, and the judges have applied to him (the witness) for the Governor's leave to execute process there: that for the trial of murder and other great offenses committed within the said Arraval, upon application to the Governor, he generally appoints the Assesseur-General of Mahon, and, for lesser offenses, the Mustastaph: and that the said John Mostyn, at the time of the seizing, imprisoning, and banishing the said Anthony, was the Governor of the said island of Minorca, by virtue of certain letters patent," etc.

Whereupon, it was insisted for the defendant that the plaintiff could not maintain any action against him on account of his proceedings as Governor within the Arraval of St. Phillip's above mentioned. The Court of Common Pleas rejected this defense, and gave judgment upon the verdict. Mostyn then sued out a writ of error from the Court of King's Bench; and, after two full arguments, by eminent counsel, the judgment was affirmed.

LORD MANSFIELD.—"TO LAY DOWN, IN AN ENGLISH COURT OF JUSTICE, SUCH A MONSTROUS PROPOSITION AS THAT A GOVERNOR, ACTING BY VIRTUE OF LETTERS PATENT UNDER THE GREAT SEAL, IS

ACCOUNTABLE ONLY TO GOD AND HIS OWN CONSCIENCE; THAT HE IS ABSOLUTELY DESPOTIC, AND CAN SPOIL, PLUNDER, AND AFFECT HIS MAJESTY'S SUBJECTS, BOTH IN THEIR LIBERTY AND PROPERTY, WITH IMPUNITY, IS A DOCTRINE THAT CAN NOT BE MAINTAINED." (Cowp. 175.)

I have said that a conqueror enforces martial law in the conquered country; but that is because he has necessarily displaced the hostile government, and is bound, therefore, to administer so much of its duties as relate to peace and good order.

No military officer can proclaim martial law in his own country, except as the constitution of the country ordains or allows. The constitution of an absolute monarchy includes the right of the sovereign to make, repeal, or suspend, at his pleasure, any and every law. But our Constitution is of a different character; and the only form of martial law it will tolerate is that, in times of rebellion and invasion, when the representatives of the people shall have declared, by statute, and in the face of their responsibility to their constituents, that the "public safety" so requires, the privilege of the writ of Habeas Corpus may be suspended for a limited time.

In Johnson *v.* Duncan, (3 Martin, 531,) Judge Derbigny said:

> "To have a correct idea of martial law in a free country, examples must not be sought in the arbitrary conduct of absolute governments. The monarch who unites in his person ALL the powers, may delegate to his generals an authority as unbounded as his own. But in a republic, where the constitution has fixed the extent and limits of every branch of the government in time of war, as well as of peace, there can exist nothing vague, uncertain, or arbitrary, in the exercise of any authority."

In opposition to these authorities, and to the indisputable grounds of argument on which they stand, the counsel for the defendant have cited the case of Luther *v.* Borden, (7 Howard, 1,) decided by the Supreme Court of the United States, at the January term, 1849. But that case, when properly examined and understood, gives them no countenance whatsoever.

The question whether a government can prescribe one law, or another, for its own subjects, is a question which depends on the constitution of that particular government. In an absolute monarchy, as Judge Derbigny has well observed, the property, and the liberty, and the life of every subject are at the discretion of the sovereign. He can grant privileges, or withhold them. He can seize property and imprison persons, or even put them to death, as well without a cause as with one. The government of an absolute monarchy, therefore, is a government of martial law: it is the very same in principle, in effect, and in modes of action. And although an absolute monarch may, at some former time, have conceded to his subjects, ever so amply or solemnly, the right to enjoy the fruits of their own labor and skill, or the right of dwelling in peace, and secure from arrest or imprisonment except in certain cases, and upon certain conditions, or the right, if you will, to breathe the air of heaven, he can at any time, nevertheless, and for any reason or no reason, revoke his concession, and take away those privileges. Such is the law of an absolute State; such are the terms of contract as implied between the subject and the sovereign in all States of that description. Charles the First revoked his assent to the Petition of Rights and Liberties; thus claiming the prerogative of an absolute monarch. More than fifty years of disturbance ensued—at times warlike, but as bloody in times of peace as in times of war—at the end of which, in 1688, Charles having lost his head, and his son, James the Second, having fled into eternal exile, it was acknowledged, on all hands, that the government of England was not an absolute monarchy, but was limited, as fundamental conditions, by the language of Magna Charta, of the Statute defining Treason, of the Petition of Rights and Liberties, of the Habeas Corpus Act, and, finally, of the combined Declaration of Rights and Act of Settlement in virtue of which William and Mary ascended the throne.

So, if absolute and unlimited power, as well as supreme power, be vested in a legislature, by the terms or necessary effect of the constitution or form of government existing in any State, the authority of such legislature to abridge the rights and the liberty of its subjects, by means of a proclamation of martial law, or otherwise, can not be doubted. It makes no difference whether such absolute, unlimited, and supreme power be vested in one man or in five hundred: the authority is the same, and may be exercised as well in the latter case as in the former. Madison repelled with scorn a mere suggestion that the government of the United States could ever *constitutionally* become a government of that description:

"The accumulation of all powers, legislative, executive, and judiciary, in the same hands, whether of one, a few, or many, and whether hereditary, self-appointed, or elective, may justly be pronounced the very definition of tyranny. Were the Federal Constitution, therefore, really chargeable with this accumulation of power, or with a mixture of powers having a dangerous tendency to such an accumulation, no further arguments would be necessary to inspire a universal reprobation of the system." (Federalist, No. 47.)

And yet, sir, it is by imputing such a character to the government of the United States, and by such imputation only, that General Halleck has arrived at the conclusion that the government can proclaim or tolerate martial law. "It is," he affirms, "a power inherent in *every* government." It is not, and can not be. It may or may not exist as allowed, or as forbidden, by the Constitution or fundamental law of each particular government. Wherefore, being expressly forbidden "within the land" of England, by the language of the Petition of Rights and Liberties, it never has been exercised within that "land" since the Stuarts were driven into exile.

The government of the United States has no "inherent" powers—none, sir, at any time, in any emergency, for any purpose. It has only the powers conferred by the Constitution as the law of its creation and existence—powers plainly expressed, or else necessarily implied. For, in addition to the fact that the Constitution declares itself to be "THE SUPREME LAW OF THE LAND" at all times, in all emergencies, and for all purposes—as well supreme in its prohibitions and in its silence, which ever means prohibition, as in its most plainly written grants—we have these two decisive declarations added as amendments, and for greater security, at the first session of the first Congress, and subsequently ratified by the several States:

> "THE ENUMERATION IN THE CONSTITUTION OF CERTAIN RIGHTS SHALL NOT BE CONSTRUED TO DENY OR DISPARAGE OTHERS RETAINED BY THE PEOPLE."
>
> "THE POWERS NOT DELEGATED TO THE UNITED STATES BY THE CONSTITUTION, NOR PROHIBITED BY IT TO THE STATES, ARE RESERVED TO THE STATES RESPECTIVELY OR TO THE PEOPLE."

Away, then, with "inherent" powers! Away, also, with that assumed right of self-defense, otherwise than by employing the powers delegated in the Constitution, and as therein prescribed, which Mr. Attorney has borrowed, as he tells us, from Daniel S. Dickinson. Sir, it was not worth borrowing. The Constitution declares in what manner, and in what manner only, the Federal Government shall defend itself. Those powers, as I have shown, are ample: they require no addition and no enlargement; but, if there must be addition, or any enlargement, let us resort to other aids than sophistry and vague assertion. I appeal, sir, to that man who was lifted by the purity of his own motives, and as the reward of his faithful consistency, to that upper heaven of PATRIOTISM where the voice of the reckless partisan is never heard, and to which the vapors of this bloody storm can not ascend—I appeal to George Washington:

> "It is important, likewise, that the habits of thinking, in a free country, should inspire caution in those intrusted with its administration to confine themselves within their respective constitutional spheres; avoiding, in the exercise of the powers of one department, to encroach upon another. *The spirit of encroachment tends to consolidate the powers of all the departments in one, and thus to create*, whatever the form of government, *a real despotism.* A just estimate of that love of power and proneness to abuse it, which predominate in the human heart, is sufficient to satisfy us of the truth of this position. The necessity of reciprocal checks in the exercise of political power, by dividing and distributing it into different depositories, and constituting each the guardian of the public weal against invasions of the

other, has been evinced by experiments, ancient and modern—some of them in our own country, and under our own eyes. *To preserve them must be as necessary as to institute them.* If, in the opinion of the people, the distribution or modification of the constitutional powers be in any particular wrong, let it be corrected by an amendment in the way in which the Constitution designates. BUT LET THERE BE NO CHANGE BY USURPATION; FOR THOUGH THIS, IN ONE INSTANCE, MAY BE THE INSTRUMENT OF GOOD, IT IS THE CUSTOMARY WEAPON BY WHICH FREE GOVERNMENTS ARE DESTROYED. THE PRECEDENT MUST, ALWAYS, GREATLY OVERBALANCE, IN PERMANENT EVIL, ANY PARTIAL OR TRANSIENT BENEFIT WHICH THE USE CAN, AT ANY TIME, YIELD."

These observations have not led me from the case of Luther and Borden, but are intended to preface my exposition of it. They furnish us a key to all mysteries.

The case was of this description:

Luther, a citizen of Massachusetts, brought his action of trespass against Borden and others, citizens of Rhode Island, in the Circuit Court of the United States, for breaking and entering his house at Warren, on the 29th of June, 1842.

Observe, at the outset, that the Federal Courts obtained jurisdiction of this controversy, not because it involved any question arising under the Constitution or laws of the United States, but solely on account of the citizenship of the parties, and as an ordinary action at common law.

The defendants justified, in substance, that there was, at the time, an insurrection of men in arms to overthrow the government of the State of Rhode Island by force; that, as a measure of defense, the LEGISLATURE of Rhode Island had declared martial law; that the plaintiff was concerned in the insurrection, and that they (the defendants) were acting as troops of the State, *under the authority of the Legislature before mentioned*, in searching the plaintiff's house in order to arrest him.

It is obvious that no question could arise, in such a case, respecting the Constitution or the laws of the United States, but only questions respecting the internal government and affairs of the State of Rhode Island. The issue which the plaintiff sought to have decided was whether a particular constitution had, or had not, been adopted by the people of that State, in May, 1842, so as to supersede the form of government established under a charter from Charles the Second, in November, 1663, and thence continued in force.

The Supreme Court of the United States inclined to the opinion that *this* could not be, in any circumstances, a judicial question; but, granting it to be such, the courts of Rhode Island had finally and effectually determined it. And their determination, inasmuch as it related, exclusively, to the organization and civil polity of their own State, must, by a rule of almost universal application, long since declared, be recognized in all other courts of justice.

The same rule had been pursued by the Senate of the United States, in deciding a contested election from Rhode Island, fifteen years before. The contestor (Potter) alleged that the contestee (Robbins) had been chosen by a legislature of which all the persons composing the Council, or Senate, continued to act and vote, illegally, after their terms of office had expired. The report in that case declares:

"It would seem to your committee a very dangerous assumption of power in one branch of Congress, or even in every department of the general government combined, to interfere with the internal regulations of the State, and to denounce the body by which these laws and resolutions were passed as a mere assemblage of citizens without any public authority whatever, and not the legislature of the State. Such a power does not belong to the Federal Government, and would, if claimed and carried out to its full extent, annihilate all the reserved rights of the States. It is a general principle of national law, applicable to all distinct and independent governments, that if there arise any disputes, in a State, on the fundamental laws and public administration, or on the prerogatives of the different powers of which it is composed, it is the business of the State *alone* to judge and determine them, in conformity to its political constitution. No government has a right to intrude into the domestic affairs of another State, and attempt to influence its deliberations or to control its action. This principle is recognized in the Constitution of the United States, by which the respective States united and formed themselves into a Federal Republic. Conceding, as we feel bound to do, to the State of Rhode Island, in common with all the other States of the Union, the power to decide for itself all questions relating to its domestic policy, there would seem to be no ground on which to rest a doubt that she has decided, in the most solemn manner, the character and powers of the body by which Mr. Robbins was chosen a Senator to Congress."

After establishing this point, in Luther *v.* Borden, and thus disposing of more than half the case, the Supreme Court of the United States, in order to illustrate the idea that such a question could not be (properly) of judicial character, cited that clause in the Federal Constitution requiring the States to guarantee each other a republican form of government, and to protect each other against invasion and domestic violence.

"Under this article of the Constitution," said Chief-Justice Taney, "it rests with CONGRESS to decide what government is the established one in a State. For, as the United States guarantee to each State a republican government, Congress must necessarily decide what government is established in the State, before it can determine whether it is republican or not. And when the Senators and Representatives of a State are admitted into the councils of the Union, the authority of the government under which they are appointed, as well as its republican character, is recognized by the proper constitutional authority. And its decision is binding on every other department of the government, and could not be questioned in a judicial tribunal." (7 How. 42.)

The Court took notice, also, of the act of Congress approved February 28, 1795, authorizing the President of the United States, on application of the legislature or executive of any State, to call forth the militia of other States in order to suppress an insurrection. That act empowers the President, as I have said, to decide whether an exigency has arisen in which the government of the United States is bound to interfere; but, so far from regarding this as one of his *constitutional* prerogatives, the Court said that Congress might deprive him of such discretion, and either retain it for particular legislation, from time to time, as occasion demanded, or confer it upon some judicial tribunal. (7 Howard, 42, 43.)

The question which of two or more claimants shall be regarded as the true government of any community, domestic or foreign, is not, and never can be, a question of law. It is, principally, a question of fact; but involves, in a large degree, political sentiment, inclination, and even interest. These are motives which address themselves to Presidents, Senators, and Representatives, in the discharge of executive and legislative duties; Courts can not be approached by them. Accordingly, at an early period in our history, it was declared that the judicial department could not recognize the independence of San Domingo until the President and the Senate had chosen to do so. (Rose *v.* Himely, 4 Cranch, 272; Hoyt *v.* Gelston, 3 Wheaton, 324.) The same declaration was made, afterward, in the case of Texas. (Kennett *.v.* Chambers, 14 Howard, 49, 50, 51.) And such is the doctrine of the British tribunals. (City of Berne *v.* Bank of England, 9 Vesey, 349.)

Of course, therefore, when the President of the United States, exercising the authority conferred on him by the act of Congress approved February 28, 1795, responded favorably to the demand of the charter government of Rhode Island, for assistance in subduing its opponents, he thus decided, as well for the legislative as for the executive department, and in the manner prescribed by law, which was the true government of the State; and by that decision, as in the case of all foreign governments, the judiciary was certainly concluded. Mr. Webster based his argument for the defendants on that proposition. (Works of Webster, vol. 6, p. 237.)

A question was made, also, whether the Legislature of Rhode Island had authority to declare martial law; not whether the Governor, or chief executive officer, could do so—for nobody pretended that, and he never attempted it. But the question was susceptible of decision, and was effectually decided, by the principles already established. The first ten amendments to the Constitution of the United States only contain limitations upon the FEDERAL Government. This has been decided many times. (Barron *v.* Mayor of Baltimore, 7 Peters, 243; Permoli *v.* First Municipality, 3 Howard, 589; Fox *v.* The State of Ohio, 5 Howard, 434, 435; Withers *v.* Buckley, 20 Howard, 89, 90; Murphy *v.* The People, 2 Cowen, 818; Barker *v.* The People, 3 Cowen, 701, 702; Livingston *v.* Mayor of New York, 8 Wendell, 100.)

The people of each State, if they wish to protect themselves against oppression and violence by their *separate* governments, must provide the necessary safeguards in their own fundamental law: and hence the Bill of Rights embodied in all the constitutions of the States recently adopted.

It could be to no purpose, therefore, in Luther *v.* Borden, that the Constitution of the United States was cited; for that did not, and could not, affect the argument one way or another. The question was whether, by the form of government prevailing in the State of Rhode Island, on the 25th of June, 1842, the Legislature of that State had, or had not, the power to declare martial law. But that, also, was a question relating entirely to the organization, internal affairs, and polity of the State; and the decision of the judicial and other authorities of Rhode Island (whether right or wrong) was conclusive on the Courts of the United States.

Mr. Justice Woodbury maintained, to be sure, that no State could declare martial law in any circumstances; but, as Chief-Justice Taney said, that proposition is too broad. Martial law, as a permanent regulation, would contravene that clause of the Federal Constitution guaranteeing to each State a republican form of government; and it would be the duty of Congress, not of the judiciary, to correct such an intolerable abuse. But, as a temporary regulation in time of tumult or war, martial law may, or may not, be declared in any State, accordingly as the Constitution of that State authorizes or forbids. (7 Howard, 45, 46.)

I agree to what the Chief-Justice said in Luther *v.* Borden, as Mr. Perry has quoted it, when that is taken—as, of course, it must be taken—in connection with other parts of his opinion. I agree that the question whether martial law can or can not be declared in any State or country, or by any branch or officer of a government, depends on the terms of its organical charter. I have not denied that the people of the several States may, if they like, so amend the Federal Constitution as to authorize Congress, or the President, or even a collector of customs, to proclaim and execute martial law. My object has been to prove that the Constitution, at present in force, contains no such authority—but many, and wise, and stringent prohibitions.

If there could be the least degree of uncertainty as to the meaning of Chief-Justice Taney, in the case of Luther *v.* Borden, that uncertainty would disappear upon reading the opinion which he delivered in the case of John Merryman, upon application for a writ of Habeas Corpus, May 28, 1861. The points decided are stated by the Chief-Justice, himself, in these words:

1. "That the President, under the Constitution of the United States, can not suspend the privilege of the writ of Habeas Corpus, nor authorize a military officer to do it."

2. "*A military officer has no right to arrest and detain a person*, not subject to the Rules and Articles of War, *for an offense against the laws of the United States, except in aid of the judicial authority, and subject to its control; and if the party is arrested by the military, it is the duty of the officer to deliver him over, immediately, to the civil authority, to be dealt with according to law.*"

As to the second point, particularly, the Chief-Justice said:

"The documents before me show that the military authority, in this case, has gone far beyond the mere suspension of the privilege of the writ of Habeas Corpus. It has, by force of arms, thrust aside the judicial authorities and officers to whom the Constitution has confided the power and duty of interpreting and administering the laws, and substituted a military government in its place, to be administered and executed by military officers. For, at the time these proceedings were had against John Merryman, the District Judge of Maryland, the Commissioner appointed under the act of Congress, the District Attorney, and the Marshal all resided in the city of Baltimore, a few miles only from the home of the prisoner. Up to that time, there had never been the slightest resistance or obstruction to the process of any Court or judicial officer of the United States, in Maryland, except by the military authority. And if a military officer, or any other person, had reason to believe that the prisoner had committed any offense against the laws of the United States, it was his duty to give information of the fact, and the evidence to support it, to the District Attorney; and it would then have become the duty of that officer to bring the matter before the District Judge or Commissioner. And, if there was sufficient legal evidence to justify his arrest, the judge or commissioner would have issued his warrant to the Marshal to arrest him; and, upon the hearing of the case, would have held him to bail, or committed him for trial, according to the character of the offense as it appeared in the testimony, or would have discharged him, immediately, if there was not sufficient evidence to support the accusation. There was no danger of any obstruction, or resistance, to the action of the civil authorities; and, therefore, no reason whatever for the interposition of the military.

"And yet, under these circumstances, a military officer, stationed in Pennsylvania, without giving any information to the District Attorney, and without any application to the judicial authorities, assumes to himself the judicial power in the district of Maryland; undertakes to decide what shall constitute the crime of treason or rebellion; what evidence (if, indeed, he required any) is sufficient to support the accusation, and justify the commitment; and commits the party, without a hearing even before himself, to close custody, in a strongly-garrisoned fort, to be there held, it would seem, during the pleasure of those who committed him.

"The Constitution provides, as I have before said, that 'no person shall be deprived of life, liberty or property, without due process of law.' It declares that 'the right of the people to be secure in their persons, houses, papers, and effects, against unreasonable searches and seizures, shall not be violated; and no warrants shall issue but upon probable cause, supported by oath or affirmation, and particularly describing the place to be searched, and the persons or things to be seized.' It provides that the party accused shall be entitled to a speedy trial, in a Court of justice.

"And these great and fundamental laws, which Congress itself could not suspend, have been disregarded and suspended, like the writ of Habeas Corpus, by a military order supported by force of arms. Such is the case now before me; and I can only say that, if the authority which the Constitution has confided to the judiciary department and judicial officers may thus, upon any pretext, or under any circumstances, be usurped by the military power, at its discretion, the people of the United States are no longer living under a government of laws, but every citizen holds life, liberty, and property at the will and pleasure of the army officer in whose military district he may happen to be found."

I can add nothing to the beauty or the force of this language: I adopt it, and all of it, without any qualification.

Mr. Perry relies, also, upon the case of Mitchell *v.* Harmony, (13 Howard, 115)—a case of this character:

Harmony was engaged in the transportation of merchandise from the United States to Chihuahua and Santa Fe, Mexico, prior to the act of Congress, approved May 13, 1846, declaring war. He left Independence, Missouri, with a train of wagons, horses, and mules, carrying goods, on the 27th of May, and before the act of Congress was known there. Mitchell was a Lieutenant-Colonel commanding a detachment of troops in Doniphan's expedition against New Mexico. This expedition overtook the plaintiff's train, and, at his request, gave it armed protection during a journey of great length. But when the command reached San Elisario, in Chihuahua, and the troops were about to proceed thence to the city of Chihuahua, distant three hundred miles, the plaintiff determined to remain where he was. Colonel Doniphan, fearing that the train and goods might fall into the hands of the enemy, and thus be of assistance to them, in time of war, directed the defendant (Mitchell) to compel the plaintiff to accompany the troops; and the plaintiff did accompany them, against his will, with all his wagons, horses, mules, goods, etc. Some of these were used for the public service, as occasion required, at the battle of Sacramento and upon the march; the residue were abandoned by the plaintiff, at Chihuahua, when the American army afterward evacuated that place, and because he could not then procure the means of transporting them elsewhere. Harmony brought an action of trespass against Colonel Mitchell, for the entire value of his train, in the Circuit Court for the Southern District of New York, and therein recovered a verdict of damages. The case was then removed to the

Supreme Court of the United States by writ of error, and the judgment was affirmed.

Mr. Perry cites this case to prove that a military commander can destroy the property of a citizen, in time of war, so as to prevent its falling into the hands of the enemy, and being of immediate advantage to him. Nobody denies that—when expressed in the language of limitation which the Supreme Court has enjoined. It is an act of appropriation for public use; and, for *that* reason, the officer is not a trespasser. Under the present Constitution of Ohio, the property of a citizen can not be taken for public use without a compensation previously made, and in money; but that was not the rule under our former Constitution, and is not the rule under the Constitution of the United States. Compensation could, and as to the United States now can, as well be made by a law subsequently enacted.* But, in order that the case may avail him, and even that it shall not be turned against him, Mr. Perry must derive from it these two propositions:

1. A citizen is entitled to *no* compensation for his property seized and destroyed by a military officer in time of war or rebellion.

2. A military officer, at such time, has unlimited and absolute discretion what property to seize or destroy; and such discretion extends not only to the place where an enemy is, or a rebellion exists, but everywhere else.

For, obviously, if the officer be a trespasser—or if the question whether he is, or is not, a trespasser can be tried in a Court of justice—Mr. Perry has taken nothing by his citation; and especially if, although the officer be acquitted of a trespass, he is acquitted upon the ground of his agency for the government, and of the government's being liable to make compensation for the property seized, or destroyed, as property taken for public use.

And now, not only did the Court decide neither of the propo-

---

* Symonds *v.* City of Cincinnati, 14 Ohio Rep. 174; Bonaparte *v.* Camden and Amboy Railroad Co., 1 Baldwin, 226; Rogers *v.* Bradshaw, 20 Johnson, 735; Jerome *v.* Ross, 7 Johns. Ch. Rep. 344; Lister *v.* Lobley, 7 Ad. and Ellis, 124.

sitions which it behooves Mr. Perry to establish, but the Court decided against both, and upon the course of reasoning which I have indicated.

The instruction of the Circuit Court to the jury was:

"That the defendant might lawfully take possession of the goods of the plaintiff to prevent them from falling into the hands of the public enemy; but, in order to justify the seizure, the danger must be immediate and impending, and not remote or contingent. And that he might, also, take them for public uses, and impress them into the public service, in case of an immediate and pressing danger, or urgent necessity, existing at the time; but not otherwise." (P. 133.)

Mr. Chief-Justice Taney—for we now have another of his opinions—said:

"The only subject for inquiry in this Court is whether the law was correctly stated in the instruction of the [Circuit] Court; and whether any thing, short of an immediate and impending danger from the public enemy, or an urgent necessity for the public service, can justify the taking of private property, by a military commander, to prevent it from falling into the hands of the enemy, or for the purpose of converting it to the use of the public.

"The instruction is objected to on the ground that it restricts the power of the officer within narrower limits than the law will justify. And that when the troops are employed in an expedition into the enemy's country, where the dangers that meet them can not always be foreseen, and where they are cut off from aid from their own government, the commanding officer must, necessarily, be intrusted with some discretionary power as to the measures he should adopt; and if he acts honestly, and to the best of his judgment, the law will protect him. *But it must be remembered that the question here is not as to the discretion he may exercise in his military operations, or in relation to those who are under his command.* His distance from home, and the duties in which he is engaged, can not enlarge his power over the property of a citizen; nor give to him, in that respect, any authority which he would not, under similar circumstances, possess at home. And where the owner has done nothing to forfeit his rights, every public officer is bound to respect them, whether he finds the property in a foreign or hostile country, or in his own.

"There are, without doubt, occasions in which private property may lawfully be taken possession of, or destroyed, to prevent it from falling into the hands of the public enemy; and, also, where a military officer, charged with a particular duty, may impress private property into the public service, or take it for public use. Unquestionably, in such cases, the government is bound to make full compensation to the owner; but the officer is not a trespasser.

"But we are clearly of opinion that, in all of these cases, the danger must be immediate and impending, or the necessity urgent for the public service, such as will not admit of delay, and where the action of the civil authority would be too late in providing the means which the occasion calls for. It is impossible to define the particular circumstances of danger, or necessity, in which this power may be lawfully exercised. Every case must depend on its own circumstances. It is the emergency that gives the right, and the emergency must be shown to exist before the taking can be justified.

"In deciding upon this necessity, however, the state of the facts as they appeared to the officer at the time he acted, must govern the decision; for he must necessarily act upon the information of others, as well as his own observation. And if, with such information as he had a right to rely upon, there is reasonable ground for believing that the peril is immediate and menacing, or the necessity urgent, he is justified in acting upon it; and the discovery, afterward, that it was false or erroneous, will not make him a trespasser. But it is not sufficient to show that he exercised an honest judgment, and took the property to promote the public service: he must show, by proof, the nature and character of the emergency, such as he had reasonable grounds to believe it to be; and it is then for a jury to say whether it was so pressing as not to admit of delay, and the occasion such, according to the information upon which he acted, that private rights must, for the time, give way to the common and public good." (Pp. 134, 135.)

I can not conceive a rebuke more peremptory than this to the doctrine which Mr. Perry asserts. Instead of declaring that a military commander, in the country of his allegiance, where the courts of civil authority are open, and their process at once available, can, upon the pretext of a rebellion existing elsewhere, and of some possible influence on the rebels, or on his own soldiers, of a citizen's exercising ordinary, peaceful, and acknowledged rights, arrogate the power of displacing the Constitution and laws of the land, and of substituting for them the secret as well as arbitrary dictates of his conscience or his pleasure, the Supreme Court of the United States, in this case of Mitchell and Harmony, has required such an officer, even in time of war, in a foreign country, where no civil authority exists, and with an enemy at hand, to deal cautiously, very cautiously, and at his peril, with the property, and, much more, with the person of a fellow citizen. "His distance from home, and the duties in which he is engaged, can not enlarge his power." Nor is it a question of his motives, or his gallantry, or his past services, or his expected usefulness: it is a question of right between man and man—as they stand together before that Majesty which is blind to all distinctions of rank, and titles, and personal or public favor.

May it please your Honor! I have now demonstrated by a vast array of authorities, judicial and historical, that no officer of the United States, civil or military, can exercise—legitimately exercise—with or without a proclamation—that arbitrary, absolute, unlimited, and irresponsible authority known as martial law. But, sir, if this were a new question—if it never had been decided, or even argued, in any instance—it could not be otherwise than perfectly plain, and impossible to be misunderstood, upon the face of the Constitution alone.

The articles which I have read, securing freedom of speech and of the press, the right of the people to assemble and consider of their grievances, immunity from seizures and searches except for probable cause, either upon actual view of a crime committed or in virtue of a warrant supported by oath or affirmation, trial upon indictment, and by an impartial jury of the district wherein the crime is alleged to have occurred, the right of compelling the attendance of witnesses, and of being defended by counsel—these articles, I say, each and all of them, are expressed in words of universal application. There is no exception made of time or place, of peace or of war, of martial law, of military law, or of any law whatsoever. The learned counsel for the defendant would interpolate exceptions which the authors of the Constitution have purposely omitted. Are we a conquered people? And, if so, who has conquered us, and in what name? On what field of battle was our liberty cloven down? Are we in rebellion? And, if not, how can we lose our rights—our own rights—by ever so great misconduct in others? Why, sir, since the Federal Government was founded, a period of more than seventy years, there has always been somewhere, in the broad expanse of our territory, opposition and even obstruction to the exercise of its duties—defiance, at times, of judicial process, or outbreaking of the violence of Indian tribes subject to our dominion, and, occasionally, invasion by foreign armies. If the argument of my learned opponents be true—if, as General Burnside appears to think, the invasion of the State of Kentucky, in some distant corner, by a squadron of "Confederate" cavalry, invests him with power to command us, in the State of Ohio, as if we were enlisted soldiers or militia-men in actual service—then, evidently, for the greater part of the time since the Constitution of the United States was ordained, its most essential provisions have not been in force, but in a condition of hopeless abeyance. For, necessarily, if Mr. Perry's argument proves any thing, it proves that martial law exists everywhere, and by constitutional intendment, without even the form of a proclamation, the moment a riot has occurred anywhere. Tell me not of the magnitude of this rebellion: that may appeal to my forbearance, or sense of expediency, but can not affect, in any degree, the question whether a particular power has or has not been delegated by the terms of a written compact. If authority to exercise martial law results (as Mr. Perry has asserted) from the mere fact of obstruction to the execution of the laws in some neighborhood, ever so remote from the place where it is attempted to be exercised, it must needs prevail in Ohio, and throughout our country, from one ocean to the other, as soon as a mob, whether of negroes or white men, shall have rescued a fugitive slave in Massachusetts, or as soon as a band of the Apaches have waylaid and slain some traveler in New Mexico.

And this marvelous exception, so contrary to the principles of a republican government, is an exception nowhere defined in the Constitution, or ever so faintly suggested. What Strafford said, in defending his life, I might well say in opposing a doctrine which, more fatally than any bill of attainder, destroys the security of every man's life, and liberty, and property, and honor. "Better it were to live under no law at all, and by the maxims of cautious prudence to conform ourselves the best we can to the arbitrary will of a master, than fancy we have a law on which we can rely, and find, at last, that this law shall inflict a punishment precedent to the promulgation, and try us by maxims unheard of till the very moment of the prosecution." *

And observe the suddenness of this change in the Constitution, as interpreted by Mr. Perry, from one extreme to another. A republic of the fairest promise, confidently reposing on the affections of the people: behold! some rebel has touched a secret spring in its frame-work, perhaps unconsciously, and the outlines of a despotism frown upon us.

Mr. Perry has quoted from General Halleck a paragraph the truth of which he does not venture to affirm, but which he calls upon others to accept as true. I will read it again:

> "During the administration of President Washington, in the Pennsylvania 'Whisky Insurrection' of 1794 and 1795, the military authorities, engaged in suppressing it, disregarded the writs which were issued by the courts for the release of the prisoners who had been captured as insurgents. General Wilkinson, under the authority of President Jefferson, during the Burr conspiracy of 1806, suspended the privilege of this writ, as against the Superior Court of New Orleans. General Jackson assumed the right to refuse obedience to the writ of Habeas Corpus, first in New Orleans, in 1814, as against the authority of Judge Hall, when the British army was approaching that city; and afterward, in Florida, as against the authority of Judge Fromentin."

It may be that some writs of Habeas Corpus were "disregarded" at the time of the whisky insurrection; but I have always

* Hume's History of England, Ch. 54.

supposed the contrary, and remain of that supposition. At all events, President Washington gave no sanction to such conduct on the part of the military officers. His instructions to them were:

"That every officer and soldier will constantly bear in mind that he comes to support the laws, and that it would be peculiarly unbecoming in him to be, in any way, the infractor of them: *that the essential principles of a free government confine the province of the military, when called forth on such occasions, to two objects:* first, to combat and subdue all who may be found IN ARMS in opposition to the national will and authority; secondly, to aid and support the CIVIL MAGISTRATES in bringing offenders to justice. THE DISPENSATION OF THIS JUSTICE BELONGS TO THE CIVIL MAGISTRATES; AND LET IT EVER BE OUR PRIDE AND OUR GLORY TO LEAVE THE SACRED DEPOSIT THERE INVIOLATE." (Irving's Life of Washington, vol. 5, ch. 25.)

The proceedings of General Wilkinson at New Orleans, in 1806, were by his own authority, and not by that of President Jefferson. This appears from the confidential message of the latter to Congress, January 22, 1807:

"By letters from General Wilkinson, of the 14th and 18th of September, which came to hand two days after date of the resolution of the House of Representatives, that is to say, on the morning of the 18th instant, I received the important affidavit a copy of which I now communicate, with extracts of so much of the letters as come within the scope of the resolution. By these, it will be seen that of three of the principal emissaries of Mr. Burr, whom the General had caused to be apprehended, one had been liberated by Habeas Corpus, and the two others, being those particularly employed in the endeavor to corrupt the General and army of the United States, have been embarked by him for our ports in the Atlantic States; probably on the consideration that an impartial trial could not be expected during the present agitations of New Orleans, and that that city was not, as yet, a safe place of confinement. *As soon as these persons shall arrive, they will be delivered to the custody of the law, and left to such course of trial, both as to place and process, as its functionaries may direct.*

The presence of the highest judicial authorities, to be assembled at this place within a few days, the means of pursuing a sounder course of proceedings here than elsewhere, and the aid of the executive means (should the judges have occasion to use them) render it equally desirable for the criminals as for the public that, *being already removed from the place where they were first apprehended*, the first regular arrest should take place here, and the course of proceedings receive here its proper direction."

The prisoners arrived at Washington City in the evening of January 22, and were immediately taken before the Circuit Court of the United States for the District of Columbia. That Court, after a regular examination, committed them for trial. They applied to the Supreme Court of the United States for a writ of Habeas Corpus in February, and were thereupon discharged. (*Ex parte* Bollman and Swartwout, 4 Cranch, 75.)

It is not true that General Jackson refused obedience to the writ of Habeas Corpus allowed by Judge Fromentin, at Pensacola, in 1821; for he had ordered the prisoner (Callava) to be discharged before he knew of the existence of any writ. But he had a quarrel with the Judge in regard to it, and absurd enough that quarrel was on both sides. (Parton's Life of Jackson, vol. 2, ch. 45.)

His conduct at New Orleans was much more serious; but, after all, it has been greatly misrepresented as well as exaggerated. There is no question that on the 16th of December, 1814, he declared the city and its environs to be under "strict" martial law; but, inasmuch as he was then acting as a military commander, in charge of the seventh military district, the precedent—granting all that has been claimed for it—can be of no avail unless sanctioned by the government of the United States as a lawful exercise of power. The truth is, however, that the government did not sanction it, and expressly disapproved it. (Letter of the Secretary of War to General Jackson, April 12, 1815.) The reason why no further notice was taken of the affair, at the time, is that Jackson submitted, like a patriot and a real soldier, as he was, the moment his error was pointed out.

He never claimed authority to suspend the privilege of Habeas

Corpus except in the city of New Orleans and its immediate neighborhood, and while invasion was actual or imminent. He never dreamed, for an instant, of such enormous and inexcusable usurpations as we now see, almost everywhere, and on nearly all occasions, practiced by military commanders. The acts of Congress then in force gave him a right to call upon the State of Louisiana for the services of every able-bodied citizen; and he had, with the assent of the State authorities, placed all who were capable of bearing arms under orders to be in readiness, as soldiers, upon brief and sudden notice. It was upon the idea that he *thus* commanded the entire population, as persons liable to military duty at once, and, therefore, subject to military law, and not upon the notion (at present so much in vogue) that a General can, by proclamation or otherwise, constitute himself an irresponsible dictator over the lives and liberties of his fellow-citizens, that Jackson assumed to act. This appears from the opinion of Judge Derbigny, in the case of Johnson *v.* Duncan, (3 Martin, 531.)

"Under the Constitution and laws of the United States, the President has a right to call, or cause to be called, into the service of the United States, even the whole militia of any part of the Union, in case of invasion. This power, exercised here by his delegate, has placed all the citizens subject to militia duty under military authority and military law. That I conceive to be the extent of the martial law; beyond which, all is usurpation of power. In that state of things, the course of judicial proceedings is certainly much shackled; but the judicial authority exists, and ought to be exercised whenever it is practicable. . . . . The proclamation of martial law, therefore, can not have had any other effect than that of placing under military authority all the citizens subject to militia service. It is in that sense *alone* that the vague expression of 'martial law' ought to be understood among us. To give it any larger extent would be trampling upon the Constitution and laws of our country."

There was another idea upon which General Jackson supposed that he might, within circumscribed boundaries, and for a limited time, exclude the operation of civil process. Judge Derbigny took notice of that:

"The counsel for the appellant, to support his assertion that, in the circumstances then existing, the Court could not administer justice, went further, and said that the city of New Orleans had become a camp, since it had pleased the General of the seventh military district to declare it so; that within the precincts of a camp there can exist no other authority than that of the commanding officer. If the premises were true, the consequence would certainly follow. But the abuse of words can not change the situation of things. A camp is a space of ground occupied by an army for their temporary habitation while they keep the field. That space has limits: it does not extend beyond the ground actually occupied by the army. The camp of the American army, during the invasion of our territory by the British, was placed at the distance of four miles below the city. During that time, the city might be considered as a besieged place, having an intrenched camp in front. But the transformation of the city itself into a camp, by the mere declaration of the General, is no more to be conceived than would the transformation of a camp into a city by the same means."

I have said that General Jackson submitted to punishment, and that cheerfully, as soon as the courts of his country declared him guilty of a violation of its Constitution and laws. He appeared before the District Court of Louisiana, March 22, 1815, in obedience to a rule to show cause why he should not be attached for contempt of its process and authority, and, on the 31st of March, after that rule had been made absolute. The successful defender of New Orleans, when an excited multitude, filling the court-room, would have rescued him from custody, and even dragged the judge from the bench, quieted the tumult with his own voice, and being fined one thousand dollars, paid the money at once. Thirty years afterward, having passed through the Presidency of the United States, and retired to private life, pecuniary embarrassments overtook him; and then Congress refunded the amount which he had paid into the public treasury, with interest—not because he was improperly fined, but because he had amply atoned, by a life of distinguished and faithful service, for what certainly was, on his part, a mere error of judgment. It was not his violation of law, but the magnanimity with which he bowed before the law, even in his hour of utmost glory, that won forever the affection and the confidence of his countrymen.

The proceedings of Wilkinson and of Jackson, at New Orleans, were both in cases of sudden emergency and of peculiar circumstances; and yet no Court has ever justified or excused them. I did not complain of the declaration of martial law in this city, last year, although I knew it to be illegal; on the contrary, I served under it. I would have served, in the circumstances, without any such declaration. But there is no necessity for martial law in Cincinnati at present. We have no enemy near at hand; our Courts are open, and are proceeding in the transaction of business as quietly, as regularly, as in a time of profound peace.

The act of March 3, 1863, confers on the President of the United States as large an authority—to say nothing more—as the Constitution will warrant. If he should deem it advisable to suspend the privilege of the writ of Habeas Corpus in any case, or in any class of cases, there is the authority. Why, then, does General Burnside attempt without law what the President has not seen fit to do by law? Is it for the purpose of treating the Congress of the United States with as much indignity as he has inflicted upon my distinguished client?

A few words in regard to another point, and with them I will conclude. Mr. Perry has complained several times, and in different connections, that Mr. Vallandigham does not deny the "charge" against him. It is, we are told, a charge of "active disloyalty" toward the government of the United States, and of "active sympathy" toward the rebels in arms. Well, sir, I know that Mr. Vallandigham denies, and that earnestly, all imputations of a criminal or a dishonorable character against him; and probably, if he knew, or if I could advise him, what Mr. Perry demands, he would insist on complying with even such a demand. But I can not comprehend—I am incapable of comprehending—what is demanded. Does Mr. Perry mean to say that there is, or can be, any crime of mere opinion or affection? Or does he mean that Mr. Vallandigham is accused of some act which ought to be denied? If so, what is it? In God's name, sir, what is it? For what was this Court established? What is the office of the District Attorney? Why are grand juries impanneled, sworn, and charged, term after term? If Mr. Vallandigham has done any thing, or even said any thing, which the law forbids, I require, as his counsel, and in his name, that he shall be accused of it, and tried for it. He can not deny until he has been accused; he can not acquit himself until he has been put on trial. Again, therefore, as his counsel—standing here, at the bar, for him—I insist on his being brought into Court for accusation. If then accused, let him be heard in defense—heard not only through my feeble lips, but by his own matchless eloquence—heard here, publicly, in the presence of all—of those who hate him as well as those who love him—of those who regard him as a traitor, and of those who believe him to be actuated by the purest motives of patriotism. He does not shrink from such an ordeal; he demands it by his petition; he challenges it in the confidence of a triumphant acquittal. But if, when brought hither, no cause of accusation is found against him, your Honor must say, and I hope will take pleasure in saying: "WHY SHOULDST THOU DEFEND THYSELF? GO IN PEACE!"

OPINION OF THE COURT

BY

HON. H. H. LEAVITT.

Ex parte—C. L. Vallandigham—Habeas Corpus.

LEAVITT, J., delivered the following opinion:

This case is before the Court on the petition of Clement L. Vallandigham, a citizen of Ohio, alleging that he was unlawfully arrested, at his home in Dayton, in this State, on the night of the 5th of May, instant, by a detachment of soldiers of the army of the United States, acting under the orders of Ambrose E. Burnside, a Major-General in the army of the United States, and brought, against his will, to the city of Cincinnati, where he has been subjected to a trial before a military commission, and is still detained in custody, and restrained of his liberty. The petitioner also avers that he is not in the land or naval service of the United States, and has not been called into active service in the militia of any State; and that his arrest, detention, and trial, as set forth in his petition, are illegal, and in violation of the Constitution of the United States. The prayer is that a writ of Habeas Corpus may issue, requiring General Burnside to produce the body of the petitioner before this Court, with the cause of his caption and detention. Accompanying the petition is a statement of the charges and specifications on which he alleges he was tried before the Military Commission. For the purposes of this decision it is not necessary to notice these charges specially, but it may be stated in brief that they impute to the prisoner the utterance of sundry disloyal opinions and statements in a public speech, at the town of Mt. Vernon, in the State of Ohio, on the 1st of May, instant, with the knowledge "that they did aid and comfort and encourage those in arms against the government, and could but induce, in his hearers, a distrust in their own government, and sympathy for those in arms against it, and a disposition to resist the laws of the land." The petitioner does not state what the judgment of the Military Commission is, nor is the Court informed whether he has been condemned or acquitted on the charges exhibited against him.

It is proper to remark here, that, on the presentation of the petition, the Court stated, to the counsel for Mr. Vallandigham, that, according to the usages of the Court, as well as of other courts of high authority, the writ was not grantable of course, and would only be allowed on a sufficient showing that it ought to issue. The Court is entirely satisfied of the correctness of the course thus indicated. The subject was fully examined by the learned Justice Swayne, when present, the presiding judge of this Court, on a petition for Habeas Corpus, presented at the last October term; a case to which further reference will be made. I shall now only note the authorities on this point, which seem to be entirely conclusive.

In the case *Ex parte* Watkins (3 Peters, 193,) which was an application to the Supreme Court for a writ of Habeas Corpus, Chief-Justice Marshall entertained no doubt as to the power of the Court to issue the writ, and stated that the only question was whether it was a case in which the power ought to be exercised. He says, in reference to that case, "the cause of imprisonment is shown as fully by the petitioner as could appear on the return of the writ; consequently, the writ ought not to be awarded, if the Court is satisfied the prisoner would be remanded to prison." The same principle is clearly and ably stated by Chief-Justice Shaw, in the case *Ex parte* Sims, before the Supreme Court of Massachusetts. (7 Cushing's Rep. 285.) See, also, Hurd on Hab. Corpus, 223, et seq.

I have no doubt of the power of this Court to issue the writ applied for. It is clearly conferred by the 14th section of the Judiciary Act of 1789; but the ruling of this Court in the case just referred to, and the authorities just cited, justify the refusal of the writ, if satisfied the petitioner would not be discharged upon a hearing after its return. The Court, therefore, directed General Burnside to be notified of the pendency of the petition, to the end that he might appear, by counsel or otherwise, to oppose the granting of the writ.

That distinguished General has accordingly presented a respectful communication to the Court, stating, generally and argumentatively, the reasons of the arrest of Mr. Vallandigham, and has also authorized able counsel to represent him in resistance of the application for the writ. And the case has been argued at great length, and with great ability, on the motion for its allowance.

It is proper to remark, further, that when the petition was presented, the Court made a distinct reference to the decision of this Court in the case of Bethuel Rupert, at October term, 1862, before noticed, as an authoritative precedent for its action on this application. On full reflection, I do not see how it is possible for me, sitting alone in the Circuit Court, to ignore the decision, made upon full consideration by Justice Swayne, with the concurrence of myself, and which, as referable to all cases involving the same principle, must be regarded as the law of this Court until reversed by a higher Court. The case of Rupert was substantially the same as that of the present petitioner. He set out in his petition, what he alleged to be an unlawful arrest by the order of a military officer, on a charge imputing to him acts of disloyalty to the government, and sympathy with the rebellion against it, and an unlawful detention and imprisonment as the result of such order. The application, however, in the case of Rupert differed from the one now before the Court, in this, that affidavits were exhibited tending to disprove the charge of disloyal conduct imputed to him; and also in this, that there was no pretense or showing by Rupert that there had been any investigation or trial by any Court of the charges against him.

The petition in this case is addressed to the *judges* of the Circuit Court, and not to a single judge of that Court. It occurs, from the absence of Mr. Justice Swayne, that the District Judge is now holding the Circuit Court, as he is authorized to do by law. But thus sitting, would it not be in violation of all settled rules of judicial practice, as well as of courtesy, for the District Judge to reverse a decision of the Circuit Court, made when both judges were on the bench? It is well known that the District Judge, though authorized to sit with the Circuit Judge in the Circuit Court, does not occupy the same official position, and that the latter judge, when present, is, *ex officio*, the presiding judge. It is obvious that confusion and uncertainty, which would greatly impair the respect due to the adjudications of the Circuit Courts of the United States, would result from the assumption of such an exercise of power by the District Judge. It would not only be disrespectful to the superior judge, but would evince in the District Judge an utter want of appreciation of his true official connection with the Circuit Court.

Now, in passing upon the application of Rupert, Mr. Justice Swayne, in an opinion of some length, though not written, distinctly held that this Court would not grant the writ of Habeas Corpus, when it appeared that the detention or imprisonment was under military authority. It is true, that Rupert was a man in humble position—unknown beyond the narrow circle in which he moved; while the present petitioner has a wide-spread fame as a prominent politician and statesman. But no one will insist that there should be any difference in the principles applicable to the two cases. If any distinction were allowable, it would be against him of admitted intelligence and distinguished talents.

I might, with entire confidence, place the grounds of action I propose in the present case upon the decision of the learned judge, in that just referred to. Even if I entertained doubts of the soundness of his views, I see no principle upon which I could be justified in treating the decision as void of authority. But the counsel of Mr. Vallandigham was not restricted in the argument of this motion to this point, but was allowed the widest latitude in the discussion of the principles involved. It seemed due to him that the Court should hear what could be urged against the legality of the arrest, and in favor of the interposition of the Court in behalf of the petitioner. And I have been greatly interested in the forcible argument which has been submitted, though unable to concur with the speaker in all his conclusions.

If it were my desire to do so, I have not now the physical strength to notice or discuss at length the grounds on which the learned counsel has attempted to prove the illegality of General Burnside's order for the arrest of Mr. Vallandigham, and the duty of the Court to grant the writ applied for. The basis of the whole argument rests on the assumption that Mr. Vallandigham, not being in the military or naval service of the government, and not, therefore, subject to the Rules and Articles of War, was not liable to arrest under or by military power. And the various provisions of the Constitution, intended to guard the citizen against unlawful arrests and imprisonments, have been cited and urged upon the attention of the Court as having a direct bearing on the point. It is hardly necessary to quote these excellent guarantees of the rights and liberties of an American citizen, as they are familiar to every reader of the Constitution. And it may be conceded that if, by a just construction of the constitutional powers of the government, in the solemn emergency now existing, they are applicable to and must control the question of the legality of the arrest of the petitioner, it can not be sustained, for the obvious reason that no warrant was issued "upon probable cause, supported by oath or affirmation," as is required in ordinary arrests for alleged crimes. But are there not other considerations of a controlling character applicable to the question? Is not the Court imperatively bound to regard the present state of the country, and, in the light which it throws upon the subject, to decide upon the expediency of interfering with the exercise of the military power as invoked in the pending application? The Court can not shut its eyes to the grave fact that war exists, involving the most imminent public danger, and threatening the subversion and destruction of the Constitution itself. In my judgment, when the life of the republic is imperiled, he mistakes his duty and obligation as a patriot who is not willing to concede to the Constitution such a capacity of adaptation to circumstances as may be necessary to meet a great emergency, and save the nation from hopeless ruin. Self-preservation is a paramount law, which a nation, as well as an individual, may find it necessary to invoke. Nothing is hazarded in saying that the great and far-seeing men who framed the Constitution of the United States supposed they were laying the foundation of our national government on an immovable basis. They did not contemplate the existence of the state of things with which the nation is now unhappily confronted, the heavy pressure of which is felt by every true patriot. They did not recognize the right of secession by one State, or any number of States, for the obvious reason that it would have been in direct conflict with the purpose in view in the adoption of the Constitution, and an incorporation of an element in the frame of the government which would inevitably result in its destruction. In their glowing visions of futurity there was no foreshadowing of a period when the people of a large geographical section would be guilty of the madness and the crime of arraying themselves in rebellion against a government under whose mild and benignant sway there was so much of hope and promise for the coming ages. We need not be surprised, therefore, that, in the organic law which they gave us, they made no specific provision for such a lamentable occurrence. They did, however, distinctly contemplate the possibility of foreign war, and vested in Congress the power to declare its existence, and "to raise and support armies," and "provide and maintain a navy." They also made provision for the suppression of insurrection and rebellion. They were aware that the grant of these powers implied all other powers necessary to give them full effect. They also declared that the President of the United States "shall be commander-in-chief of the army and navy and of the militia of the several States when called into actual service," and they placed upon him the solemn obligation "to take care that the laws be faithfully executed." In reference to a local rebellion, in which the laws of the Union were obstructed, the act of the 28th of February, 1795, was passed, providing in substance, that whenever, in any State, the civil authorities of the Union were unable to enforce the laws, the President shall be empowered to call out such military force as might be necessary for the emergency. Fortunately for the country this law was in force when several States of the Union repudiated their allegiance to the national government, and placed themselves in armed rebellion against it. It was sufficiently comprehensive in its terms to meet such an occurrence, although it was not a case within the contemplation of Congress when the law was enacted. It was under this statute that the President issued his proclamation of the 15th of April, 1861. From that time the country has been in a state of war, the history and progress of which are familiar to all. More than two years have elapsed, during which the treasure of the nation has been lavishly contributed, and blood has freely flowed, and this formidable rebellion is not yet subdued. The energies of the loyal people of the Union are to be put to further trials, and, in all probability, the enemy is yet to be encountered on many a bloody field.

It is not to be disguised, then, that our country is in imminent peril, and that the crisis demands of every American citizen a hearty support of all proper means for the restoration of the Union and the return of an honorable peace. Those placed by the people at the head of the government, it may well be presumed, are earnestly and sincerely devoted to its preservation and perpetuity. The President may not be the man of our choice, and the measures of his administration may not be such as all can fully approve. But these are minor considerations, and can absolve no man from the paramount obligation of lending his aid for the salvation of his country. All should feel that no evil they can be called on to endure, as the result of war, is comparable with the subversion of our chosen government, and the horrors which must follow from such a catastrophe.

I have referred thus briefly to the present crisis of the country as having a bearing on the question before the Court. It is clearly not a time when any one connected with the judicial department of the government should allow himself, except from the most stringent obligations of duty, to embarrass or thwart the Executive in his efforts to deliver the country from the dangers which press so heavily upon it. Now, the question which I am called upon to decide is, whether General Burnside, as an agent of the executive department of the government, has transgressed his authority in ordering the arrest of Mr. Vallandigham. If the theory of his counsel is sustainable, that there can be no legal arrest except by warrant, based on an affidavit of probable cause, the conclusion would be clear that the arrest was illegal. But I do not think I am bound to regard the inquiry as occupying this narrow base. General Burnside, by the order of the President, has been designated and appointed to take the military supervision of the Department of the Ohio, composed of the States of Kentucky, Ohio, Indiana, Illinois, and Michigan. The precise extent of his authority, in this responsible position, is not known to the Court. It may, however, be properly assumed, as a fair presumption, that the President has clothed him with all the powers necessary to the efficient discharge of his duties, in the station to which he has been called. He is the representative and agent of the President, within the limits of his department. In time of war, the President is not above the Constitution, but derives his power expressly from the provision of that instrument, declaring that he shall be commander-in-chief of the army and navy. The Constitution does not specify the powers he may rightfully exercise in this character, nor are they defined by legislation. No one denies, however, that the President, in this character, is invested with very high powers, which it is well known have been called into exercise on various occasions during the present rebellion. A memorable instance is seen in the emancipation proclamation, issued by the President as commander-in-chief, and which he justifies as a military necessity. It is, perhaps, not easy to define what acts are properly within this designation, but they must, undoubtedly, be limited to such as are necessary to the protection and preservation of the government and the Constitution, which the President has sworn to support and defend. And in deciding what he may rightfully do under this power, where there is no express legislative declaration, the President is guided solely by his own judgment and discretion, and is only amenable for an abuse of his authority by impeachment, prosecuted according to the requirements of the Constitution. The occasion which justifies the exercise of this power exists only from the necessity of the case; and when the necessity exists, there is a clear justification of the act.

If this view of the power of the President is correct, it undoubtedly implies the right to arrest persons, who, by their mischievous acts of disloyalty, impede or endanger the military operations of the government. And, if the necessity exists, I see no reason why the power does not attach to the officer or General in command of a military department. The only reason why the appointment is made is, that the President can not discharge the duties in person. He, therefore, constitutes an agent to represent him, clothed with the necessary power for the efficient supervision of the military interests of the government throughout the department. And it is not necessary that martial law should be proclaimed or exist, to enable the General in command to perform the duties assigned to him. Martial law is well defined by an able jurist to be "the will of a military commander, operating without any restraint, save his judgment, upon the lives, upon the persons, upon the entire social and individual condition of all over whom this law extends." It can not be claimed that this law was in operation in General Burnside's department when Mr. Vallandigham was arrested. Nor is it necessary that it should have been in force to justify the arrest. The power vested by virtue of the authority conferred by the appointment of the President. Under that appointment, General Burnside assumed command of this department. That he was a man eminently fitted for the position, there is no room for a doubt. He had achieved, during his brief military career, a national reputation as a wise, discreet, patriotic and brave General. He not only enjoyed the confidence and respect of the President and Secretary of War, but of the whole country. He has nobly laid his party preferences and predilections upon the altar of his country, and consecrated his life to her service. It was known that the widely-extended department, with the military supervision of which he was charged, was one of great importance, and demanded great vigilance and ability in the administration of its military concerns. Kentucky was a border State, in which there was a large element of disaffection toward the national government, and sympathy with those in rebellion against it. Formidable invasions have been attempted, and are now threatened. Four of the States have a river border, and are in perpetual danger of invasion. The enforcement of the late conscription law was foreseen as a positive necessity. In Ohio, Indiana, and Illinois, a class of mischievous politicians had succeeded in poisoning the minds of a portion of the community with the rankest feelings of disloyalty. Artful men, disguising their latent treason under hollow pretensions of devotion to the Union, were striving to disseminate their pestilent heresies among the masses of the people. The evil was one of alarming magnitude, and threatened seriously to impede the military operations of the government, and greatly to protract the suppression of the rebellion. General Burnside was not slow to perceive the dangerous consequences of these disloyal efforts, and resolved, if possible, to suppress them. In the exercise of his discretion, he issued the order—No. 38—which has been brought to the notice of the Court. I shall not comment on that order, or say any thing more in vindication of its expediency. I refer to it only because General Burnside, in his manly and patriotic communication to the Court, has stated fully his motives and reasons for issuing it; and, also, that it was for its supposed violation that he ordered the arrest of Mr. Vallandigham. He has done this under his responsibility as the commanding General of this department, and in accordance with what he supposed to be the power vested in him by the appointment of the President. It was virtually the act of the executive department under the power vested in the President by the Constitution; and I am unable to perceive on what principle a judicial tribunal can be invoked to annul or reverse it. In the judgment of the commanding General, the emergency required it, and whether he acted wisely or discreetly is not properly a subject for judicial review.

It is worthy of remark here, that this arrest was not made by General Burnside under any claim or pretension that he had authority to dispose of or punish the party arrested, according to his own will, without trial and proof of the facts alleged as the ground for the arrest, but with a view to an investigation by a Military Court or Commission. Such an investigation has taken place, the result of which has not been made known to this Court. Whether the Military Commission for the trial of the charges against Mr. Vallandigham was legally constituted and had jurisdiction of the case, is not a question before this Court. There is clearly no authority in this Court, on the pending motion, to revise or reverse the proceedings of the Military Commission, if they were before the Court. The sole question is, whether the arrest was legal; and, as before remarked, its legality depends on the necessity which existed for making it; and of that necessity, for the reason stated, this Court can not judicially determine. General Burnside is unquestionably amenable to the executive department for his conduct. If he has acted arbitrarily and upon insufficient reasons, it is within the power, and would be the duty of the President, not only to annul his acts, but to visit him with decisive marks of his disapprobation. To the President, as commander-in-chief of the army, he must answer for his official conduct. But, under our Constitution, which studiously seeks to keep the executive, legislative, and judicial departments of the government from all interference and conflict with each other, it would be an unwarrantable exercise of the judicial power to decide that a co-ordinate branch of the government, acting under its high responsibilities, had violated the Constitution, in its letter or its spirit, by authorizing the arrest in question. Especially in these troublous times, when the national life is in peril, and when union and harmony among the different branches of the government are so imperatively demanded, such interference would find no excuse or vindication. Each department of the government must, to some extent, act on a presumption that a co-ordinate branch knows its powers and duties, and will not transcend them. If the doctrine is to obtain, that every one charged with, and guilty of, acts of mischievous disloyalty, not within the scope of the criminal laws of the land, in custody under the military authority, is to be set free by courts or judges on Habeas Corpus, and that there is no power by which he may be temporarily placed where he can not perpetrate mischief, it requires no argument to prove that the most alarming conflicts must follow, and the action of the government be most seriously impaired. I dare not, in my judicial position, assume the fearful responsibility implied in the sanction of such a doctrine.

And here, without subjecting myself to the charge of trenching upon the domain of political discussion, I may be indulged in the remark, that there is too much of the pestilential leaven of disloyalty in the community. There is a class of men in the loyal States who seem to have no just appreciation of the deep criminality of those who are in arms, avowedly for the overthrow of the government, and the establishment of a Southern Confederacy. They have not, I fear, risen to any right estimate of their duties and obligations, as American citizens, to a government which has strewn its blessings with a profuse hand, and is felt only in the benefits it bestows. I may venture the assertion that the page of history will be searched in vain for an example of a rebellion so wholly destitute of excuse or vindication, and so dark with crime, as that which our bleeding country is now called upon to confront, and for the suppression of which all her energies are demanded. Its cause is to be found in the unhallowed ambition of political aspirants and agitators, who boldly avow as their aim, not the establishment of a government for the better security of human rights, but one in which all political power is to be concentrated in an odious and despotic oligarchy. It is, indeed, consolatory to know that in most sections of the North those who sympathize with the rebellion are not so numerous or formidable as the apprehensions of some would seem to indicate. It may be assumed, I trust, that in most of the Northern States reliable and unswerving patriotism is the rule, and disloyalty and treason the exception. But there should be no division of sentiment upon this momentous question. Men should know, and lay the truth to heart, that there is a course of conduct not involving overt treason, or any offense technically defined by statute, and not, therefore, subject to punishment as such, which, nevertheless, implies moral guilt and a gross offense against their country. Those who live under the protection and enjoy the blessings of our benignant government, must learn that they can not stab its vitals with impunity. If they cherish hatred and hostility to it, and desire its subversion, let them withdraw from its jurisdiction, and seek the fellowship and protection of those with whom they are in sympathy. If they remain *with* us, while they are not *of* us, they must be subject to such a course of dealing as the great law of self-preservation prescribes and will enforce. And let them not complain, if the stringent doctrine of military necessity should find them to be the legitimate subjects of its action. I have no fears that the recognition of this doctrine will lead to an arbitrary invasion of the personal security or personal liberty of the citizen. It is rare, indeed, that a charge of disloyalty will be made upon insufficient grounds. But if there should be an occasional mistake, such an occurrence is not to be put in competition with the preservation of the life of the nation. And I confess I am but little moved by the eloquent appeals of those who, while they indignantly denounce violations of personal liberty, look with no horror upon a despotism as unmitigated as the world has ever witnessed.

But I can not pursue this subject further. I have been compelled by circumstances to present my views in the briefest way. I am aware there are points made by the learned counsel representing Mr. Vallandigham, to which I have not adverted. I have had neither time nor strength for a more elaborate consideration of the questions involved in this application. For the reasons which I have attempted to set forth, I am led clearly to the conclusion that I can not judicially pronounce the order of General Burnside for the arrest of Mr. Vallandigham as a nullity, and must, therefore, hold that no sufficient ground has been exhibited for granting the writ applied for. In reaching this result, I have not found it necessary to refer to the authorities which have been cited, and which are not controverted, for the obvious reason that they do not apply to the theory of this case, as understood and affirmed by the Court. And I may properly add here, that I am fortified in my conclusion by the fact, just brought to my notice, that the Legislature of Ohio, at its late session, has passed two statutes, in which the validity and legality of arrests in this State under military authority are distinctly sanctioned. This is a clear indication of the opinion of that body, that the rights and liberties of the people are not put in jeopardy by the exercise of the power in question, and is, moreover, a concession that the present state of the country requires and justifies its exercise. It is an intimation that the people of our patriotic State will sanction such a construction of the Constitution as, without a clear violation of its letter, will adapt it to the existing emergency.

There is one other consideration to which I may, perhaps, properly refer, not as a reason for refusing the writ applied for, but for the purpose of saying that, if granted, there is no probability that it would be available in relieving Mr. Vallandigham from his present position. It is, at least, morally certain it would not be obeyed. And I confess I am somewhat reluctant to authorize a process, knowing it would not be respected, and that the Court is powerless to enforce obedience. Yet, if satisfied there were sufficient grounds for the allowance of the writ, the consideration to which I have adverted would not be conclusive against it.

For these reasons I am constrained to refuse the writ.

Franklin, Benjamin.

Life and Writings of Benjamin Franklin. Containing the Memoirs written by himself, and continued by his grandson and others. With his Social Epistolary Correspondence, Philosophical, Political and Moral Letters and Essays, and his Diplomatic Transactions as Agent at London and Minister Plenipotentiary at Versailles. Augmented by much matter not contained in any former edition. With a postliminious Preface, by WILLIAM DUANE, 2 vols., 8vo., cloth, $5.

Franklin's Works.

10 vols., 8vo., $15.

Benton's Thirty Years' View.

Thirty Years' View; or, A History of the Working of the American Government for Thirty Years, from 1820 to 1850; chiefly taken from the Congress Debates, the private papers of General Jackson, and the speeches of ex-Senator Benton, with his actual view of men and affairs. With Historical Notes and Illustrations, and some Notices of eminent deceased cotemporaries. By THOS. H. BENTON. Two very large vols., 8vo., cloth, $6.

Benton's Debates of Congress.

Abridgment of the Debates of Congress, from 1789 to 1856. From Gales and Seaton's Annals of Congress; from their Register of Debates; and from the Official Reported Debates, by John C. Rives. By the Author of "The Thirty Years' View." 16 vols. Published by subscription. Cloth, per vol., $3.50.

Webster's Life and Works.

The Speeches, Forensic Arguments, and Diplomatic Papers of Daniel Webster, with a Notice of his Life and Works, by EDWARD EVERETT. Eleventh Edition. 6 vols., 8vo., cloth, with portraits; price, $12.

Webster's Private Correspondence.

The Private Correspondence of Daniel Webster, with the Autobiography. Edited by his son, FLETCHER WEBSTER. 2 vols., 8vo., cloth; portraits; price, $4.50.

Cushing's Parliamentary Law.

Elements of the Law and Practice of Legislative Assemblies in the United States of America. Second Edition. By Hon. LUTHER STEARNS CUSHING. Royal 8vo.; price, $5.

Wheaton's International Law.

Elements of International Law. By the late Hon. HENRY WHEATON, LL.D. Seventh edition, revised, annotated, and brought down to the present time, with a Biographical Notice of Mr. Wheaton, and an account of the Diplomatic Transactions in which he was concerned. By Hon. WILLIAM BEACH LAWRENCE, formerly Charge d'Affaires at London. 8vo.; price, $7.50.

Goodrich's Science of Government.

The Science of Government as Exhibited in the Institutions of the United States of America. By CHARLES B. GOODRICH. 8vo., cloth; price, $1.25.

Duer's Constitutional Jurisprudence.

A Course of Lectures on the Constitutional Jurisprudence of the United States. Delivered annually in Columbia College, New York, by WILLIAM ALEXANDER DUER, LL.D., late President of that Institution. The second edition, revised, enlarged, and adapted to professional, as well as general use. 12mo., cloth; price, $1.75.

Story on the Constitution.

Commentaries on the Constitution of the United States; with a Preliminary Review of the Constitutional History of the Colonies and States, before the Adoption of the Constitution. By Hon. JOSEPH STORY, LL.D. Third Edition. 2 vols., 8vo., sheep; price, $7.50.

Sparks's Writings of Washington.

The Writings of George Washington: being his Correspondence, Addresses, Messages, and other Papers, Official and Private. Selected and published from the Original Manuscripts; with a Life of the Author, Notes, and Illustrations. By Hon. JARED SPARKS. 12 vols., 8vo., cloth; with Portraits; price, $18.

Sparks's Life of Washington.

The Life of George Washington. By Hon. JARED SPARKS. New Edition. 8vo., cloth; with Portraits; price, $1.50.

Eliot's History of Liberty.

History of Liberty. Part I, The Ancient Romans; Part II, The Early Christians. By Samuel Eliot. 4 vols., 12mo., cloth; price, $5.

Story's Miscellaneous Writings.

The Miscellaneous Writings of Hon. Joseph Story. Edited by his son, W. W. STORY. 8vo., cloth; price, $3.

Lawrence on Visitation and Search.

Visitation and Search; or, An Historical Sketch of the British Claim to exercise a Maritime Police over the Vessels of all Nations, in Peace as well as War, etc. By Hon. WILLIAM BEACH LAWRENCE. 8vo., cloth, $1.

Biographical History of Congress.

Comprising Memoirs of Members of the Congress of the United States, together with a History of Internal Improvements, from the foundation of the Government to the present time. By HENRY G. WHEELER. With Portraits and Facsimile Autographs. 2 vols., 8vo., muslin, $3 per volume.

A series of biographical sketches of the members of Congress, divested of party bias, and drawn from authentic sources; thus embodying in a succinct and attractive form much of the cotemporary history and political progress of the country.

Aaron Burr's Memoirs,

With Miscellaneous Correspondence. By M. L. DAVIS. Portraits. 2 vols., 8vo., muslin, $3.75.

The extraordinary history of Aaron Burr is here displayed by Mr. Davis with great integrity and ability. The work is full of instruction to public men. Perhaps no one has illustrated in a more striking manner the fate of unprincipled ambition, the prostitution of great talents, the work of a splendid career. To the common reader the Memoirs have much of the interest of tragedy.—GRISWOLD.

Hume's History of England.

The History of England, from the Invasion of Julius Cæsar to the Revolution of 1688. By DAVID HUME. A new Edition, with the Author's last Corrections and Improvements. To which is prefixed a short account of his Life, written by himself. Reprinted in large type, from the last London trade edition. 6 vols., 8vo., cloth ; price, $9.

Bowen's Political Economy.

The Principles of Political Economy, applied to the Condition, the Resources, and the Institutions of the American people. By FRANCIS BOWEN, Alvord Professor of Moral Philosophy and Civil Polity in Harvard College. Second Edition. 8vo., cloth, $2.25.

Boeckh's Athenians.

The Public Economy of the Athenians. By AUGUSTUS BOECKH. Translated from the second German Edition. With Notes and copious Index, by ANTHONY LAMB. Portrait. 8vo., cloth; price, $4.

Bancroft's History.

A History of the United States, from the Discovery of the American Continent. By Hon. GEORGE BANCROFT. With Portraits, Maps, etc. Vols. I to VIII. 8vo., cloth; price, $16.

Curtis's History of the Constitution.

History of the Origin, Formation, and Adoption of the Constitution of the United States. By GEORGE TICKNOR CURTIS. Complete in two large and handsome octavo volumes. Muslin, $5.

Hallam's Constitutional History of England.

From the Accession of Henry VII to the death of George II. 8vo., sheep extra, $2.

Mr. Hallam is far better qualified than any other writer of our times for the task he has accomplished. He has great industry and great acuteness; his knowledge is extensive, various, and profound; his mind is equally distinguished by the amplitude of its grasp and by the delicacy of its touch. On a general survey, we do not scruple to pronounce the "Constitutional History" the most important book that we ever read.—*Macaulay.*

This is a production of the greatest value, and distinguished, like his other works, for research, judgment, taste, and elegance.—*Chancellor Kent.*

Goodrich's British Eloquence.

Select British Eloquence; embracing the best Speeches entire of the most eminent Orators of Great Britain for the last two Centuries; with Sketches of their Lives, an Estimate of their Genius, and Notes, Critical and Explanatory. By CHAUNCEY A. GOODRICH, D. D., Professor in Yale College. 8vo., muslin, $4; sheep extra, $4.50.

Hildreth's History of the United States.

First Series. From the First Settlement of the Country to the Adoption of the Federal Constitution. 3 vols., 8vo., muslin, $7.50; sheep extra, $8.25.

Second Series. From the Adoption of the Federal Constitution to the end of the Sixteenth Congress. 3 vols., 8vo., muslin, $7.50; sheep extra, $8.25.

Burke's Complete Works.

The Complete Works of Edmund Burke. With a Memoir. Portrait. 3 vols., 8vo., sheep extra, $5.50.

Federalist, The,

Or the New Constitution. Written, 1788, by Mr. HAMILTON, Mr. MADISON, and Mr. JAY. With an Appendix. 8vo., pp. 496, $1.75.

Elliott's Debates.

Elliott's Debates on the Federal Constitution. 5 vols., 8vo., law sheep, $15.

Dr. Allibone's Dictionary of Authors.

A Critical Dictionary of English Literature, and English and American Authors, Living and Deceased, from the earliest accounts to the middle of the Nineteenth Century, containing upward of thirty thousand Biographies and Literary Notices. By S. AUSTIN ALLIBONE, LL.D. Vol. II, completing the work, will be published during next year. Superroyal octavo, cloth, beveled. Vol. I, $5.

The Military Law of the United States,

Relating to the Army, Volunteer Militia, and to Bounty Lands and Pensions, from the foundation of the Government, 1776, to 1863. A new Edition, thoroughly revised and much enlarged, embracing all the Military Laws of the last Congress. Compiled by JOHN F. CALLAN, Clerk to the Military Committee, United States Senate. Law sheep, 8vo., $5.

A Military Dictionary.

Comprising Information on Raising and Keeping Troops; Actual Service; Makeshifts and Improved Material; and Law, Government, Regulations and Administration relating to Land Forces. By Lt.-Col. HENRY L. SCOTT, U. S. A. One large volume, 8vo. Profusely Illustrated. Half morocco, $5.

Military Law and Courts-Martial.

By Capt. S. V. BENET, U. S. Ordnance, Assistant Professor of Ethics, U. S. Military Academy. Second Edition. 1 vol., 8vo., law sheep, $3.

Parton's Jackson.

The Life of Andrew Jackson, President of the United States. By JAMES PARTON. 3 vols., crown 8vo. With Portraits on Steel. Cloth, Subscribers' Edition, $7.50; library sheep, extra, $9.

Abbott's Austria.

The Empire of Austria, its Rise and Present Power. By JOHN S. C. ABBOTT, with Steel Portrait. Crown 8vo., cloth, $1.75.

Abbott's Russia.

The Empire of Russia, its Rise and Present Power. By JOHN S. C. ABBOTT. Crown 8vo., cloth, $1.75.

Abbott's Italy.

The Empire of Italy, its Rise and Present Power. By JOHN S. C. ABBOTT. Crown 8vo., $1.75.

Aaron Burr's Private Journal,

During his Residence in Europe; with Selections from his Correspondence. Edited by M. L. DAVIS. 2 vols., 8vo., muslin, $5.50.

Life and Times of Aaron Burr,

Vice-President of the United States. By JAMES PARTON. With Portraits. Crown 8vo., $2.

Alison's History of Europe.

First Series. From the Commencement of the French Revolution in 1789, to the Restoration of the Bourbons, in 1815. In addition to the Notes on Chapter LXXVI, which correct the errors of the Original Work concerning the United States, a copious Analytical Index has been appended to this American Edition. 4 vols., 8vo., muslin, $7.50.

Alison's History of Europe.

Second Series. From the Fall of Napoleon, in 1815, to the Accession of Louis Napoleon, in 1852. A new Series. 4 vols., 8vo., muslin, $7.50.

Appleton.

Appleton's Cyclopædia of American Eloquence: A collection of Speeches and Addresses by the most eminent Orators of America; with Biographical Sketches and Illustrative Notes. By FRANK MOORE. Two handsome volumes, large 8vo., embellished with the finest steel-plate Portraits. Cloth, $5; sheep, $6.

CONTENTS: James Otis, Patrick Henry, R. H. Lee, W. H. Drayton, Joseph Warren, James Wilson, William Livingston, Fisher Ames, John Rutledge, Madison, Jay, Randolph, Hamilton, Hancock, Adams, Washington, Elias Boudinot, John Dickinson, etc.

Benton (Thos. H.)

Dred Scott Case. Historical and Legal Examination of that part of the Decision of the Supreme Court of the United States in the Dred Scott Case, which declares the Unconstitutionality of the Missouri Compromise Act, and the Self-extension of the Constitution to Territories, carrying Slavery along with it. With an Appendix. One vol., 8vo., cloth, $1.25.

Gibbon's Rome.

History of the Decline and Fall of the Roman Empire. By EDWARD GIBBON. With Notes by Rev. H. H. MILMAN and M. GUIZOT. With Maps and Engravings. A new, cheap Edition, with Notes, by Rev. H. H. MILMAN. To which is added a complete Index of the whole work, and a Portrait of the Author. Riverside Edition. 6 vols., 12mo., cloth, $9.

Lanman (Charles.)

Dictionary of the United States Congress; containing Biographical Sketches of its Members from the Foundation of the Government. With an Appendix. Compiled as a Manual of Reference for the Legislator and Statesman. 8vo., cloth, $2.

Grote.

Grote's History of Greece. 12 vols., 12mo., muslin, $12.

The author has now incontestibly won for himself the title of *the* historian of Greece.—*Quarterly Review.*

Our Slave States.

By FREDERICK LAW OLMSTEAD. 3 vols., 12mo. 1. Olmstead's Sea-board Slave States. 2. Olmstead's Texas. 3. Olmstead's Back Country. 3 vols., 12mo., cloth. Per set, $4.50.

The Rebellion Record.

A Diary of American Events. Edited by FRANK MOORE. Five volumes, royal 8vo., with 59 Portraits on Steel, with Maps and full Indices. Price, in cloth, $21; sheep, $22.50; half calf, antique, $27.50; half morocco, $27.50.

Irving's Works.

16 vols., 12mo., cloth, $24; half calf, $37; calf, $44.

Irving's Life of Washington.

5 vols., 12mo., cloth, $7.50; sheep, $8.50; half calf, $12.50; calf, $15.

Marshall's Life of Washington.

2 vols., 8vo., $4.

Encyclopædia Britannica.

Eighth Edition. A Dictionary of Arts, Sciences, and General Literature. In 22 vols., 4to. Illustrated with upward of five thousand Engravings on Wood and Steel. $150.

Appleton's New American Cyclopædia

Of Universal Knowledge. 16 vols., royal 8vo., cloth, $56; sheep, $64.

Appleton's Cyclopædia of Biography,

Foreign and American. Edited by Rev. Dr. HAWKS. Royal 8vo. With over 600 engravings. $4.50.

Garland's Life of John Randolph.

1 vol., 8vo. Portraits. $1.75.

Brande's Encyclopædia of Science, Literature, and Art.

1 vol., 8vo., sheep, $5.

Macaulay's History of England.

5 vols., 8vo., $7,50; 5 vols., 12mo., $2.50.

The Annual Cyclopædia.

Being a Supplement to the New American Cyclopædia. Per vol., cloth, $3.50; sheep, $4.

Prescott's Works.

15 vols., 8vo., cloth, $37.50.

Sparks's Correspondence of the Revolution.

Being Letters from Eminent Men to George Washington, from the time of his taking Command of the American Army to the end of his Life. Edited by Hon. JARED SPARKS. 4 vols., 8vo., cloth; price, $9; royal 8vo., cloth, $12.

www.ingramcontent.com/pod-product-compliance
Lightning Source LLC
LaVergne TN
LVHW010230110826
845151LV00004B/1243

9781425525880